THEORY
TEST
FOR CAR DRIVERS

D0307532

THEORY TEST

FOR CAR DRIVERS

The official revision questions
and answers for car drivers from
the Driving Standards Agency

The British School of Motoring
Fanum House
Basing View
Basingstoke
Hampshire RG21 4EA

ISBN: 978-0-7495-7173-3

Colour separation by Wellcom, London
Printed and bound by Leo Paper Products, China

Front cover (top right): © MBI/Alamy

A04713

Contents

Getting Your Licence

You want to pass your driving test and take advantage of the freedom and mobility that driving a car can give you. The following three things will help you to achieve your goal.

- Acquire knowledge of the rules of the road by learning The Highway Code.
- Take the right attitude. Be careful, courteous and considerate to all other road users.
- Learn and understand the skills of driving by taking lessons from a trained and qualified driving instructor.

This book has been designed to help you become a careful and safe driver and help you take the first steps towards achieving your goal – preparing for your Theory Test.

Six essential steps to getting your licence

1 Get your provisional licence
You can apply online for your provisional licence at www.direct.gov.uk/motoring or apply using form D1 available from Post Offices.

The driving licence is issued in the form of a two-part document: a photocard and a paper counterpart.

You must be at least 17 before you can legally begin learning to drive and you must be in possession of the correct licence documents. Take care when completing all the forms. Many licences cannot be issued for the required date because of errors or omissions on the application. You will need to provide proof of identity, such as a UK passport.

2 Learn The Highway Code
The Highway Code is essential reading for all drivers and not just those learning to drive. It sets out all the rules for good driving, as well as the rules for other road users such as pedestrians and motorcycle riders. When you have learned the rules you will be able to answer most of the questions in the Theory Test and be ready to start learning the driving skills you will need to pass your Practical Test.

3 Apply for and take the Theory Test
The driving test is in two parts, the Theory Test and the Practical Test. Once you have a valid provisional licence you may take the Theory Test at any time, but you must pass it before you are allowed to apply for the Practical Test. It is important, however, not to take your Theory Test too early in your course of practical lessons. This is because you need the experience of meeting real hazards while you are learning to drive, to help you pass the hazard perception element of the Theory Test.

You can book your Theory Test by post, by phone or online using a debit or credit card. Application forms are available from the DSA by calling the telephone number below.

Post: DSA, PO BOX 381, M50 3UW
Phone: 0300 200 1122
Welsh speakers: 0300 200 1133
Minicom: 0300 200 1166
Fax: 0300 200 1177
Online: www.direct.gov.uk/theorytest

4 Learn to drive

It is recommended that you learn to drive with an Approved Driving Instructor (ADI). Only an ADI may legally charge for providing tuition. A fully qualified ADI must display a green badge on the windscreen of the car while teaching you. Some trainee driving instructors display a pink badge on the windscreen.

Choose an instructor or driving school by asking friends or relatives for recommendations. Price is important, so find out whether the school offers any discounts for blocks or courses of lessons paid in advance; if you decide to pay in advance, make sure the driving school is reputable. If lesson prices are very low, ask yourself 'why?' Check how long the lesson will last. And don't forget to ask about the car you'll be learning to drive in. Is it modern and reliable? Is it insured? Does it have dual controls?

The most efficient and cost-effective way to learn to drive is to accept that there is no short-cut approach to learning the necessary skills. Agree with your instructor on a planned course of tuition suited to your needs, take regular lessons, and don't skip weeks and expect to pick up where you left off. Ensure the full official syllabus is covered and, as your skills develop, get as much driving practice on the road as possible with a relative or friend – but make sure they are legally able to supervise your practice. They must be over 21 years of age and have held a full driving licence for at least three years.

5 Apply for and take the Practical Test

Once you have passed the Theory Test, and with your instructor's guidance based on your progress, you can plan ahead for a suitable test date for the Practical Test.

You can book your Practical Test online at www.direct.gov.uk/practicaltest or by calling 0300 200 1122 between 8am and 6pm Monday to Friday. You can pay for your test using a credit or debit card and the person who books the test must be the cardholder. If you need to, you can change your practical test appointment by calling the same number or online at www.direct.gov.uk.

Make sure you have the following details to hand when booking your Practical Test:

- Theory Test pass certificate number
- driver number shown on your licence
- driving school code number (if known)
- your preferred date
- unacceptable days or periods
- if you can accept a test at short notice
- disability or any special circumstances
- your credit/debit card details.

Saturday and weekday evening tests are available at some driving test centres. The fee is higher than for a driving test during normal working hours on weekdays. Evening tests are available during the summer months only.

You can book your Practical Test by post, by phone or online using a debit or credit card. Application forms are available from the DSA by calling the number below.

Post: DSA, PO Box 280, Newcastle upon Tyne NE99 1FP
Phone: 0300 200 1122
Welsh speakers: 0300 200 1133
Minicom: 0300 200 1144
Fax: 0300 200 1155
Online: www.direct.gov.uk/practicaltest

6 Apply for your full driving licence

If you have a photocard provisional driving licence issued after 1 March 2004, and pass your driving test, the examiner can issue your full driving licence immediately. The DVLA will send your new full licence by post within four weeks of passing your practical test.

If you don't have a photocard provisional driving licence, you need to send your Pass Certificate and your provisional licence to the DVLA in Swansea, within two years of passing your Practical Test.

After the Practical Test

The Driving Standards Agency (DSA) and the insurance industry recognize and seek to reward those drivers who enhance their basic skills and widen their experience by taking further training in the form of the Pass Plus scheme.

This is a six-module syllabus that covers town and rural driving, night driving, driving in adverse weather conditions and driving on dual carriageways and motorways. It offers you the opportunity to gain more driving experience with the help of an instructor. Insurance companies may be prepared to offer discounts to new drivers who have completed the course. There is no test to take at the end of the course.

More information

For more information on learning to drive, including the Theory Test (multiple-choice questions and hazard perception), the Practical Test and Pass Plus, visit www.direct.gov.uk/motoring.

About the
Theory Test

Revising for the Theory Test

The Theory Test is all about making you a safer driver and it is a good idea to prepare for the Theory Test at the same time as you develop your skills behind the wheel for the Practical Test. By preparing for both tests at the same time, you will reinforce your knowledge and understanding of all aspects of driving and improve your chances of passing both tests first time.

How to use this book

This book is designed to help you prepare for the multiple-choice questions part of the Theory Test and contains all the official revision questions from the DSA. From January 2012 the test will consist of 50 unseen theory test questions based on the topics shown here (see pages 19–259). The real test questions will no longer be published but you can use this book to help you revise for the test.

The questions are arranged into the Theory Test topics, such as Safety Margins and Hazard Awareness. Each topic has its own colour band to help you find your way through the book.

Start your revision by picking a topic; you don't have to study the topics in order. Study each question carefully to make sure you understand what it is asking you and how many answers you need to mark. Look carefully at any diagram or photograph before reading the explanatory information and deciding on your answer(s).

All the answers are given in the back of this book (see pages 267–271).

Remember

- Learning the Highway Code and taking lessons with an ADI (approved driving instructor) are the best way to prepare for your Theory Test.
- Don't attempt too many questions at once.
- Don't try to learn the questions and answers by heart; the real test questions are not available for you to practice and are different from the revision questions given in this book.

Questions marked **NI** are **not** found in Theory Tests in Northern Ireland.

1 Each question tells you how many boxes to tick to answer the question.

21 Mark *one* answer

You are travelling along this narrow country road. When passing the cyclist you should go

3 Look carefully at any photograph, symbol or diagram given within the question.

☐ **A** slowly, sounding the horn as you pass
☐ **B** quickly, leaving plenty of room
☐ **C** slowly, leaving plenty of room
☐ **D** quickly, sounding the horn as you pass

2 Read through all the possible answers.

Look well ahead and only pull out if it is safe. You will need to use all of the road to pass the cyclist, so be extra-cautious. Look out for entrances to fields where tractors or other farm machinery could be waiting to pull out.

4 Each question is accompanied by an explanation that will help you understand the theory behind the question and what answer may be appropriate. Make sure you read through this text before answering the question. Please note that this text will not appear in your live Theory Test.

What to Expect in the Theory Test

The Theory Test consists of two parts: 50 multiple-choice questions and hazard perception. You have to pass both parts in order to pass your Theory Test. You will receive your test scores at the end of the test. Even if you only failed on one part of the Theory Test, you still have to take both parts again next time.

Multiple-choice questions

You will have 57 minutes to complete the question part of the test using a touch-screen and all the questions are multiple-choice. The 50 questions appear on the screen one at a time and you can return to any of the questions within the 57 minutes to re-check or change your answers. You have to score a minimum of 43 out of 50 to pass. The Government may change the pass mark from time to time. Your driving school or the DSA will be able to tell you if there has been a change.

Each question has four, five or six possible answers. You must mark the boxes with the correct answer(s). Each question tells you how many answers to mark. Don't worry about accidentally missing marking an answer because you'll be reminded that you haven't ticked enough boxes before moving on to the next question.

Study each question carefully and look carefully at any diagram, drawing or photograph. Before you look at the answers given, decide what you think the correct answer(s) might be. Read through the options and then select the answer(s) that matches the one you had decided on. If you follow this system, you will avoid being confused by answers that appear to be similar.

You can answer the questions in any order you choose by moving forwards and backwards through the questions. You can also change your answer(s) if necessary and flag questions you're unsure about, then go back to them later in the test. Your remaining time is shown on the screen.

Case study questions

Typically, five of the 50 questions will take the form of a case study. All five questions will be based on a single driving situation and appear one at a time.

Case studies are designed to test that you not only know your car theory but also that you understand how to apply your knowledge when faced with a given driving situation.

The case study in your Theory Test could be based on any driving scenario and ask questions from a range of topics in the DSA's database of questions.

The sample case study on the following pages demonstrates how the case study questions may appear in your live test, so you'll know what to expect.

CASE STUDY 1

You need to go to the airport to pick up a relative that has been on holiday. The journey will take you on various roads including both A-roads and motorways.

As you start your journey it begins to rain and continues to get heavier as you drive.

You have not driven to the airport before but you have planned your route before leaving and feel confident about the journey.

1. You are following a vehicle on a wet road. You should leave a time gap of at least

Mark one answer

☐ one second

☐ two seconds

☐ three seconds

☐ four seconds

Back	Flag	Review	Next

CASE STUDY 1

You need to go to the airport to pick up a relative that has been on holiday. The journey will take you on various roads including both A-roads and motorways.

As you start your journey it begins to rain and continues to get heavier as you drive.

You have not driven to the airport before but you have planned your route before leaving and feel confident about the journey.

2. What does this sign mean?

Mark one answer

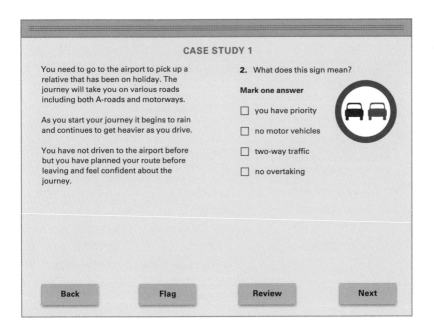

☐ you have priority

☐ no motor vehicles

☐ two-way traffic

☐ no overtaking

Back	Flag	Review	Next

CASE STUDY 1

You need to go to the airport to pick up a relative that has been on holiday. The journey will take you on various roads including both A-roads and motorways.

As you start your journey it begins to rain and continues to get heavier as you drive.

You have not driven to the airport before but you have planned your route before leaving and feel confident about the journey.

3. You have just gone through deep water. To dry off the brakes you should

Mark one answer

- [ ] accelerate and keep to a high speed for a short time
- [ ] go slowly while gently applying the brakes
- [ ] avoid using the brakes at all for a few miles
- [ ] stop for at least an hour to allow them time to dry

Back   Flag   Review   Next

CASE STUDY 1

You need to go to the airport to pick up a relative that has been on holiday. The journey will take you on various roads including both A-roads and motorways.

As you start your journey it begins to rain and continues to get heavier as you drive.

You have not driven to the airport before but you have planned your route before leaving and feel confident about the journey.

4. A bus has stopped at a bus stop ahead of you. Its right-hand indicator is flashing. You should

Mark one answer

- [ ] flash your headlights and slow down
- [ ] slow down and give way if it is safe to do so
- [ ] sound your horn and keep going
- [ ] slow down and then sound your horn

Back   Flag   Review   Next

CASE STUDY 1

You need to go to the airport to pick up a relative that has been on holiday. The journey will take you on various roads including both A-roads and motorways.

As you start your journey it begins to rain and continues to get heavier as you drive.

You have not driven to the airport before but you have planned your route before leaving and feel confident about the journey.

5. Where you see street lights but no speed limit signs the limit is usually

Mark one answer

☐ 30mph

☐ 40mph

☐ 50mph

☐ 60mph

Back	Flag	Review	Next

Answers to sample case study questions:
1 D **2** D **3** B **4** B **5** A

Hazard perception

The video clips element of the Theory Test is known as hazard perception. Its aim is to find out how good you are at noticing hazards developing on the road ahead. The test will also show how much you know about the risks to you as a driver, the risks to your passengers and the risks to other road users.

Who do you think have the most accidents – new or experienced drivers? New drivers have just had lessons, so they should remember how to drive safely, but in fact statistics show that new drivers have the most accidents.

Learner drivers need training in how to spot hazards because they are often so busy thinking about the car's controls that they forget to watch the road and traffic. Losing concentration for even a second could prove fatal to you or another road user.

Proper training can help you to recognize more of the hazards that you will meet when driving and to spot those hazards earlier, so you are less likely to have an accident.

Your driving instructor has been trained to help you learn hazard perception skills and can give you plenty of practice in what to look out for when driving, how to anticipate hazards, and what action to take to deal with hazards of all kinds.

What is a hazard?

A hazard is anything that might cause you to change speed or direction when driving. The hazard perception element of the Theory Test is about spotting developing hazards. This is one of the key skills of good driving and is also called anticipation. Anticipating hazards, such as car doors opening or children running into the road, means looking out for them in advance and taking the appropriate action.

As you get more driving experience you will start to learn about the times and places where you are most likely to meet hazards. An example of this is the rush hour. You know people take more risks when they are in a hurry. Maybe they have to drop their children at school before going to work. Perhaps they are late for a meeting or want to get home. So you have to be prepared for bad driving, for example another driver pulling out in front of you.

You won't be able to practise with the real video clips used in the official test, of course, but training books and practice videos are widely available.

What to expect in the hazard perception test

After answering the multiple-choice questions, you will be given a short break before you begin the hazard perception part of the test. The hazard perception test lasts for about 20 minutes. Before you start you will be given some instructions explaining how the test works; you'll also get a chance to practise with the computer and mouse before you start. This is to make sure that you know what to expect on the test and that you are happy with what you have to do.

Next you will see 14 film clips of real street scenes with traffic such as cars, pedestrians, cyclists, etc. The scenes are shot from the point of view of a driver in

a car. You have to notice potential hazards that are developing on the road ahead – that is, problems that could lead to an incident. As soon as you notice a hazard developing, click the mouse. You will have plenty of time to see the hazard

Above: Click the mouse when you spot potential hazards – the pedestrian crossing the side road and the cyclist approaching a parked vehicle (ringed in yellow). Click again as the hazard develops when the cyclist (ringed in red) moves out to overtake the parked vehicle.

Note that the computer has checks built in to show anyone trying to cheat – for example someone who keeps clicking the mouse all the time. Be aware that, unlike the Theory Test questions, you will not have an opportunity to go back to an earlier clip and change your response, so you need to concentrate throughout the test.

and the sooner you notice it, the more marks you score.

Each clip has at least one hazard in it but some clips may have more than one hazard. You have to score a minimum of 44 out of 75 to pass, but the pass mark may change so check with your instructor or the DSA before sitting your test.

Further information

For more practical information on learning to drive including the Theory Test, Practical Test and Pass Plus visit www.direct.gov.uk/drivingtest.

Theory Test Revision Questions

Contents

1 Mark *one* answer
Before you make a U-turn in the road, you should

- ☐ **A** give an arm signal as well as using your indicators
- ☐ **B** signal so that other drivers can slow down for you
- ☑ **C** look over your shoulder for a final check
- ☐ **D** select a higher gear than normal

If you want to make a U-turn, slow down and ensure that the road is clear in both directions. Make sure that the road is wide enough to carry out the manoeuvre safely.

2 Mark *three* answers
As you approach this bridge you should

- ☐ **A** move into the middle of the road to get a better view
- ☐ **B** slow down
- ☐ **C** get over the bridge as quickly as possible
- ☐ **D** consider using your horn
- ☐ **E** find another route
- ☐ **F** beware of pedestrians

This sign gives you a warning. The brow of the hill prevents you seeing oncoming traffic so you must be cautious. The bridge is narrow and there may not be enough room for you to pass an oncoming vehicle at this point. There is no footpath, so pedestrians may be walking in the road. Consider the hidden hazards and be ready to react if necessary.

3 Mark *one* answer
In which of these situations should you avoid overtaking?

- ☐ **A** Just after a bend
- ☐ **B** In a one-way street
- ☐ **C** On a 30mph road
- ☐ **D** Approaching a dip in the road

As you begin to think about overtaking, ask yourself if it's really necessary. If you can't see well ahead stay back and wait for a safer place to pull out.

4 Mark *one* answer
This road marking warns

- ☐ **A** drivers to use the hard shoulder
- ☐ **B** overtaking drivers there is a bend to the left
- ☐ **C** overtaking drivers to move back to the left
- ☐ **D** drivers that it is safe to overtake

You should plan your overtaking to take into account any hazards ahead. In this picture the marking indicates that you are approaching a junction. You will not have time to overtake and move back into the left safely.

5 Mark *one* answer
Your mobile phone rings while you are travelling. You should

- ☐ **A** stop immediately
- ☐ **B** answer it immediately
- ☐ **C** pull up in a suitable place
- ☐ **D** pull up at the nearest kerb

The safest option is to switch off your mobile phone before you set off, and use a message service. Even hands-free systems are likely to distract your attention. Don't endanger other road users. If you need to make a call, pull up in a safe place when you can, you may need to go some distance before you can find one. It's illegal to use a hand-held mobile or similar device when driving or riding, except in a genuine emergency.

6 Mark *one* answer
Why are these yellow lines painted across the road?

- ☐ **A** To help you choose the correct lane
- ☐ **B** To help you keep the correct separation distance
- ☐ **C** To make you aware of your speed
- ☐ **D** To tell you the distance to the roundabout

These lines are often found on the approach to a roundabout or a dangerous junction. They give you extra warning to adjust your speed. Look well ahead and do this in good time.

7 Mark *one* answer
You are approaching traffic lights that have been on green for some time. You should

- ☐ **A** accelerate hard
- ☐ **B** maintain your speed
- ☐ **C** be ready to stop
- ☐ **D** brake hard

The longer traffic lights have been on green, the greater the chance of them changing. Always allow for this on approach and be prepared to stop.

8 Mark *one* answer
Which of the following should you do before stopping?

- ☐ **A** Sound the horn
- ☐ **B** Use the mirrors
- ☐ **C** Select a higher gear
- ☐ **D** Flash your headlights

Before pulling up check the mirrors to see what is happening behind you. Also assess what is ahead and make sure you give the correct signal if it helps other road users.

9 Mark *one* answer
When following a large vehicle you should keep well back because this

- ☐ **A** allows you to corner more quickly
- ☐ **B** helps the large vehicle to stop more easily
- ☐ **C** allows the driver to see you in the mirrors
- ☐ **D** helps you to keep out of the wind

If you're following a large vehicle but are so close to it that you can't see the exterior mirrors, the driver can't see you.
    Keeping well back will also allow you to see the road ahead by looking past either side of the large vehicle.

10 Mark *one* answer

When you see a hazard ahead you should use the mirrors. Why is this?

☐ **A** Because you will need to accelerate out of danger
☐ **B** To assess how your actions will affect following traffic
☐ **C** Because you will need to brake sharply to a stop
☐ **D** To check what is happening on the road ahead

You should be constantly scanning the road for clues about what is going to happen next. Check your mirrors regularly, particularly as soon as you spot a hazard. What is happening behind may affect your response to hazards ahead.

11 Mark *one* answer

You are waiting to turn right at the end of a road. Your view is obstructed by parked vehicles. What should you do?

☐ **A** Stop and then move forward slowly and carefully for a proper view
☐ **B** Move quickly to where you can see so you only block traffic from one direction
☐ **C** Wait for a pedestrian to let you know when it is safe for you to emerge
☐ **D** Turn your vehicle around immediately and find another junction to use

At junctions your view is often restricted by buildings, trees or parked cars. You need to be able to see in order to judge a safe gap. Edge forward slowly and keep looking all the time. Don't cause other road users to change speed or direction as you emerge.

12 Mark *two* answers

Objects hanging from your interior mirror may

☐ **A** restrict your view
☐ **B** improve your driving
☐ **C** distract your attention
☐ **D** help your concentration

Ensure that you can see clearly through the windscreen of your vehicle. Stickers or hanging objects could affect your field of vision or draw your eyes away from the road.

13 Mark *four* answers

Which of the following may cause loss of concentration on a long journey?

☐ **A** Loud music
☐ **B** Arguing with a passenger
☐ **C** Using a mobile phone
☐ **D** Putting in a cassette tape
☐ **E** Stopping regularly to rest
☐ **F** Pulling up to tune the radio

You should not allow yourself to be distracted when driving. You need to concentrate fully in order to be safe on the road. Loud music could mask other sounds, such as the audible warning of an emergency vehicle. Any distraction which causes you to take your hands off the steering wheel or your eyes off the road could be dangerous.

14 Mark *two* answers
On a long motorway journey boredom can cause you to feel sleepy. You should

☐ **A** leave the motorway and find a safe place to stop
☐ **B** keep looking around at the surrounding landscape
☐ **C** drive faster to complete your journey sooner
☐ **D** ensure a supply of fresh air into your vehicle
☐ **E** stop on the hard shoulder for a rest

Plan your journey to include suitable rest stops. You should take all possible precautions against feeling sleepy while driving. Any lapse of concentration could have serious consequences.

15 Mark *two* answers
You are driving at dusk. You should switch your lights on

☐ **A** even when street lights are not lit
☐ **B** so others can see you
☐ **C** only when others have done so
☐ **D** only when street lights are lit

Your headlights and tail lights help others on the road to see you. It may be necessary to turn on your lights during the day if visibility is reduced, for example due to heavy rain. In these conditions the light might fade before the street lights are timed to switch on. Be seen to be safe.

16 Mark *two* answers
You are most likely to lose concentration when driving if you

☐ **A** use a mobile phone
☐ **B** listen to very loud music
☐ **C** switch on the heated rear window
☐ **D** look at the door mirrors

Distractions which cause you to take your hands off the steering wheel or your eyes off the road are potentially dangerous. You must be in full control of your vehicle at all times.

17 Mark *four* answers
Which FOUR are most likely to cause you to lose concentration while you are driving?

☐ **A** Using a mobile phone
☐ **B** Talking into a microphone
☐ **C** Tuning your car radio
☐ **D** Looking at a map
☐ **E** Checking the mirrors
☐ **F** Using the demisters

It's easy to be distracted. Planning your journey before you set off is important. A few sensible precautions are to tune your radio to stations in your area of travel, take planned breaks, and plan your route. Except for emergencies it is illegal to use a hand-held mobile phone while driving. Even using a hands-free kit can distract your attention.

18 Mark *one* answer
You should ONLY use a mobile phone when

- ☐ **A** receiving a call
- ☐ **B** suitably parked
- ☐ **C** driving at less than 30mph
- ☐ **D** driving an automatic vehicle

It is illegal to use a hand-held mobile phone while driving, except in a genuine emergency. Even using hands-free kit can distract your attention. Park in a safe and convenient place before receiving or making a call or using text messaging. Then you will also be free to take notes or refer to papers.

19 Mark *one* answer
You are driving on a wet road. You have to stop your vehicle in an emergency. You should

- ☐ **A** apply the handbrake and footbrake together
- ☐ **B** keep both hands on the wheel
- ☐ **C** select reverse gear
- ☐ **D** give an arm signal

As you drive, look well ahead and all around so that you're ready for any hazards that might occur. There may be occasions when you have to stop in an emergency. React as soon as you can whilst keeping control of the vehicle.

20 Mark *three* answers
When you are moving off from behind a parked car you should

- ☐ **A** look round before you move off
- ☐ **B** use all the mirrors on the vehicle
- ☐ **C** look round after moving off
- ☐ **D** use the exterior mirrors only
- ☐ **E** give a signal if necessary
- ☐ **F** give a signal after moving off

Before moving off you should use all the mirrors to check if the road is clear. Look round to check the blind spots and give a signal if it is necessary to warn other road users of your intentions.

21 Mark *one* answer
You are travelling along this narrow country road. When passing the cyclist you should go

- ☐ **A** slowly, sounding the horn as you pass
- ☐ **B** quickly, leaving plenty of room
- ☐ **C** slowly, leaving plenty of room
- ☐ **D** quickly, sounding the horn as you pass

Look well ahead and only pull out if it is safe. You will need to use all of the road to pass the cyclist, so be extra-cautious. Look out for entrances to fields where tractors or other farm machinery could be waiting to pull out.

22 Mark *one* answer
Your vehicle is fitted with a hand-held telephone. To use the telephone you should

☐ **A** reduce your speed
☐ **B** find a safe place to stop
☐ **C** steer the vehicle with one hand
☐ **D** be particularly careful at junctions

Your attention should be on your driving at all times. Except in a genuine emergency never attempt to use a hand-held phone while on the move. It's illegal and very dangerous. Your eyes could wander from the road and at 60mph your vehicle will travel about 27 metres (89 feet) every second.

23 Mark *one* answer
To answer a call on your mobile phone while travelling you should

☐ **A** reduce your speed wherever you are
☐ **B** stop in a proper and convenient place
☐ **C** keep the call time to a minimum
☐ **D** slow down and allow others to overtake

No phone call is important enough to risk endangering lives. It's better to switch your phone off completely when driving. If you must be contactable plan your route to include breaks so you can catch up on messages in safety. Always choose a safe and convenient place to take a break, such as a lay-by or service area.

24 Mark *one* answer
You lose your way on a busy road. What is the best action to take?

☐ **A** Stop at traffic lights and ask pedestrians
☐ **B** Shout to other drivers to ask them the way
☐ **C** Turn into a side road, stop and check a map
☐ **D** Check a map, and keep going with the traffic flow

It's easy to lose your way in an unfamiliar area. If you need to check a map or ask for directions, first find a safe place to stop.

25 Mark *one* answer
Windscreen pillars can obstruct your view. You should take particular care when

☐ **A** driving on a motorway
☐ **B** driving on a dual carriageway
☐ **C** approaching a one-way street
☐ **D** approaching bends and junctions

Windscreen pillars can obstruct your view, particularly at bends and junctions. Look out for other road users, particularly cyclists and pedestrians, as they can be hard to see.

26 Mark *one* answer
You cannot see clearly behind when reversing. What should you do?

☐ **A** Open your window to look behind
☐ **B** Open the door and look behind
☐ **C** Look in the nearside mirror
☐ **D** Ask someone to guide you

If you want to turn your car around try to find a place where you have good all-round vision. If this isn't possible and you're unable to see clearly, then get someone to guide you.

27 Mark *one* answer
What does the term 'blind spot' mean for a driver?

☐ **A** An area covered by your right-hand mirror
☐ **B** An area not covered by your headlights
☐ **C** An area covered by your left-hand mirror
☐ **D** An area not covered by your mirrors

Modern vehicles provide the driver with well-positioned mirrors which are essential to safe driving. However, they cannot see every angle of the scene behind and to the sides of the vehicle. This is why it is essential that you check over your shoulder, so that you are aware of any hazards not reflected in your mirrors.

28 Mark *one* answer
Your vehicle is fitted with a hands-free phone system. Using this equipment whilst driving

☐ **A** is quite safe as long as you slow down
☐ **B** could distract your attention from the road
☐ **C** is recommended by The Highway Code
☐ **D** could be very good for road safety

Using a hands-free system doesn't mean that you can safely drive and use a mobile phone. This type of mobile phone can still distract your attention from the road. As a driver, it is your responsibility to keep yourself and other road users safe at all times.

29 Mark *one* answer
Using a hands-free phone is likely to

☐ **A** improve your safety
☐ **B** increase your concentration
☐ **C** reduce your view
☐ **D** divert your attention

Unlike someone in the car with you, the person on the other end of the line is unable to see the traffic situations you are dealing with. They will not stop speaking to you even if you are approaching a hazardous situation. You need to be concentrating on your driving all of the time, but especially so when dealing with a hazard.

30 Mark *one* answer
What is the safest way to use a mobile phone in your vehicle?

☐ **A** Use hands-free equipment
☐ **B** Find a suitable place to stop
☐ **C** Drive slowly on a quiet road
☐ **D** Direct your call through the operator

It's illegal to use a hand-held mobile phone while driving, except in genuine emergencies. Even using hands-free kit is very likely to take your mind off your driving. If the use of a mobile causes you to drive in a careless or dangerous manner, you could be prosecuted for those offences. The penalties include an unlimited fine, disqualification and up to two years' imprisonment.

31 Mark *one* answer

Your mobile phone rings while you are on the motorway. Before answering you should

☐ **A** reduce your speed to 30mph
☐ **B** pull up on the hard shoulder
☐ **C** move into the left-hand lane
☐ **D** stop in a safe place

When driving on motorways, you can't just pull up to answer your mobile phone. Do not stop on the hard shoulder or slip road. To avoid being distracted it's safer to switch it off when driving. If you need to be contacted plan your journey to include breaks at service areas so you can pick up any messages when you stop.

32 Mark *one* answer

You are turning right onto a dual carriageway. What should you do before emerging?

☐ **A** Stop, apply the handbrake and then select a low gear
☐ **B** Position your vehicle well to the left of the side road
☐ **C** Check that the central reservation is wide enough for your vehicle
☐ **D** Make sure that you leave enough room for a vehicle behind

Before emerging right onto a dual carriageway make sure that the central reserve is deep enough to protect your vehicle. If it's not, you should treat it as one road and check that it's clear in both directions before pulling out. Neglecting to do this could place part or all of your vehicle in the path of approaching traffic and cause a collision.

33 Mark *one* answer

You are waiting to emerge from a junction. The windscreen pillar is restricting your view. What should you be particularly aware of?

☐ **A** Lorries
☐ **B** Buses
☐ **C** Motorcyclists
☐ **D** Coaches

Windscreen pillars can completely block your view of pedestrians, motorcyclists and pedal cyclists. You should particularly watch out for these road users; don't just rely on a quick glance. Where possible make eye contact with them so you can be sure they have seen you too.

34 Mark *one* answer

When emerging from junctions, which is most likely to obstruct your view?

☐ **A** Windscreen pillars
☐ **B** Steering wheel
☐ **C** Interior mirror
☐ **D** Windscreen wipers

Windscreen pillars can block your view, particularly at junctions. Those road users most at risk of not being seen are cyclists, motorcyclists and pedestrians. Never rely on just a quick glance.

35 Mark *one* answer
Your vehicle is fitted with a navigation system. How should you avoid letting this distract you while driving?

☐ **A** Keep going and input your destination into the system
☐ **B** Keep going as the system will adjust to your route
☐ **C** Stop immediately to view and use the system
☐ **D** Stop in a safe place before using the system

Vehicle navigation systems can be useful when driving on unfamiliar routes. However they can also distract you and cause you to lose control if you look at or adjust them while driving. Pull up in a convenient and safe place before adjusting them.

36 Mark *one* answer
You are driving on a motorway and want to use your mobile phone. What should you do?

☐ **A** Try to find a safe place on the hard shoulder
☐ **B** Leave the motorway and stop in a safe place
☐ **C** Use the next exit and pull up on the slip road
☐ **D** Move to the left lane and reduce your speed

Except in a genuine emergency you MUST NOT use your mobile phone when driving. If you need to use it leave the motorway and find a safe place to stop. Even a hands-free phone can distract your attention. Use your voicemail to receive calls. Driving requires all of your attention, all of the time.

37 Mark one answer
You must not use a hand-held phone while driving. Using a hands-free system

☐ **A** is acceptable in a vehicle with power steering
☐ **B** will significantly reduce your field of vision
☐ **C** will affect your vehicle's electronic systems
☐ **D** is still likely to distract your attention from the road

While driving your concentration is required all the time. Even using a hands-free kit can still distract your attention from the road. Any distraction, however brief, is potentially dangerous and could cause you to lose control. Except in a genuine emergency, it is an offence to use a hand-held phone while driving.

38 Mark *one* answer
At a pelican crossing the flashing amber light means you MUST

- ☐ **A** stop and wait for the green light
- ☐ **B** stop and wait for the red light
- ☐ **C** give way to pedestrians waiting to cross
- ☐ **D** give way to pedestrians already on the crossing

Pelican crossings are signal-controlled crossings operated by pedestrians. Push-button controls change the signals. Pelican crossings have no red-and-amber stage before green. Instead, they have a flashing amber light, which means you MUST give way to pedestrians already on the crossing, but if it is clear, you may continue.

39 Mark *one* answer
You should never wave people across at pedestrian crossings because

- ☐ **A** there may be another vehicle coming
- ☐ **B** they may not be looking
- ☐ **C** it is safer for you to carry on
- ☐ **D** they may not be ready to cross

If people are waiting to use a pedestrian crossing, slow down and be prepared to stop. Don't wave them across the road since another driver may not have seen them, not have seen your signal and may not be able to stop safely.

40 Mark *one* answer
'Tailgating' means

- ☐ **A** using the rear door of a hatchback car
- ☐ **B** reversing into a parking space
- ☐ **C** following another vehicle too closely
- ☐ **D** driving with rear fog lights on

'Tailgating' is used to describe this dangerous practice, often seen in fast-moving traffic and on motorways. Following the vehicle in front too closely is dangerous because it

- restricts your view of the road ahead
- leaves you no safety margin if the vehicle in front slows down or stops suddenly.

41 Mark *one* answer
Following this vehicle too closely is unwise because

- ☐ **A** your brakes will overheat
- ☐ **B** your view ahead is increased
- ☐ **C** your engine will overheat
- ☐ **D** your view ahead is reduced

Staying back will increase your view of the road ahead. This will help you to see any hazards that might occur and allow you more time to react.

42 Mark *one* answer
You are following a vehicle on a wet road. You should leave a time gap of at least

- ☐ **A** one second
- ☐ **B** two seconds
- ☐ **C** three seconds
- ☐ **D** four seconds

Wet roads will reduce your tyres' grip on the road. The safe separation gap of at least two seconds in dry conditions should be doubled in wet weather.

43 Mark *one* answer
A long, heavily-laden lorry is taking a long time to overtake you. What should you do?

- ☐ **A** Speed up
- ☐ **B** Slow down
- ☐ **C** Hold your speed
- ☐ **D** Change direction

A long lorry with a heavy load will need more time to pass you than a car, especially on an uphill stretch of road. Slow down and allow the lorry to pass.

44 Mark *three* answers
Which of the following vehicles will use blue flashing beacons?

- ☐ **A** Motorway maintenance
- ☐ **B** Bomb disposal
- ☐ **C** Blood transfusion
- ☐ **D** Police patrol
- ☐ **E** Breakdown recovery

When you see emergency vehicles with blue flashing beacons, move out of the way as soon as it is safe to do so.

45 Mark *three* answers
Which THREE of these emergency services might have blue flashing beacons?

- ☐ **A** Coastguard
- ☐ **B** Bomb disposal
- ☐ **C** Gritting lorries
- ☐ **D** Animal ambulances
- ☐ **E** Mountain rescue
- ☐ **F** Doctors' cars

When attending an emergency these vehicles will be travelling at speed. You should help their progress by pulling over and allowing them to pass. Do so safely. Don't stop suddenly or in a dangerous position.

46 Mark *one* answer
When being followed by an ambulance showing a flashing blue beacon you should

- ☐ **A** pull over as soon as safely possible to let it pass
- ☐ **B** accelerate hard to get away from it
- ☐ **C** maintain your speed and course
- ☐ **D** brake harshly and immediately stop in the road

Pull over in a place where the ambulance can pass safely. Check that there are no bollards or obstructions in the road that will prevent it from doing so.

47 Mark *one* answer
What type of emergency vehicle is fitted with a green flashing beacon?

☐ **A** Fire engine
☐ **B** Road gritter
☐ **C** Ambulance
☐ **D** Doctor's car

A green flashing beacon on a vehicle means the driver or passenger is a doctor on an emergency call. Give way to them if it's safe to do so. Be aware that the vehicle may be travelling quickly or may stop in a hurry.

48 Mark *one* answer
A flashing green beacon on a vehicle means

☐ **A** police on non-urgent duties
☐ **B** doctor on an emergency call
☐ **C** road safety patrol operating
☐ **D** gritting in progress

If you see a vehicle with a flashing green beacon approaching, allow it to pass when you can do so safely. Be aware that someone's life could depend on the driver making good progress through traffic.

49 Mark *one* answer
Diamond-shaped signs give instructions to

☐ **A** tram drivers
☐ **B** bus drivers
☐ **C** lorry drivers
☐ **D** taxi drivers

These signs only apply to trams. They are directed at tram drivers but you should know their meaning so that you're aware of the priorities and are able to anticipate the actions of the driver.

50 Mark *one* answer
On a road where trams operate, which of these vehicles will be most at risk from the tram rails?

☐ **A** Cars
☐ **B** Cycles
☐ **C** Buses
☐ **D** Lorries

The narrow wheels of a bicycle can become stuck in the tram rails, causing the cyclist to stop suddenly, wobble or even lose balance altogether. The tram lines are also slippery which could cause a cyclist to slide or fall off.

51 Mark *one* answer
What should you use your horn for?

☐ **A** To alert others to your presence
☐ **B** To allow you right of way
☐ **C** To greet other road users
☐ **D** To signal your annoyance

Your horn must not be used between 11.30pm and 7am in a built-up area or when you are stationary, unless a moving vehicle poses a danger. Its function is to alert other road users to your presence.

52 Mark *one* answer
You are in a one-way street and want to turn right. You should position yourself

☐ **A** in the right-hand lane
☐ **B** in the left-hand lane
☐ **C** in either lane, depending on the traffic
☐ **D** just left of the centre line

If you're travelling in a one-way street and wish to turn right you should take up a position in the right-hand lane. This will enable other road users not wishing to turn to proceed on the left. Indicate your intention and take up your position in good time.

53 Mark *one* answer
You wish to turn right ahead. Why should you take up the correct position in good time?

☐ **A** To allow other drivers to pull out in front of you
☐ **B** To give a better view into the road that you're joining
☐ **C** To help other road users know what you intend to do
☐ **D** To allow drivers to pass you on the right

If you wish to turn right into a side road take up your position in good time. Move to the centre of the road when it's safe to do so. This will allow vehicles to pass you on the left. Early planning will show other traffic what you intend to do.

54 Mark *one* answer
At which type of crossing are cyclists allowed to ride across with pedestrians?

☐ **A** Toucan
☐ **B** Puffin
☐ **C** Pelican
☐ **D** Zebra

A toucan crossing is designed to allow pedestrians and cyclists to cross at the same time. Look out for cyclists approaching the crossing at speed.

55 Mark *one* answer
You are travelling at the legal speed limit. A vehicle comes up quickly behind, flashing its headlights. You should

- ☐ **A** accelerate to make a gap behind you
- ☐ **B** touch the brakes sharply to show your brake lights
- ☐ **C** maintain your speed to prevent the vehicle from overtaking
- ☐ **D** allow the vehicle to overtake

Don't enforce the speed limit by blocking another vehicle's progress. This will only lead to the other driver becoming more frustrated. Allow the other vehicle to pass when you can do so safely.

56 Mark *one* answer
You should ONLY flash your headlights to other road users

- ☐ **A** to show that you are giving way
- ☐ **B** to show that you are about to turn
- ☐ **C** to tell them that you have right of way
- ☐ **D** to let them know that you are there

You should only flash your headlights to warn others of your presence. Don't use them to greet others, show impatience or give priority to other road users. They could misunderstand your signal.

57 Mark *one* answer
You are approaching unmarked crossroads. How should you deal with this type of junction?

- ☐ **A** Accelerate and keep to the middle
- ☐ **B** Slow down and keep to the right
- ☐ **C** Accelerate looking to the left
- ☐ **D** Slow down and look both ways

Be extra-cautious, especially when your view is restricted by hedges, bushes, walls and large vehicles etc. In the summer months these junctions can become more difficult to deal with when growing foliage may obscure your view.

58 Mark *one* answer
You are approaching a pelican crossing. The amber light is flashing. You must

- ☐ **A** give way to pedestrians who are crossing
- ☐ **B** encourage pedestrians to cross
- ☐ **C** not move until the green light appears
- ☐ **D** stop even if the crossing is clear

While the pedestrians are crossing don't encourage them to cross by waving or flashing your headlights: other road users may misunderstand your signal. Don't harass them by creeping forward or revving your engine.

59 Mark *one* answer
The conditions are good and dry. You could use the 'two-second rule'

☐ **A** before restarting the engine after it has stalled
☐ **B** to keep a safe gap from the vehicle in front
☐ **C** before using the 'Mirror-Signal-Manoeuvre' routine
☐ **D** when emerging on wet roads

To measure this, choose a fixed reference point such as a bridge, sign or tree. When the vehicle ahead passes the object, say to yourself 'Only a fool breaks the two-second rule.' If you reach the object before you finish saying this, you're TOO CLOSE.

60 Mark *one* answer
At a puffin crossing, which colour follows the green signal?

☐ **A** Steady red
☐ **B** Flashing amber
☐ **C** Steady amber
☐ **D** Flashing green

Puffin crossings have infra-red sensors which detect when pedestrians are crossing and hold the red traffic signal until the crossing is clear. The use of a sensor means there is no flashing amber phase as there is with a pelican crossing.

61 Mark *one* answer
You are in a line of traffic. The driver behind you is following very closely. What action should you take?

☐ **A** Ignore the following driver and continue to travel within the speed limit
☐ **B** Slow down, gradually increasing the gap between you and the vehicle in front
☐ **C** Signal left and wave the following driver past
☐ **D** Move over to a position just left of the centre line of the road

It can be worrying to see that the car behind is following you too closely. Give yourself a greater safety margin by easing back from the vehicle in front.

62 Mark *one* answer
A vehicle has a flashing green beacon. What does this mean?

☐ **A** A doctor is answering an emergency call
☐ **B** The vehicle is slow-moving
☐ **C** It is a motorway police patrol vehicle
☐ **D** The vehicle is carrying hazardous chemicals

A doctor attending an emergency may show a green flashing beacon on their vehicle. Give way to them when you can do so safely as they will need to reach their destination quickly. Be aware that they might pull over suddenly.

63 Mark *one* answer

A bus has stopped at a bus stop ahead of you. Its right-hand indicator is flashing. You should

- ☐ **A** flash your headlights and slow down
- ☐ **B** slow down and give way if it is safe to do so
- ☐ **C** sound your horn and keep going
- ☐ **D** slow down and then sound your horn

Give way to buses whenever you can do so safely, especially when they signal to pull away from bus stops. Look out for people leaving the bus and crossing the road.

64 Mark *one* answer

You are driving on a clear night. There is a steady stream of oncoming traffic. The national speed limit applies. Which lights should you use?

- ☐ **A** Full beam headlights
- ☐ **B** Sidelights
- ☐ **C** Dipped headlights
- ☐ **D** Fog lights

Use the full beam headlights only when you can be sure that you won't dazzle other road users.

65 Mark *one* answer

You are driving behind a large goods vehicle. It signals left but steers to the right. You should

- ☐ **A** slow down and let the vehicle turn
- ☐ **B** drive on, keeping to the left
- ☐ **C** overtake on the right of it
- ☐ **D** hold your speed and sound your horn

Large, long vehicles need extra room when making turns at junctions. They may move out to the right in order to make a left turn. Keep well back and don't attempt to pass on the left.

66 Mark *one* answer

You are driving along this road. The red van cuts in close in front of you. What should you do?

- ☐ **A** Accelerate to get closer to the red van
- ☐ **B** Give a long blast on the horn
- ☐ **C** Drop back to leave the correct separation distance
- ☐ **D** Flash your headlights several times

There are times when other drivers make incorrect or ill-judged decisions. Be tolerant and try not to retaliate or react aggressively. Always consider the safety of other road users, your passengers and yourself.

67 Mark *one* answer

You are waiting in a traffic queue at night. To avoid dazzling following drivers you should

- ☐ **A** apply the handbrake only
- ☐ **B** apply the footbrake only
- ☐ **C** switch off your headlights
- ☐ **D** use both the handbrake and footbrake

You should consider drivers behind as brake lights can dazzle. However, if you are driving in fog it's safer to keep your foot on the footbrake. In this case it will give the vehicle behind extra warning of your presence.

68 Mark *one* answer

You are driving in traffic at the speed limit for the road. The driver behind is trying to overtake. You should

- ☐ **A** move closer to the car ahead, so the driver behind has no room to overtake
- ☐ **B** wave the driver behind to overtake when it is safe
- ☐ **C** keep a steady course and allow the driver behind to overtake
- ☐ **D** accelerate to get away from the driver behind

Keep a steady course to give the driver behind an opportunity to overtake safely. If necessary, slow down. Reacting incorrectly to another driver's impatience can lead to danger.

69 Mark *one* answer

A bus lane on your left shows no times of operation. This means it is

- ☐ **A** not in operation at all
- ☐ **B** only in operation at peak times
- ☐ **C** in operation 24 hours a day
- ☐ **D** only in operation in daylight hours

Don't drive or park in a bus lane when it's in operation. This can cause disruption to traffic and delays to public transport.

70 Mark *two* answers

You are driving along a country road. A horse and rider are approaching. What should you do?

- ☐ **A** Increase your speed
- ☐ **B** Sound your horn
- ☐ **C** Flash your headlights
- ☐ **D** Drive slowly past
- ☐ **E** Give plenty of room
- ☐ **F** Rev your engine

It's important that you reduce your speed. Passing too closely at speed could startle the horse and unseat the rider.

71 Mark *one* answer
A person herding sheep asks you to stop. You should

- ☐ **A** ignore them as they have no authority
- ☐ **B** stop and switch off your engine
- ☐ **C** continue on but drive slowly
- ☐ **D** try and get past quickly

Allow the sheep to clear the road before you proceed. Animals are unpredictable and startle easily; they could turn and run into your path or into the path of another moving vehicle.

72 Mark *one* answer
When overtaking a horse and rider you should

- ☐ **A** sound your horn as a warning
- ☐ **B** go past as quickly as possible
- ☐ **C** flash your headlights as a warning
- ☐ **D** go past slowly and carefully

Horses can become startled by the sound of a car engine or the rush of air caused by passing too closely. Keep well back and only pass when it is safe; leave them plenty of room. You may have to use the other side of the road to go past: if you do, first make sure there is no oncoming traffic.

73 Mark *one* answer
You are approaching a zebra crossing. Pedestrians are waiting to cross. You should

- ☐ **A** give way to the elderly and infirm only
- ☐ **B** slow down and prepare to stop
- ☐ **C** use your headlights to indicate they can cross
- ☐ **D** wave at them to cross the road

Look out on the approach especially for children and older pedestrians. They may walk across without looking. Zebra crossings have flashing amber beacons on both sides of the road, black and white stripes on the crossing and white zigzag markings on both sides of the crossing. Where you can see pedestrians waiting to cross, slow down and prepare to stop.

74 Mark *one* answer
A vehicle pulls out in front of you at a junction. What should you do?

- ☐ **A** Swerve past it and sound your horn
- ☐ **B** Flash your headlights and drive up close behind
- ☐ **C** Slow down and be ready to stop
- ☐ **D** Accelerate past it immediately

Try to be ready for the unexpected. Plan ahead and learn to anticipate hazards. You'll then give yourself more time to react to any problems that might occur.

Be tolerant of the behaviour of other road users who don't behave correctly.

75 Mark *one* answer

You stop for pedestrians waiting to cross at a zebra crossing. They do not start to cross. What should you do?

☐ **A** Be patient and wait
☐ **B** Sound your horn
☐ **C** Carry on
☐ **D** Wave them to cross

If you stop for pedestrians and they don't start to cross don't wave them across or sound your horn. This could be dangerous if another vehicle is approaching which hasn't seen or heard your signal.

76 Mark *one* answer

You are following this lorry. You should keep well back from it to

☐ **A** give you a good view of the road ahead
☐ **B** stop following traffic from rushing through the junction
☐ **C** prevent traffic behind you from overtaking
☐ **D** allow you to hurry through the traffic lights if they change

By keeping well back you will increase your width of vision around the rear of the lorry. This will allow you to see further down the road and be prepared for any hazards.

77 Mark *one* answer

You are approaching a red light at a puffin crossing. Pedestrians are on the crossing. The red light will stay on until

☐ **A** you start to edge forward on to the crossing
☐ **B** the pedestrians have reached a safe position
☐ **C** the pedestrians are clear of the front of your vehicle
☐ **D** a driver from the opposite direction reaches the crossing

The electronic device will automatically detect that the pedestrians have reached a safe position. Don't proceed until the green light shows it is safe for vehicles to do so.

78 Mark *one* answer

Which instrument panel warning light would show that headlights are on full beam?

☐ A   ☐ B

☐ C   ☐ D

You should be aware of where all the warning lights and visual aids are on the vehicle you are driving. If you are driving a vehicle for the first time you should take time to check all the controls.

79 Mark *one* answer
At puffin crossings, which light will not show to a driver?

☐ **A** Flashing amber ☐ **B** Red
☐ **C** Steady amber ☐ **D** Green

A flashing amber light is shown at pelican crossings, but puffin crossings are different. They are controlled electronically and automatically detect when pedestrians are on the crossing. The phase is shortened or lengthened according to the position of the pedestrians.

80 Mark *one* answer
You should leave at least a two-second gap between your vehicle and the one in front when conditions are

☐ **A** wet ☐ **B** good
☐ **C** damp ☐ **D** foggy

In good, dry conditions an alert driver, who's driving a vehicle with tyres and brakes in good condition, needs to keep a distance of at least two seconds from the car in front.

81 Mark *one* answer
You are driving at night on an unlit road behind another vehicle. You should

☐ **A** flash your headlights
☐ **B** use dipped beam headlights
☐ **C** switch off your headlights
☐ **D** use full beam headlights

If you follow another vehicle with your headlights on full beam they could dazzle the driver. Leave a safe distance and ensure that the light from your dipped beam falls short of the vehicle in front.

82 Mark *one* answer
You are driving a slow-moving vehicle on a narrow winding road. You should

☐ **A** keep well out to stop vehicles overtaking dangerously
☐ **B** wave following vehicles past you if you think they can overtake quickly
☐ **C** pull in safely when you can, to let following vehicles overtake
☐ **D** give a left signal when it is safe for vehicles to overtake you

Try not to hold up a queue of traffic. Other road users may become impatient and this could lead to reckless actions. If you're driving a slow-moving vehicle and the road is narrow, look for a safe place to pull in. DON'T wave other traffic past since this could be dangerous if you or they haven't seen an oncoming vehicle.

83 Mark *two* answers
You have a loose filler cap on your diesel fuel tank. This will

☐ **A** waste fuel and money
☐ **B** make roads slippery for other road users
☐ **C** improve your vehicles' fuel consumption
☐ **D** increase the level of exhaust emissions

Diesel fuel is especially slippery if spilled on a wet road. At the end of a dry spell of weather you should be aware that the road surfaces may have a high level of diesel spillage that hasn't been washed away by rain.

84 Mark *one* answer
To avoid spillage after refuelling, you should make sure that

☐ **A** your tank is only three quarters full
☐ **B** you have used a locking filler cap
☐ **C** you check your fuel gauge is working
☐ **D** your filler cap is securely fastened

When learning to drive it is a good idea to practise filling your car with fuel. Ask your instructor if you can use a petrol station and fill the fuel tank yourself. You need to know where the filler cap is located on the car you are driving in order to park on the correct side of the pump. Take care not to overfill the tank or spill fuel. Make sure you secure the filler cap as soon as you have replaced the fuel nozzle.

85 Mark *one* answer
If your vehicle uses diesel fuel, take extra care when refuelling. Diesel fuel when spilt is

☐ **A** sticky
☐ **B** odourless
☐ **C** clear
☐ **D** slippery

If you are using diesel, or are at a pump which has a diesel facility, be aware that there may be spilt fuel on the ground. Fuel contamination on the soles of your shoes may cause them to slip when using the foot pedals.

86 Mark *one* answer
What style of driving causes increased risk to everyone?

☐ **A** Considerate
☐ **B** Defensive
☐ **C** Competitive
☐ **D** Responsible

Competitive driving increases the risks to everyone and is the opposite of responsible, considerate and defensive driving. Defensive driving is about questioning the actions of other road users and being prepared for the unexpected. Don't be taken by surprise.

87 Mark *one* answer
Young, inexperienced and newly qualified drivers can often be involved in crashes. This is due to

☐ **A** being too cautious at junctions
☐ **B** driving in the middle of their lane
☐ **C** showing off and being competitive
☐ **D** staying within the speed limit

Newly qualified, and particularly young drivers, are more vulnerable in the first year after passing the test. Inexperience plays a part in this but it's essential to have the correct attitude. Be responsible and always show courtesy and consideration to other road users.

88 Mark *two* answers
Which TWO are badly affected if the tyres are under-inflated?

☐ **A** Braking
☐ **B** Steering
☐ **C** Changing gear
☐ **D** Parking

Your tyres are your only contact with the road so it is very important to ensure that they are free from defects, have sufficient tread depth and are correctly inflated. Correct tyre pressures help reduce the risk of skidding and provide a safer and more comfortable drive or ride.

89 Mark *one* answer
You must NOT sound your horn

☐ **A** between 10pm and 6am in a built-up area
☐ **B** at any time in a built-up area
☐ **C** between 11.30pm and 7am in a built-up area
☐ **D** between 11.30pm and 6am on any road

Vehicles can be noisy. Every effort must be made to prevent excessive noise, especially in built-up areas at night. Don't
• rev the engine
• sound the horn
unnecessarily.
It is illegal to sound your horn in a built-up area between 11.30pm and 7am, except when another vehicle poses a danger.

90 Mark *three* answers
The pictured vehicle is 'environmentally friendly' because it

☐ **A** reduces noise pollution
☐ **B** uses diesel fuel
☐ **C** uses electricity
☐ **D** uses unleaded fuel
☐ **E** reduces parking spaces
☐ **F** reduces town traffic

Trams are powered by electricity and therefore do not emit exhaust fumes. They are also much quieter than petrol or diesel engined vehicles and can carry a large number of passengers.

91 Mark *one* answer
Supertrams or Light Rapid Transit (LRT) systems are environmentally friendly because

☐ **A** they use diesel power
☐ **B** they use quieter roads
☐ **C** they use electric power
☐ **D** they do not operate during rush hour

This means that they do not emit toxic fumes, which add to city pollution problems. They are also a lot quieter and smoother to ride on.

92 Mark *one* answer
'Red routes' in major cities have been introduced to

- ☐ **A** raise the speed limits
- ☐ **B** help the traffic flow
- ☐ **C** provide better parking
- ☐ **D** allow lorries to load more freely

Traffic jams today are often caused by the volume of traffic. However, inconsiderate parking can lead to the closure of an inside lane or traffic having to wait for oncoming vehicles. Driving slowly in traffic increases fuel consumption and causes a build-up of exhaust fumes.

93 Mark *one* answer
Road humps, chicanes, and narrowings are

- ☐ **A** always at major road works
- ☐ **B** used to increase traffic speed
- ☐ **C** at toll-bridge approaches only
- ☐ **D** traffic calming measures

Traffic calming measures help keep vehicle speeds low in congested areas where there are pedestrians and children. A pedestrian is much more likely to survive a collision with a vehicle travelling at 20mph than at 40mph.

94 Mark *one* answer
The purpose of a catalytic converter is to reduce

- ☐ **A** fuel consumption
- ☐ **B** the risk of fire
- ☐ **C** toxic exhaust gases
- ☐ **D** engine wear

Catalytic converters are designed to reduce a large percentage of toxic emissions. They work more efficiently when the engine has reached its normal working temperature.

95 Mark *one* answer
Catalytic converters are fitted to make the

- ☐ **A** engine produce more power
- ☐ **B** exhaust system easier to replace
- ☐ **C** engine run quietly
- ☐ **D** exhaust fumes cleaner

Harmful gases in the exhaust system pollute the atmosphere. These gases are reduced by up to 90% if a catalytic converter is fitted. Cleaner air benefits everyone, especially people who live or work near congested roads.

96 Mark *one* answer
It is essential that tyre pressures are checked regularly. When should this be done?

- ☐ **A** After any lengthy journey
- ☐ **B** After travelling at high speed
- ☐ **C** When tyres are hot
- ☐ **D** When tyres are cold

When you check the tyre pressures do so when the tyres are cold. This will give you a more accurate reading. The heat generated from a long journey will raise the pressure inside the tyre.

97 Mark *one* answer
When should you NOT use your horn in a built-up area?

☐ **A** Between 8pm and 8am
☐ **B** Between 9pm and dawn
☐ **C** Between dusk and 8am
☐ **D** Between 11.30pm and 7am

By law you must not sound your horn in a built-up area between 11.30pm and 7am. The exception to this is when another road user poses a danger.

98 Mark *one* answer
You will use more fuel if your tyres are

☐ **A** under-inflated
☐ **B** of different makes
☐ **C** over-inflated
☐ **D** new and hardly used

Check your tyre pressures frequently – normally once a week. If pressures are lower than those recommended by the manufacturer, there will be more 'rolling resistance'. The engine will have to work harder to overcome this, leading to increased fuel consumption.

99 Mark *two* answers
How should you dispose of a used battery?

☐ **A** Take it to a local authority site
☐ **B** Put it in the dustbin
☐ **C** Break it up into pieces
☐ **D** Leave it on waste land
☐ **E** Take it to a garage
☐ **F** Burn it on a fire

Batteries contain acid which is hazardous and must be disposed of safely.

100 Mark *one* answer
What is most likely to cause high fuel consumption?

☐ **A** Poor steering control
☐ **B** Accelerating around bends
☐ **C** Staying in high gears
☐ **D** Harsh braking and accelerating

Accelerating and braking gently and smoothly will help to save fuel, reduce wear on your vehicle and is better for the environment.

101 Mark *one* answer
The fluid level in your battery is low. What should you top it up with?

☐ **A** Battery acid
☐ **B** Distilled water
☐ **C** Engine oil
☐ **D** Engine coolant

Some modern batteries are maintenance-free. Check your vehicle handbook and, if necessary, make sure that the plates in each battery cell are covered.

102 Mark *one* answer
You are parked on the road at night. Where must you use parking lights?

☐ **A** Where there are continuous white lines in the middle of the road
☐ **B** Where the speed limit exceeds 30mph
☐ **C** Where you are facing oncoming traffic
☐ **D** Where you are near a bus stop

When parking at night, park in the direction of the traffic. This will enable other road users to see the reflectors on the rear of your vehicle. Use your parking lights if the speed limit is over 30mph.

103 Mark *three* answers

Motor vehicles can harm the environment. This has resulted in

- ☐ **A** air pollution
- ☐ **B** damage to buildings
- ☐ **C** less risk to health
- ☐ **D** improved public transport
- ☐ **E** less use of electrical vehicles
- ☐ **F** using up of natural resources

Exhaust emissions are harmful to health. Together with vibration from heavy traffic this can result in damage to buildings. Most petrol and diesel fuels come from a finite and non-renewable source. Anything you can do to reduce your use of these fuels will help the environment.

104 Mark *three* answers

Excessive or uneven tyre wear can be caused by faults in which THREE of the following?

- ☐ **A** The gearbox
- ☐ **B** The braking system
- ☐ **C** The accelerator
- ☐ **D** The exhaust system
- ☐ **E** Wheel alignment
- ☐ **F** The suspension

Regular servicing will help to detect faults at an early stage and this will avoid the risk of minor faults becoming serious or even dangerous.

105 Mark *one* answer

You need to top up your battery. What level should you fill to?

- ☐ **A** The top of the battery
- ☐ **B** Half-way up the battery
- ☐ **C** Just below the cell plates
- ☐ **D** Just above the cell plates

Top up the battery with distilled water and make sure each cell plate is covered.

106 Mark *one* answer

You are parking on a two-way road at night. The speed limit is 40mph. You should park on the

- ☐ **A** left with parking lights on
- ☐ **B** left with no lights on
- ☐ **C** right with parking lights on
- ☐ **D** right with dipped headlights on

At night all vehicles must display parking lights when parked on a road with a speed limit greater than 30mph. They should be close to the kerb, facing in the direction of the traffic flow and not within a distance as specified in The Highway Code.

107 Mark *one* answer

Before starting a journey it is wise to plan your route. How can you do this?

- ☐ **A** Look at a map
- ☐ **B** Contact your local garage
- ☐ **C** Look in your vehicle handbook
- ☐ **D** Check your vehicle registration document

Planning your journey before you set out can help to make it much easier, more pleasant and may help to ease traffic congestion. Look at a map to help you to do this. You may need different scale maps depending on where and how far you're going. Printing or writing out the route can also help.

108 Mark *one* answer ⬛ NI

It can help to plan your route before starting a journey. You can do this by contacting

- ☐ **A** your local filling station
- ☐ **B** a motoring organisation
- ☐ **C** the Driver Vehicle Licensing Agency
- ☐ **D** your vehicle manufacturer

Most motoring organisations will give you a detailed plan of your trip showing directions and distance. Some will also include advice on rest and fuel stops. The Highways Agency website will also give you information on roadworks and incidents and gives expected delay times.

109 Mark *one* answer

How can you plan your route before starting a long journey?

- ☐ **A** Check your vehicle's workshop manual
- ☐ **B** Ask your local garage
- ☐ **C** Use a route planner on the internet
- ☐ **D** Consult your travel agents

Various route planners are available on the internet. Most of them give you various options allowing you to choose the most direct, quickest or scenic route. They can also include rest and fuel stops and distances. Print them off and take them with you.

110 Mark *one* answer

Planning your route before setting out can be helpful. How can you do this?

- ☐ **A** Look in a motoring magazine
- ☐ **B** Only visit places you know
- ☐ **C** Try to travel at busy times
- ☐ **D** Print or write down the route

Print or write down your route before setting out. Some places are not well signed so using place names and road numbers may help you avoid problems en route. Try to get an idea of how far you're going before you leave. You can also use it to re-check the next stage at each rest stop.

111 Mark *one* answer

Why is it a good idea to plan your journey to avoid busy times?

☐ **A** You will have an easier journey
☐ **B** You will have a more stressful journey
☐ **C** Your journey time will be longer
☐ **D** It will cause more traffic congestion

No one likes to spend time in traffic queues. Try to avoid busy times related to school or work travel. As well as moving vehicles you should also consider congestion caused by parked cars, buses and coaches around schools.

112 Mark *one* answer

Planning your journey to avoid busy times has a number of advantages. One of these is

☐ **A** your journey will take longer
☐ **B** you will have a more pleasant journey
☐ **C** you will cause more pollution
☐ **D** your stress level will be greater

Having a pleasant journey can have safety benefits. You will be less tired and stressed and this will allow you to concentrate more on your driving or riding.

113 Mark *one* answer

It is a good idea to plan your journey to avoid busy times. This is because

☐ **A** your vehicle will use more fuel
☐ **B** you will see less road works
☐ **C** it will help to ease congestion
☐ **D** you will travel a much shorter distance

Avoiding busy times means that you are not adding needlessly to traffic congestion. Other advantages are that you will use less fuel and feel less stressed.

114 Mark *one* answer

By avoiding busy times when travelling

☐ **A** you are more likely to be held up
☐ **B** your journey time will be longer
☐ **C** you will travel a much shorter distance
☐ **D** you are less likely to be delayed

If possible, avoid the early morning and late afternoon and early evening 'rush hour'. Doing this should allow you to travel in a more relaxed frame of mind, concentrate solely on what you're doing and arrive at your destination feeling less stressed.

115 Mark *one* answer

It can help to plan your route before starting a journey. Why should you also plan an alternative route?

☐ **A** Your original route may be blocked
☐ **B** Your maps may have different scales
☐ **C** You may find you have to pay a congestion charge
☐ **D** Because you may get held up by a tractor

It can be frustrating and worrying to find your planned route is blocked by roadworks or diversions. If you have planned an alternative you will feel less stressed and more able to concentrate fully on your driving or riding. If your original route is mostly on motorways it's a good idea to plan an alternative using non-motorway roads. Always carry a map with you just in case you need to refer to it.

116 Mark *one* answer

As well as planning your route before starting a journey, you should also plan an alternative route. Why is this?

☐ **A** To let another driver overtake
☐ **B** Your first route may be blocked
☐ **C** To avoid a railway level crossing
☐ **D** In case you have to avoid emergency vehicles

It's a good idea to plan an alternative route in case your original route is blocked for any reason. You're less likely to feel worried and stressed if you've got an alternative in mind. This will enable you to concentrate fully on your driving or riding. Always carry a map that covers the area you will travel in.

117 Mark *one* answer

You are making an appointment and will have to travel a long distance. You should

☐ **A** allow plenty of time for your journey
☐ **B** plan to go at busy times
☐ **C** avoid all national speed limit roads
☐ **D** prevent other drivers from overtaking

Always allow plenty of time for your journey in case of unforeseen problems. Anything can happen, punctures, breakdowns, road closures, diversions etc. You will feel less stressed and less inclined to take risks if you are not 'pushed for time'.

118 Mark *one* answer

Rapid acceleration and heavy braking can lead to

☐ **A** reduced pollution
☐ **B** increased fuel consumption
☐ **C** reduced exhaust emissions
☐ **D** increased road safety

Using the controls smoothly can reduce fuel consumption by about 15% as well as reducing wear and tear on your vehicle. Plan ahead and anticipate changes of speed well in advance. This will reduce the need to accelerate rapidly or brake sharply.

119 Mark *one* answer

What percentage of all emissions does road transport account for?

☐ **A** 10%
☐ **B** 20%
☐ **C** 30%
☐ **D** 40%

Transport is an essential part of modern life but it does have environmental effects. In heavily populated areas traffic is the biggest source of air pollution. Eco-safe driving and riding will reduce emissions and can make a surprising difference to local air quality.

120 Mark *one* answer

Which of these, if allowed to get low, could cause you to crash?

☐ **A** Anti-freeze level
☐ **B** Brake fluid level
☐ **C** Battery water level
☐ **D** Radiator coolant level

You should carry out frequent checks on all fluid levels but particularly brake fluid. As the brake pads or shoes wear down the brake fluid level will drop. If it drops below the minimum mark on the fluid reservoir, air could enter the hydraulic system and lead to a loss of braking efficiency or complete brake failure.

121 Mark *one* answer

New petrol-engined cars must be fitted with catalytic converters. The reason for this is to

☐ **A** control exhaust noise levels
☐ **B** prolong the life of the exhaust system
☐ **C** allow the exhaust system to be recycled
☐ **D** reduce harmful exhaust emissions

We should all be concerned about the effect traffic has on our environment. Fumes from vehicles are polluting the air around us. Catalytic converters act like a filter, removing some of the toxic waste from exhaust gases.

122 Mark *one* answer

What can cause heavy steering?

☐ **A** Driving on ice
☐ **B** Badly worn brakes
☐ **C** Over-inflated tyres
☐ **D** Under-inflated tyres

If your tyre pressures are low this will increase the drag on the road surface and make the steering feel heavy. Your vehicle will also use more fuel. Incorrectly inflated tyres can affect the braking, cornering and handling of your vehicle to a dangerous level.

123 Mark *two* answers

Driving with under-inflated tyres can affect

☐ **A** engine temperature
☐ **B** fuel consumption
☐ **C** braking
☐ **D** oil pressure

Keeping your vehicle's tyres correctly inflated is a legal requirement.
Driving with correctly inflated tyres will use less fuel and your vehicle will brake more safely.

124 Mark *two* answers

Excessive or uneven tyre wear can be caused by faults in the

☐ **A** gearbox   ☐ **B** braking system
☐ **C** suspension   ☐ **D** exhaust system

Uneven wear on your tyres can be caused by the condition of your vehicle. Having it serviced regularly will ensure that the brakes, steering and wheel alignment are maintained in good order.

125 Mark *one* answer

The main cause of brake fade is

☐ **A** the brakes overheating
☐ **B** air in the brake fluid
☐ **C** oil on the brakes
☐ **D** the brakes out of adjustment

If your vehicle is fitted with drum brakes they can get hot and lose efficiency. This happens when they're used continually, such as on a long, steep, downhill stretch of road. Using a lower gear will assist the braking and help prevent the vehicle gaining momentum.

126 Mark *one* answer

Your anti-lock brakes warning light stays on. You should

☐ **A** check the brake fluid level
☐ **B** check the footbrake free play
☐ **C** check that the handbrake is released
☐ **D** have the brakes checked immediately

Consult the vehicle handbook or garage before driving the vehicle. Only drive to a garage if it is safe to do so. If you're not sure get expert help.

127 Mark *one* answer

While driving, this warning light on your dashboard comes on. It means

☐ **A** a fault in the braking system
☐ **B** the engine oil is low
☐ **C** a rear light has failed
☐ **D** your seat belt is not fastened

Don't ignore this warning light. A fault in your braking system could have dangerous consequences.

128 Mark *one* answer

It is important to wear suitable shoes when you are driving. Why is this?

☐ **A** To prevent wear on the pedals
☐ **B** To maintain control of the pedals
☐ **C** To enable you to adjust your seat
☐ **D** To enable you to walk for assistance if you break down

When you're going to drive, ensure that you're wearing suitable clothing.
  Comfortable shoes will ensure that you have proper control of the foot pedals.

129 Mark *one* answer

What will reduce the risk of neck injury resulting from a collision?

☐ **A** An air-sprung seat
☐ **B** Anti-lock brakes
☐ **C** A collapsible steering wheel
☐ **D** A properly adjusted head restraint

If you're involved in a collision, head restraints will reduce the risk of neck injury. They must be properly adjusted. Make sure they aren't positioned too low, in a crash this could cause damage to the neck.

130 Mark *one* answer

You are testing your suspension. You notice that your vehicle keeps bouncing when you press down on the front wing. What does this mean?

☐ **A** Worn tyres
☐ **B** Tyres under-inflated
☐ **C** Steering wheel not located centrally
☐ **D** Worn shock absorbers

If you find that your vehicle bounces as you drive around a corner or bend in the road, the shock absorbers might be worn. Press down on the front wing and, if the vehicle continues to bounce, take it to be checked by a qualified mechanic.

131 Mark *one* answer

A roof rack fitted to your car will

☐ **A** reduce fuel consumption
☐ **B** improve the road handling
☐ **C** make your car go faster
☐ **D** increase fuel consumption

If you are carrying anything on a roof rack, make sure that any cover is securely fitted and does not flap about while driving. Aerodynamically designed roof boxes are available which reduce wind resistance and, in turn, fuel consumption.

132 Mark *one* answer

It is illegal to drive with tyres that

☐ **A** have been bought second-hand
☐ **B** have a large deep cut in the side wall
☐ **C** are of different makes
☐ **D** are of different tread patterns

When checking your tyres for cuts and bulges in the side walls, don't forget the inner walls (i.e. those facing each other under the vehicle).

133 Mark *one* answer

The legal minimum depth of tread for car tyres over three quarters of the breadth is

☐ **A** 1mm   ☐ **B** 1.6mm
☐ **C** 2.5mm   ☐ **D** 4mm

Tyres must have sufficient depth of tread to give them a good grip on the road surface. The legal minimum for cars is 1.6mm.
    This depth should be across the central three quarters of the breadth of the tyre and around the entire circumference.

134 Mark *one* answer
You are carrying two 13-year-old children and their parents in your car. Who is responsible for seeing that the children wear seat belts?

☐ **A** The children's parents
☐ **B** You, the driver
☐ **C** The front-seat passenger
☐ **D** The children

Seat belts save lives and reduce the risk of injury. If you are carrying passengers under 14 years of age it's your responsibility as the driver to ensure that their seat belts are fastened or they are seated in an approved child restraint.

135 Mark *one* answer
When a roof rack is not in use it should be removed. Why is this?

☐ **A** It will affect the suspension
☐ **B** It is illegal
☐ **C** It will affect your braking
☐ **D** It will waste fuel

We are all responsible for the environment we live in. If each driver takes responsibility for conserving fuel, together it will make a difference.

136 Mark *three* answers
How can you, as a driver, help the environment?

☐ **A** By reducing your speed
☐ **B** By gentle acceleration
☐ **C** By using leaded fuel
☐ **D** By driving faster
☐ **E** By harsh acceleration
☐ **F** By servicing your vehicle properly

Rapid acceleration and heavy braking lead to greater fuel consumption. They also increase wear and tear on your vehicle.

Having your vehicle regularly serviced means your engine will maintain its efficiency, produce cleaner emissions and lengthen its life.

137 Mark *three* answers
To help the environment, you can avoid wasting fuel by

☐ **A** having your vehicle properly serviced
☐ **B** making sure your tyres are correctly inflated
☐ **C** not over-revving in the lower gears
☐ **D** driving at higher speeds where possible
☐ **E** keeping an empty roof rack properly fitted
☐ **F** servicing your vehicle less regularly

If you don't have your vehicle serviced regularly, the engine will not burn all the fuel efficiently. This will cause excess gases to be discharged into the atmosphere.

138 Mark *three* answers
To reduce the volume of traffic on the roads you could

- ☐ **A** use public transport more often
- ☐ **B** share a car when possible
- ☐ **C** walk or cycle on short journeys
- ☐ **D** travel by car at all times
- ☐ **E** use a car with a smaller engine
- ☐ **F** drive in a bus lane

Walking or cycling are good ways to get exercise. Using public transport also gives the opportunity for exercise if you walk to the railway station or bus stop. Leave the car at home whenever you can.

139 Mark *three* answers
Which THREE of the following are most likely to waste fuel?

- ☐ **A** Reducing your speed
- ☐ **B** Carrying unnecessary weight
- ☐ **C** Using the wrong grade of fuel
- ☐ **D** Under-inflated tyres
- ☐ **E** Using different brands of fuel
- ☐ **F** A fitted, empty roof rack

Wasting fuel costs you money and also causes unnecessary pollution. Ensuring your tyres are correctly inflated, avoiding carrying unnecessary weight, and removing a roof rack that is not in use, will all help to reduce your fuel consumption.

140 Mark *three* answers
Which THREE things can you, as a road user, do to help the environment?

- ☐ **A** Cycle when possible
- ☐ **B** Drive on under-inflated tyres
- ☐ **C** Use the choke for as long as possible on a cold engine
- ☐ **D** Have your vehicle properly tuned and serviced
- ☐ **E** Watch the traffic and plan ahead
- ☐ **F** Brake as late as possible without skidding

Although the car is a convenient form of transport it can also cause damage to health and the environment, especially when used on short journeys. Before you travel consider other types of transport. Walking and cycling are better for your health and public transport can be quicker, more convenient and less stressful than driving.

141 Mark *one* answer
To help protect the environment you should NOT

- ☐ **A** remove your roof rack when unloaded
- ☐ **B** use your car for very short journeys
- ☐ **C** walk, cycle, or use public transport
- ☐ **D** empty the boot of unnecessary weight

Try not to use your car as a matter of routine. For shorter journeys, consider walking or cycling instead – this is much better for both you and the environment.

142 Mark *three* answers
Which THREE does the law require you to keep in good condition?

☐ **A** Gears
☐ **B** Transmission
☐ **C** Headlights
☐ **D** Windscreen
☐ **E** Seat belts

Other things to check include lights: get someone to help you check the brake lights and indicators. Battery: a lot of these are now maintenance-free. Steering: check for play in the steering. Oil, water and suspension also need checking. Always check that the speedometer is working once you've moved off.

143 Mark *one* answer
Driving at 70mph uses more fuel than driving at 50mph by up to

☐ **A** 10%
☐ **B** 30%
☐ **C** 75%
☐ **D** 100%

Your vehicle will use less fuel if you avoid heavy acceleration. The higher the engine revs, the more fuel you will use. Using the same gear, a vehicle travelling at 70mph will use up to 30% more fuel to cover the same distance, than at 50mph. However, don't travel so slowly that you inconvenience or endanger other road users.

144 Mark *one* answer
Your vehicle pulls to one side when braking. You should

☐ **A** change the tyres around
☐ **B** consult your garage as soon as possible
☐ **C** pump the pedal when braking
☐ **D** use your handbrake at the same time

The brakes on your vehicle must be effective and properly adjusted. If your vehicle pulls to one side when braking, take it to be checked by a qualified mechanic. Don't take risks.

145 Mark *one* answer
Unbalanced wheels on a car may cause

☐ **A** the steering to pull to one side
☐ **B** the steering to vibrate
☐ **C** the brakes to fail
☐ **D** the tyres to deflate

If your wheels are out of balance it will cause the steering to vibrate at certain speeds. It is not a fault that will rectify itself. You will have to take your vehicle to a garage or tyre fitting firm as this is specialist work.

146 Mark *two* answers
Turning the steering wheel while your car is stationary can cause damage to the

☐ **A** gearbox   ☐ **B** engine
☐ **C** brakes   ☐ **D** steering
☐ **E** tyres

Turning the steering wheel when the car is not moving can cause unnecessary wear to the tyres and steering mechanism. This is known as 'dry' steering.

147 Mark *one* answer
**You have to leave valuables in your car.
It would be safer to**

☐ **A** put them in a carrier bag
☐ **B** park near a school entrance
☐ **C** lock them out of sight
☐ **D** park near a bus stop

If you have to leave valuables in your car, always lock them out of sight. If you can see them, so can a thief.

148 Mark *one* answer
How could you deter theft from your car when leaving it unattended?

☐ **A** Leave valuables in a carrier bag
☐ **B** Lock valuables out of sight
☐ **C** Put valuables on the seats
☐ **D** Leave valuables on the floor

If you can see valuables in your car so can a thief. If you can't take them with you lock them out of sight or you risk losing them, as well as having your car damaged.

149 Mark *one* answer
Which of the following may help to deter a thief from stealing your car?

☐ **A** Always keeping the headlights on
☐ **B** Fitting reflective glass windows
☐ **C** Always keeping the interior light on
☐ **D** Etching the car number on the windows

Having your car registration number etched on all your windows is a cheap and effective way to deter professional car thieves.

150 Mark *one* answer
Which of the following should not be kept in your vehicle?

☐ **A** A first aid kit
☐ **B** A road atlas
☐ **C** The tax disc
☐ **D** The vehicle documents

Never leave the vehicle's documents inside it. They would help a thief dispose of the vehicle more easily.

151 Mark *one* answer
What should you do when leaving your vehicle?

☐ **A** Put valuable documents under the seats
☐ **B** Remove all valuables
☐ **C** Cover valuables with a blanket
☐ **D** Leave the interior light on

When leaving your vehicle unattended it is best to take valuables with you. If you can't, then lock them out of sight in the boot. If you can see valuables in your car, so can a thief.

152 Mark *one* answer
Which of these is most likely to deter the theft of your vehicle?

☐ **A** An immobiliser
☐ **B** Tinted windows
☐ **C** Locking wheel nuts
☐ **D** A sun screen

An immobiliser makes it more difficult for your vehicle to be driven off by a thief. It is a particular deterrent to opportunist thieves.

153 Mark *one* answer

When parking and leaving your car you should

☐ **A** park under a shady tree
☐ **B** remove the tax disc
☐ **C** park in a quiet road
☐ **D** engage the steering lock

When you leave your car always engage the steering lock. This increases the security of your vehicle, as the ignition key is needed to release the steering lock.

154 Mark *one* answer

When leaving your vehicle parked and unattended you should

☐ **A** park near a busy junction
☐ **B** park in a housing estate
☐ **C** remove the key and lock it
☐ **D** leave the left indicator on

An unlocked car is an open invitation to thieves. Leaving the keys in the ignition not only makes your car easy to steal, it could also invalidate your insurance.

155 Mark *two* answers

Which TWO of the following will improve fuel consumption?

☐ **A** Reducing your road speed
☐ **B** Planning well ahead
☐ **C** Late and harsh braking
☐ **D** Driving in lower gears
☐ **E** Short journeys with a cold engine
☐ **F** Rapid acceleration

Harsh braking, constant gear changes and harsh acceleration increase fuel consumption. An engine uses less fuel when travelling at a constant low speed.

You need to look well ahead so you are able to anticipate hazards early. Easing off the accelerator and timing your approach, at junctions, for example, could actually improve the fuel consumption of your vehicle.

156 Mark *one* answer

You service your own vehicle. How should you get rid of the old engine oil?

☐ **A** Take it to a local authority site
☐ **B** Pour it down a drain
☐ **C** Tip it into a hole in the ground
☐ **D** Put it into your dustbin

It is illegal to pour engine oil down any drain. Oil is a pollutant and harmful to wildlife. Dispose of it safely at an authorised site.

157 Mark *one* answer

Why do MOT tests include a strict exhaust emission test?

☐ **A** To recover the cost of expensive garage equipment
☐ **B** To help protect the environment against pollution
☐ **C** To discover which fuel supplier is used the most
☐ **D** To make sure diesel and petrol engines emit the same fumes

Emission tests are carried out to ensure your vehicle's engine is operating efficiently. This ensures the pollution produced by the engine is kept to a minimum. If your vehicle is not serviced regularly, it may fail the annual MOT test.

158 Mark *three* answers

To reduce the damage your vehicle causes to the environment you should

☐ **A** use narrow side streets
☐ **B** avoid harsh acceleration
☐ **C** brake in good time
☐ **D** anticipate well ahead
☐ **E** use busy routes

By looking well ahead and recognising hazards early you can avoid last-minute harsh braking. Watch the traffic flow and look well ahead for potential hazards so you can control your speed accordingly. Avoid over-revving the engine and accelerating harshly as this increases wear to the engine and uses more fuel.

159 Mark *one* answer

Your vehicle has a catalytic converter. Its purpose is to reduce

☐ **A** exhaust noise
☐ **B** fuel consumption
☐ **C** exhaust emissions
☐ **D** engine noise

Catalytic converters reduce the harmful gases given out by the engine. The gases are changed by a chemical process as they pass through a special filter.

160 Mark *two* answers

A properly serviced vehicle will give

☐ **A** lower insurance premiums
☐ **B** you a refund on your road tax
☐ **C** better fuel economy
☐ **D** cleaner exhaust emissions

When you purchase your vehicle, check at what intervals you should have it serviced. This can vary depending on model and manufacturer. Use the service manual and keep it up to date. The cost of a service may well be less than the cost of running a poorly maintained vehicle.

161 Mark *one* answer

You enter a road where there are road humps. What should you do?

- ☐ **A** Maintain a reduced speed throughout
- ☐ **B** Accelerate quickly between each one
- ☐ **C** Always keep to the maximum legal speed
- ☐ **D** Drive slowly at school times only

The humps are there for a reason – to reduce the speed of the traffic. Don't accelerate harshly between them as this means you will only have to brake harshly to negotiate the next hump. Harsh braking and accelerating uses more fuel.

162 Mark *one* answer

When should you especially check the engine oil level?

- ☐ **A** Before a long journey
- ☐ **B** When the engine is hot
- ☐ **C** Early in the morning
- ☐ **D** Every 6,000 miles

During long journeys an engine can use more oil than on shorter trips. Insufficient oil is potentially dangerous: it can lead to excessive wear and expensive repairs.

Most cars have a dipstick to allow the oil level to be checked. If not, you should refer to the vehicle's handbook. Also make checks on
- • fuel
- • water
- • tyres.

163 Mark *one* answer

You are having difficulty finding a parking space in a busy town. You can see there is space on the zigzag lines of a zebra crossing. Can you park there?

- ☐ **A** No, unless you stay with your car
- ☐ **B** Yes, in order to drop off a passenger
- ☐ **C** Yes, if you do not block people from crossing
- ☐ **D** No, not in any circumstances

It's an offence to park there. You will be causing an obstruction by obscuring the view of both pedestrians and drivers.

164 Mark *one* answer

When leaving your car unattended for a few minutes you should

- ☐ **A** leave the engine running
- ☐ **B** switch the engine off but leave the key in
- ☐ **C** lock it and remove the key
- ☐ **D** park near a traffic warden

Always switch off the engine, remove the key and lock your car, even if you are only leaving it for a few minutes.

165 Mark *one* answer

When parking and leaving your car for a few minutes you should

- ☐ **A** leave it unlocked
- ☐ **B** lock it and remove the key
- ☐ **C** leave the hazard warning lights on
- ☐ **D** leave the interior light on

Always remove the key and lock your car even if you only leave it for a few minutes.

166 Mark *one* answer

When leaving your vehicle where should you park if possible?

- ☐ **A** Opposite a traffic island
- ☐ **B** In a secure car park
- ☐ **C** On a bend
- ☐ **D** At or near a taxi rank

Whenever possible leave your car in a secure car park. This will help stop thieves.

167 Mark *three* answers

In which THREE places would parking your vehicle cause danger or obstruction to other road users?

- ☐ **A** In front of a property entrance
- ☐ **B** At or near a bus stop
- ☐ **C** On your driveway
- ☐ **D** In a marked parking space
- ☐ **E** On the approach to a level crossing

Don't park your vehicle where parking restrictions apply. Think carefully before you slow down and stop. Look at road markings and signs to ensure that you aren't parking illegally.

168 Mark *three* answers

In which THREE places would parking cause an obstruction to others?

- ☐ **A** Near the brow of a hill
- ☐ **B** In a lay-by
- ☐ **C** Where the kerb is raised
- ☐ **D** Where the kerb has been lowered for wheelchairs
- ☐ **E** At or near a bus stop

Think about the effect your parking will have on other road users. Don't forget that not all vehicles are the size of a car. Large vehicles will need more room to pass and might need more time too.

Parking out of the view of traffic, such as before the brow of a hill, causes unnecessary risks. Think before you park.

169 Mark *one* answer

You are away from home and have to park your vehicle overnight. Where should you leave it?

- ☐ **A** Opposite another parked vehicle
- ☐ **B** In a quiet road
- ☐ **C** Opposite a traffic island
- ☐ **D** In a secure car park

When leaving your vehicle unattended, use a secure car park whenever possible.

170 Mark *one* answer

The most important reason for having a properly adjusted head restraint is to

☐ **A** make you more comfortable
☐ **B** help you to avoid neck injury
☐ **C** help you to relax
☐ **D** help you to maintain your driving position

The restraint should be adjusted so that it gives maximum protection to the head and neck. This will help in the event of a rear-end collision.

171 Mark *two* answers

As a driver you can cause more damage to the environment by

☐ **A** choosing a fuel-efficient vehicle
☐ **B** making a lot of short journeys
☐ **C** driving in as high a gear as possible
☐ **D** accelerating as quickly as possible
☐ **E** having your vehicle regularly serviced

For short journeys it may be quicker to walk, or cycle, which is far better for your health. Time spent stationary in traffic with the engine running is damaging to health, the environment and expensive in fuel costs.

172 Mark *one* answer

As a driver, you can help reduce pollution levels in town centres by

☐ **A** driving more quickly
☐ **B** over-revving in a low gear
☐ **C** walking or cycling
☐ **D** driving short journeys

Using a vehicle for short journeys means the engine does not have time to reach its normal running temperature. When an engine is running below its normal running temperature it produces increased amounts of pollution. Walking and cycling do not create pollution and have health benefits as well.

173 Mark *one* answer

How can you reduce the chances of your car being broken into when leaving it unattended?

☐ **A** Take all valuables with you
☐ **B** Park near a taxi rank
☐ **C** Place any valuables on the floor
☐ **D** Park near a fire station

When leaving your car take all valuables with you if you can, otherwise lock them out of sight.

174 Mark *one* answer

How can you help to prevent your car radio being stolen?

☐ **A** Park in an unlit area
☐ **B** Hide the radio with a blanket
☐ **C** Park near a busy junction
☐ **D** Install a security-coded radio

A security-coded radio can deter thieves as it is likely to be of little use when removed from the vehicle.

175 Mark *one* answer

You are parking your car. You have some valuables which you are unable to take with you. What should you do?

☐ **A** Park near a police station
☐ **B** Put them under the driver's seat
☐ **C** Lock them out of sight
☐ **D** Park in an unlit side road

Your vehicle is like a shop window for thieves. Either remove all valuables or lock them out of sight.

176 Mark *one* answer

Wherever possible, which one of the following should you do when parking at night?

☐ **A** Park in a quiet car park
☐ **B** Park in a well-lit area
☐ **C** Park facing against the flow of traffic
☐ **D** Park next to a busy junction

If you are away from home, try to avoid leaving your vehicle unattended in poorly-lit areas. If possible park in a secure, well-lit car park.

177 Mark *one* answer

How can you lessen the risk of your vehicle being broken into at night?

☐ **A** Leave it in a well-lit area
☐ **B** Park in a quiet side road
☐ **C** Don't engage the steering lock
☐ **D** Park in a poorly-lit area

Having your vehicle broken into or stolen can be very distressing and inconvenient. Avoid leaving your vehicle unattended in poorly-lit areas.

178 Mark *one* answer

To help keep your car secure you could join a

☐ **A** vehicle breakdown organisation
☐ **B** vehicle watch scheme
☐ **C** advanced driver's scheme
☐ **D** car maintenance class

The vehicle watch scheme helps reduce the risk of having your car stolen. By displaying high visibility vehicle watch stickers in your car you are inviting the police to stop your vehicle if seen in use between midnight and 5am.

179 Mark *one* answer

On a vehicle, where would you find a catalytic converter?

☐ **A** In the fuel tank
☐ **B** In the air filter
☐ **C** On the cooling system
☐ **D** On the exhaust system

Although carbon dioxide is still produced, a catalytic converter reduces the toxic and polluting gases by up to 90%. Unleaded fuel must be used in vehicles fitted with a catalytic converter.

180 Mark *one* answer
When leaving your car to help keep it secure you should

- ☐ **A** leave the hazard warning lights on
- ☐ **B** lock it and remove the key
- ☐ **C** park on a one-way street
- ☐ **D** park in a residential area

To help keep your car secure when you leave it, you should always remove the key from the ignition, lock it and take the key with you. Don't make it easy for thieves.

181 Mark *one* answer
You will find that driving smoothly can

- ☐ **A** reduce journey times by about 15%
- ☐ **B** increase fuel consumption by about 15%
- ☐ **C** reduce fuel consumption by about 15%
- ☐ **D** increase journey times by about 15%

Not only will you save about 15% of your fuel by driving smoothly, but you will also reduce the amount of wear and tear on your vehicle as well as reducing pollution. You will also feel more relaxed and have a more pleasant journey.

182 Mark *one* answer
You can save fuel when conditions allow by

- ☐ **A** using lower gears as often as possible
- ☐ **B** accelerating sharply in each gear
- ☐ **C** using each gear in turn
- ☐ **D** missing out some gears

Missing out intermediate gears when appropriate, helps to reduce the amount of time spent accelerating and decelerating – the time when your vehicle uses most fuel.

183 Mark *one* answer
How can driving in an eco-safe manner help protect the environment?

- ☐ **A** Through the legal enforcement of speed regulations
- ☐ **B** By increasing the number of cars on the road
- ☐ **C** Through increased fuel bills
- ☐ **D** By reducing exhaust emissions

Eco-safe driving is all about becoming a more environmentally-friendly driver. This will make your journeys more comfortable as well as considerably reducing your fuel bills and reducing emissions that can damage the environment.

184 Mark *one* answer
What does eco-safe driving achieve?

- ☐ **A** Increased fuel consumption
- ☐ **B** Improved road safety
- ☐ **C** Damage to the environment
- ☐ **D** Increased exhaust emissions

The emphasis is on hazard awareness and planning ahead. By looking well ahead you will have plenty of time to deal with hazards safely and won't need to brake sharply. This will also reduce damage to the environment.

185 Mark *one* answer

How can missing out some gear changes save fuel?

☐ **A** By reducing the amount of time you are accelerating
☐ **B** Because there is less need to use the footbrake
☐ **C** By controlling the amount of steering
☐ **D** Because coasting is kept to a minimum

Missing out some gears helps to reduce the amount of time you are accelerating and this saves fuel. You don't always need to change up or down through each gear. As you accelerate between each gear more fuel is injected into the engine than if you had maintained constant acceleration. Fewer gear changes means less fuel used.

186 Mark *one* answer

Missing out some gears saves fuel by reducing the amount of time you spend

☐ **A** braking
☐ **B** coasting
☐ **C** steering
☐ **D** accelerating

It is not always necessary to change up or down through each gear. Missing out intermediate gears helps to reduce the amount of time you are accelerating. Because fuel consumption is at its highest when accelerating this can save fuel.

187 Mark *one* answer

You are checking your trailer tyres. What is the legal minimum tread depth over the central three quarters of its breadth?

☐ **A** 1mm
☐ **B** 1.6mm
☐ **C** 2mm
☐ **D** 2.6mm

Trailers and caravans may be left in storage over the winter months and tyres can deteriorate. It's important to check their tread depth and also the pressures and general condition. The legal tread depth applies to the central three quarters of its breadth over its entire circumference.

188 Mark *one* answer

Fuel consumption is at its highest when you are

☐ **A** braking
☐ **B** coasting
☐ **C** accelerating
☐ **D** steering

Always try to use the accelerator smoothly. Taking your foot off the accelerator allows the momentum of the car to take you forward, especially when going downhill. This can save a considerable amount of fuel without any loss of control over the vehicle.

189 Mark *one* answer
Car passengers MUST wear a seat belt/restraint if one is available, unless they are

- ☐ **A** under 14 years old
- ☐ **B** under 1.5 metres (5 feet) in height
- ☐ **C** sitting in the rear seat
- ☐ **D** exempt for medical reasons

If you have adult passengers it is their responsibility to wear a seat belt, but you should still remind them to use them as they get in the car. It is your responsibility to ensure that all children in your car are secured with an appropriate restraint.

190 Mark *one* answer
Car passengers MUST wear a seat belt if one is available, unless they are

- ☐ **A** in a vehicle fitted with air bags
- ☐ **B** travelling within a congestion charging zone
- ☐ **C** sitting in the rear seat
- ☐ **D** exempt for medical reasons

When adult passengers are travelling in a vehicle, it is their own responsibility to wear a seat belt. However, you should still remind them to use a seat belt.

191 Mark *one* answer
You are driving the children of a friend home from school. They are both under 14 years old. Who is responsible for making sure they wear a seat belt or approved child restraint where required?

- ☐ **A** An adult passenger
- ☐ **B** The children
- ☐ **C** You, the driver
- ☐ **D** Your friend

Passengers should always be secured and safe. Children should be encouraged to fasten their seat belts or approved restraints themselves from an early age so that it becomes a matter of routine. As the driver you must check that they are fastened securely. It's your responsibility.

192 Mark *one* answer
You have too much oil in your engine. What could this cause?

- ☐ **A** Low oil pressure
- ☐ **B** Engine overheating
- ☐ **C** Chain wear
- ☐ **D** Oil leaks

Too much oil in the engine will create excess pressure and could damage engine seals and cause oil leaks. Any excess oil should be drained off.

193 Mark *one* answer

You are carrying a 5-year-old child in the back seat of your car. They are under 1.35 metres (4 feet 5 inches). A correct child restraint is NOT available. They MUST

☐ **A** sit behind the passenger seat
☐ **B** use an adult seat belt
☐ **C** share a belt with an adult
☐ **D** sit between two other children

Usually a correct child restraint MUST be used. In a few exceptional cases if one is not available an adult seat belt MUST be used. In a collision unrestrained objects and people can cause serious injury or even death.

194 Mark *one* answer

You are carrying a child using a rear-facing baby seat. You want to put it on the front passenger seat. What MUST you do before setting off?

☐ **A** Deactivate all front and rear airbags
☐ **B** Make sure any front passenger airbag is deactivated
☐ **C** Make sure all the child safety locks are off
☐ **D** Recline the front passenger seat

You MUST deactivate any frontal passenger airbag when using a rear-facing baby seat in a front passenger seat. It is ILLEGAL if you don't. If activated in a crash it could cause serious injury or death. Ensure you follow the manufacturers instructions. In some cars this is now done automatically.

195 Mark *one* answer

You are carrying an 11-year-old child in the back seat of your car. They are under 1.35 metres (4 feet 5 inches) in height. You MUST make sure that

☐ **A** they sit between two belted people
☐ **B** they can fasten their own seat belt
☐ **C** a suitable child restraint is available
☐ **D** they can see clearly out of the front window

It is your responsibility as a driver to ensure that children are secure and safe in your vehicle. Make sure you are familiar with the rules. In a few very exceptional cases when a child restraint is not available, an adult seat belt MUST be used. Child restraints and seat belts save lives!

196 Mark *one* answer

You are parked at the side of the road. You will be waiting for some time for a passenger. What should you do?

☐ **A** Switch off the engine
☐ **B** Apply the steering lock
☐ **C** Switch off the radio
☐ **D** Use your headlights

If your vehicle is stationary and is likely to remain so for some time, switch off the engine. We should all try to reduce global warming and pollution.

197 Mark *one* answer

You are using a rear-facing baby seat. You want to put it on the front passenger seat which is protected by a frontal airbag. What MUST you do before setting off?

☐ **A** Deactivate the airbag
☐ **B** Turn the seat to face sideways
☐ **C** Ask a passenger to hold the baby
☐ **D** Put the child in an adult seat belt

If the airbag activates near a baby seat, it could cause serious injury or even death to the child. It is illegal to fit a rear-facing baby seat into a passenger seat protected by an active frontal airbag. You MUST secure it in a different seat or deactivate the relevant airbag. Follow the manufacturers advice when fitting a baby seat.

198 Mark *one* answer

You are carrying a five-year-old child in the back seat of your car. They are under 1.35 metres (4 feet 5 inches) in height. They MUST use an adult seat belt ONLY if

☐ **A** a correct child restraint is not available
☐ **B** it is a lap type belt
☐ **C** they sit between two adults
☐ **D** it can be shared with another adult

You should make all efforts to ensure a correct child restraint is used, with very few exceptions. If in specific circumstances one is not available, then an adult seat belt MUST be used. Unrestrained objects, including people, can be thrown violently around in a collision, and may cause serious injury or even death!

199 Mark *one* answer

You are leaving your vehicle parked on a road unattended. When may you leave the engine running?

☐ **A** If you will be parking for less than five minutes
☐ **B** If the battery keeps going flat
☐ **C** When parked in a 20mph zone
☐ **D** Never if you are away from the vehicle

When you leave your vehicle parked on a road, switch off the engine and secure the vehicle. Make sure there aren't any valuables visible, shut all the windows, lock the vehicle, set the alarm if it has one and use an anti-theft device such as a steering wheel lock.

200 Mark *one* answer
Braking distances on ice can be

☐ **A** twice the normal distance
☐ **B** five times the normal distance
☐ **C** seven times the normal distance
☐ **D** ten times the normal distance

In icy and snowy weather, your stopping distance will increase by up to ten times compared to good, dry conditions.

Take extra care when braking, accelerating and steering, to cut down the risk of skidding.

201 Mark *one* answer
Freezing conditions will affect the distance it takes you to come to a stop. You should expect stopping distances to increase by up to

☐ **A** two times
☐ **B** three times
☐ **C** five times
☐ **D** ten times

Your tyre grip is greatly reduced on icy roads and you need to allow up to ten times the normal stopping distance.

202 Mark *one* answer
In windy conditions you need to take extra care when

☐ **A** using the brakes
☐ **B** making a hill start
☐ **C** turning into a narrow road
☐ **D** passing pedal cyclists

You should always give cyclists plenty of room when overtaking. When it's windy, a sudden gust could blow them off course.

203 Mark *one* answer
When approaching a right-hand bend you should keep well to the left. Why is this?

☐ **A** To improve your view of the road
☐ **B** To overcome the effect of the road's slope
☐ **C** To let faster traffic from behind overtake
☐ **D** To be positioned safely if you skid

Doing this will give you an earlier view around the bend and enable you to see any hazards sooner.

It also reduces the risk of collision with an oncoming vehicle that may have drifted over the centre line while taking the bend.

204 Mark *one* answer
You have just gone through deep water. To dry off the brakes you should

☐ **A** accelerate and keep to a high speed for a short time
☐ **B** go slowly while gently applying the brakes
☐ **C** avoid using the brakes at all for a few miles
☐ **D** stop for at least an hour to allow them time to dry

Water on the brakes will act as a lubricant, causing them to work less efficiently. Using the brakes lightly as you go along will dry them out.

205 Mark *two* answers

In very hot weather the road surface can become soft. Which TWO of the following will be most affected?

☐ **A** The suspension
☐ **B** The grip of the tyres
☐ **C** The braking
☐ **D** The exhaust

Only a small part of your tyres is in contact with the road. This is why you must consider the surface on which you're travelling, and alter your speed to suit the road conditions.

206 Mark *one* answer

Where are you most likely to be affected by a side wind?

☐ **A** On a narrow country lane
☐ **B** On an open stretch of road
☐ **C** On a busy stretch of road
☐ **D** On a long, straight road

In windy conditions, care must be taken on exposed roads. A strong gust of wind can blow you off course. Watch out for other road users who are particularly likely to be affected, such as cyclists, motorcyclists, high-sided lorries and vehicles towing trailers.

207 Mark *one* answer

In good conditions, what is the typical stopping distance at 70mph?

☐ **A** 53 metres (175 feet)
☐ **B** 60 metres (197 feet)
☐ **C** 73 metres (240 feet)
☐ **D** 96 metres (315 feet)

Note that this is the typical stopping distance. It will take at least this distance to think, brake and stop in good conditions. In poor conditions it will take much longer.

208 Mark *one* answer

What is the shortest overall stopping distance on a dry road at 60mph?

☐ **A** 53 metres (175 feet)
☐ **B** 58 metres (190 feet)
☐ **C** 73 metres (240 feet)
☐ **D** 96 metres (315 feet)

This distance is the equivalent of 18 car lengths. Try pacing out 73 metres and then look back. It's probably further than you think.

209 Mark *one* answer

You are following a vehicle at a safe distance on a wet road. Another driver overtakes you and pulls into the gap you have left. What should you do?

- ☐ **A** Flash your headlights as a warning
- ☐ **B** Try to overtake safely as soon as you can
- ☐ **C** Drop back to regain a safe distance
- ☐ **D** Stay close to the other vehicle until it moves on

Wet weather will affect the time it takes for you to stop and can affect your control. Your speed should allow you to stop safely and in good time. If another vehicle pulls into the gap you've left, ease back until you've regained your stopping distance.

210 Mark *one* answer

You are travelling at 50mph on a good, dry road. What is your typical overall stopping distance?

- ☐ **A** 36 metres (118 feet)
- ☐ **B** 53 metres (175 feet)
- ☐ **C** 75 metres (245 feet)
- ☐ **D** 96 metres (315 feet)

Even in good conditions it will usually take you further than you think to stop. Don't just learn the figures, make sure you understand how far the distance is.

211 Mark *one* answer

You are on a good, dry, road surface. Your brakes and tyres are good. What is the typical overall stopping distance at 40mph?

- ☐ **A** 23 metres (75 feet)
- ☐ **B** 36 metres (118 feet)
- ☐ **C** 53 metres (175 feet)
- ☐ **D** 96 metres (315 feet)

Stopping distances are affected by a number of variable factors. These include the type, model and condition of your vehicle, road and weather conditions, and your reaction time. Look well ahead for hazards and leave enough space between you and the vehicle in front. This should allow you to pull up safely if you have to, without braking sharply.

212 Mark *one* answer

What should you do when overtaking a motorcyclist in strong winds?

- ☐ **A** Pass close
- ☐ **B** Pass quickly
- ☐ **C** Pass wide
- ☐ **D** Pass immediately

In strong winds riders of two-wheeled vehicles are particularly vulnerable. When you overtake them allow plenty of room. Always check to the left as you pass.

213 Mark *one* answer

You are overtaking a motorcyclist in strong winds? What should you do?

☐ **A** Allow extra room
☐ **B** Give a thank you wave
☐ **C** Move back early
☐ **D** Sound your horn

It is easy for motorcyclists to be blown off course. Always give them plenty of room if you decide to overtake, especially in strong winds. Decide whether you need to overtake at all. Always check to the left as you pass.

214 Mark *one* answer

Overall stopping distance is made up of thinking and braking distance. You are on a good, dry road surface with good brakes and tyres. What is the typical BRAKING distance from 50mph?

☐ **A** 14 metres (46 feet)
☐ **B** 24 metres (80 feet)
☐ **C** 38 metres (125 feet)
☐ **D** 55 metres (180 feet)

Be aware this is just the braking distance. You need to add the thinking distance to this to give the OVERALL STOPPING DISTANCE. At 50mph the typical thinking distance will be 15 metres (50 feet), plus a braking distance of 38 metres (125 feet), giving an overall stopping distance of 53 metres (175 feet). The distance could be greater than this depending on your attention and response to any hazards. These figures are a general guide.

215 Mark *one* answer

In heavy motorway traffic the vehicle behind you is following too closely. How can you lower the risk of a collision?

☐ **A** Increase your distance from the vehicle in front
☐ **B** Operate the brakes sharply
☐ **C** Switch on your hazard lights
☐ **D** Move onto the hard shoulder and stop

On busy roads traffic may still travel at high speeds despite being close together. Don't follow too closely to the vehicle in front. If a driver behind seems to be 'pushing' you, gradually increase your distance from the vehicle in front by slowing down gently. This will give you more space in front if you have to brake, and lessen the risk of a collision involving several vehicles.

216 Mark *one* answer
You are following other vehicles in fog. You have your lights on. What else can you do to reduce the chances of being in a collision?

- ☐ **A** Keep close to the vehicle in front
- ☐ **B** Use your main beam instead of dipped headlights
- ☐ **C** Keep up with the faster vehicles
- ☐ **D** Reduce your speed and increase the gap in front

When it's foggy use dipped headlights. This will help you see and be seen by other road users. If visibility is seriously reduced consider using front and rear fog lights. Keep a sensible speed and don't follow the vehicle in front too closely. If the road is wet and slippery you'll need to allow twice the normal stopping distance.

217 Mark *three* answers
To avoid a collision when entering a contraflow system, you should

- ☐ **A** reduce speed in good time
- ☐ **B** switch lanes at any time to make progress
- ☐ **C** choose an appropriate lane in good time
- ☐ **D** keep the correct separation distance
- ☐ **E** increase speed to pass through quickly
- ☐ **F** follow other motorists closely to avoid long queues

In a contraflow system you will be travelling close to oncoming traffic and sometimes in narrow lanes. You should obey the temporary speed limit signs, get into the correct lane at the proper time and keep a safe separation distance from the vehicle ahead. When traffic is at a very low speed, merging in turn is recommended if it's safe and appropriate.

218 Mark *one* answer
What is the most common cause of skidding?

- ☐ **A** Worn tyres
- ☐ **B** Driver error
- ☐ **C** Other vehicles
- ☐ **D** Pedestrians

A skid happens when the driver changes the speed or direction of their vehicle so suddenly that the tyres can't keep their grip on the road.
   Remember that the risk of skidding on wet or icy roads is much greater than in dry conditions.

219 Mark *one* answer
You are driving on an icy road. How can you avoid wheel-spin?

- ☐ **A** Drive at a slow speed in as high a gear as possible
- ☐ **B** Use the handbrake if the wheels start to slip
- ☐ **C** Brake gently and repeatedly
- ☐ **D** Drive in a low gear at all times

If you're travelling on an icy road extra caution will be required to avoid loss of control. Keeping your speed down and using the highest gear possible will reduce the risk of the tyres losing their grip on this slippery surface.

220 Mark *one* answer
Skidding is mainly caused by

- ☐ **A** the weather ☐ **B** the driver
- ☐ **C** the vehicle ☐ **D** the road

You should always consider the conditions and drive accordingly.

221 Mark *two* answers
You are driving in freezing conditions. What should you do when approaching a sharp bend?

- ☐ **A** Slow down before you reach the bend
- ☐ **B** Gently apply your handbrake
- ☐ **C** Firmly use your footbrake
- ☐ **D** Coast into the bend
- ☐ **E** Avoid sudden steering movements

Harsh use of the accelerator, brakes or steering are likely to lead to skidding, especially on slippery surfaces. Avoid steering and braking at the same time.

In icy conditions it's very important that you constantly assess what's ahead, so that you can take appropriate action in plenty of time.

222 Mark *one* answer
You are turning left on a slippery road. The back of your vehicle slides to the right. You should

- ☐ **A** brake firmly and not turn the steering wheel
- ☐ **B** steer carefully to the left
- ☐ **C** steer carefully to the right
- ☐ **D** brake firmly and steer to the left

Steer into the skid but be careful not to overcorrect with too much steering. Too much movement may lead to a skid in the opposite direction. Skids don't just happen, they are caused. The three important factors in order are: the driver, the vehicle and the road conditions.

223 Mark *four* answers
Before starting a journey in freezing weather you should clear ice and snow from your vehicle's

- ☐ **A** aerial
- ☐ **B** windows
- ☐ **C** bumper
- ☐ **D** lights
- ☐ **E** mirrors
- ☐ **F** number plates

Don't travel unless you have no choice. Making unnecessary journeys in bad weather can increase the risk of having a collision. It's important that you can see and be seen. Make sure any snow or ice is cleared from lights, mirrors, number plates and windows.

224 Mark *one* answer
You are trying to move off on snow. You should use

- ☐ **A** the lowest gear you can
- ☐ **B** the highest gear you can
- ☐ **C** a high engine speed
- ☐ **D** the handbrake and footbrake together

If you attempt to move off in a low gear, such as first, the engine will rev at a higher speed. This could cause the wheels to spin and dig further into the snow.

225 Mark *one* answer
When driving in falling snow you should

☐ **A** brake firmly and quickly
☐ **B** be ready to steer sharply
☐ **C** use sidelights only
☐ **D** brake gently in plenty of time

Braking on snow can be extremely dangerous. Be gentle with both the accelerator and brake to prevent wheel-spin.

---

226 Mark *one* answer
The MAIN benefit of having four-wheel drive is to improve

☐ **A** road holding
☐ **B** fuel consumption
☐ **C** stopping distances
☐ **D** passenger comfort

By driving all four wheels there is improved grip, but this does not replace the skills you need to drive safely. The extra grip helps road holding when travelling on slippery or uneven roads.

---

227 Mark *one* answer
You are about to go down a steep hill. To control the speed of your vehicle you should

☐ **A** select a high gear and use the brakes carefully
☐ **B** select a high gear and use the brakes firmly
☐ **C** select a low gear and use the brakes carefully
☐ **D** select a low gear and avoid using the brakes

When going down a steep hill your vehicle will speed up. This will make it more difficult for you to stop. Select a lower gear to give you more engine braking and control. Use this in combination with careful use of the brakes.

228 Mark *two* answers
You wish to park facing DOWNHILL. Which TWO of the following should you do?

☐ **A** Turn the steering wheel towards the kerb
☐ **B** Park close to the bumper of another car
☐ **C** Park with two wheels on the kerb
☐ **D** Put the handbrake on firmly
☐ **E** Turn the steering wheel away from the kerb

Turning the wheels towards the kerb will allow it to act as a chock, preventing any forward movement of the vehicle. It will also help to leave it in gear, or select Park if you have an automatic.

---

229 Mark *one* answer
You are driving in a built-up area. You approach a speed hump. You should

☐ **A** move across to the left-hand side of the road
☐ **B** wait for any pedestrians to cross
☐ **C** slow your vehicle right down
☐ **D** stop and check both pavements

Many towns have speed humps to slow down traffic. Slow down when driving over them. If you go too fast they may affect your steering and suspension, causing you to lose control or even damaging it. Be aware of pedestrians in these areas.

230 Mark *one* answer

You are on a long, downhill slope. What should you do to help control the speed of your vehicle?

☐ **A** Select neutral
☐ **B** Select a lower gear
☐ **C** Grip the handbrake firmly
☐ **D** Apply the parking brake gently

Selecting a low gear when travelling downhill will help you to control your speed. The engine will assist the brakes and help prevent your vehicle gathering speed.

231 Mark *one* answer

Anti-lock brakes prevent wheels from locking. This means the tyres are less likely to

☐ **A** aquaplane
☐ **B** skid
☐ **C** puncture
☐ **D** wear

If an anti-lock braking system is fitted it activates automatically when maximum braking pressure is applied or when it senses that the wheels are about to lock. It prevents the wheels from locking so you can continue to steer the vehicle during braking. It does not remove the need for good driving practices such as anticipation and correct speed for the conditions.

232 Mark *one* answer

Anti-lock brakes reduce the chances of a skid occurring particularly when

☐ **A** driving down steep hills
☐ **B** braking during normal driving
☐ **C** braking in an emergency
☐ **D** driving on good road surfaces

The anti-lock braking system will operate when the brakes have been applied harshly.
It will reduce the chances of your car skidding, but it is not a miracle cure for careless driving.

233 Mark *one* answer

Vehicles fitted with anti-lock brakes

☐ **A** are impossible to skid
☐ **B** can be steered while you are braking
☐ **C** accelerate much faster
☐ **D** are not fitted with a handbrake

Preventing the wheels from locking means that the vehicle's steering and stability can be maintained, leading to safer stopping. However, you must ensure that the engine does not stall, as this could disable the power steering. Look in your vehicle handbook for the correct method when stopping in an emergency.

234 Mark *two* answers

Anti-lock brakes may not work as effectively if the road surface is

☐ **A** dry
☐ **B** loose
☐ **C** wet
☐ **D** good
☐ **E** firm

Poor contact with the road surface could cause one or more of the tyres to lose grip on the road. This is more likely to happen when braking in poor weather conditions, when the road surface is uneven or has loose chippings.

235 Mark *one* answer

Anti-lock brakes are of most use when you are

☐ **A** braking gently
☐ **B** driving on worn tyres
☐ **C** braking excessively
☐ **D** driving normally

Anti-lock brakes will not be required when braking normally. Looking well down the road and anticipating possible hazards could prevent you having to brake late and harshly. Knowing that you have anti-lock brakes is not an excuse to drive in a careless or reckless way.

236 Mark *one* answer

Driving a vehicle fitted with anti-lock brakes allows you to

☐ **A** brake harder because it is impossible to skid
☐ **B** drive at higher speeds
☐ **C** steer and brake at the same time
☐ **D** pay less attention to the road ahead

When stopping in an emergency anti-lock brakes will help you continue to steer when braking. In poor weather conditions this may be less effective. You need to depress the clutch pedal to prevent the car stalling as most power steering systems use an engine-driven pump and will only operate when the engine is running. Look in your vehicle handbook for the correct method when stopping in an emergency.

237 Mark *one* answer

Anti-lock brakes can greatly assist with

☐ **A** a higher cruising speed
☐ **B** steering control when braking
☐ **C** control when accelerating
☐ **D** motorway driving

If the wheels of your vehicle lock they will not grip the road and you will lose steering control. In good conditions the anti-lock system will prevent the wheels locking and allow you to retain steering control.

238 Mark *one* answer
You are driving a vehicle fitted with anti-lock brakes. You need to stop in an emergency. You should apply the footbrake

☐ **A** slowly and gently
☐ **B** slowly but firmly
☐ **C** rapidly and gently
☐ **D** rapidly and firmly

Look well ahead down the road as you drive and give yourself time and space to react safely to any hazards. You may have to stop in an emergency due to a misjudgement by another driver or a hazard arising suddenly such as a child running out into the road. In this case, if your vehicle has anti-lock brakes, you should apply the brakes immediately and keep them firmly applied until you stop.

239 Mark *two* answers
Your vehicle has anti-lock brakes, but they may not always prevent skidding. This is most likely to happen when driving

☐ **A** in foggy conditions
☐ **B** on surface water
☐ **C** on loose road surfaces
☐ **D** on dry tarmac
☐ **E** at night on unlit roads

In very wet weather water can build up between the tyre and the road surface. As a result your vehicle actually rides on a thin film of water and your tyres will not grip the road. Gravel or shingle surfaces also offer less grip and can present problems when braking. An anti-lock braking system may be ineffective in these conditions.

240 Mark *one* answer
You are driving along a country road. You see this sign. AFTER dealing safely with the hazard you should always

☐ **A** check your tyre pressures
☐ **B** switch on your hazard warning lights
☐ **C** accelerate briskly
☐ **D** test your brakes

Deep water can affect your brakes, so you should check that they're working properly before you build up speed again. Before you do this, remember to check your mirrors and consider what's behind you.

241 Mark *one* answer
You are driving in heavy rain. Your steering suddenly becomes very light. You should

☐ **A** steer towards the side of the road
☐ **B** apply gentle acceleration
☐ **C** brake firmly to reduce speed
☐ **D** ease off the accelerator

If the steering becomes light in these conditions it is probably due to a film of water that has built up between your tyres and the road surface. Easing off the accelerator should allow your tyres to displace the film of water and they should then regain their grip on the road.

242 Mark *one* answer
The roads are icy. You should drive slowly

☐ **A** in the highest gear possible
☐ **B** in the lowest gear possible
☐ **C** with the handbrake partly on
☐ **D** with your left foot on the brake

Driving at a slow speed in a high gear will reduce the likelihood of wheel-spin and help your vehicle maintain the best possible grip.

243 Mark *one* answer
You are driving along a wet road. How can you tell if your vehicle is aquaplaning?

☐ **A** The engine will stall
☐ **B** The engine noise will increase
☐ **C** The steering will feel very heavy
☐ **D** The steering will feel very light

If you drive at speed in very wet conditions your steering may suddenly feel 'light'. This means that the tyres have lifted off the surface of the road and are skating on the surface of the water. This is known as aquaplaning. Reduce speed by easing off the accelerator, but don't brake until your steering returns to normal.

244 Mark *two* answers
How can you tell if you are driving on ice?

☐ **A** The tyres make a rumbling noise
☐ **B** The tyres make hardly any noise
☐ **C** The steering becomes heavier
☐ **D** The steering becomes lighter

Drive extremely carefully when the roads are icy. When travelling on ice, tyres make virtually no noise and the steering feels unresponsive.

In icy conditions, avoid harsh braking, acceleration and steering.

245 Mark *one* answer
You are driving along a wet road. How can you tell if your vehicle's tyres are losing their grip on the surface?

☐ **A** The engine will stall
☐ **B** The steering will feel very heavy
☐ **C** The engine noise will increase
☐ **D** The steering will feel very light

If you drive at speed in very wet conditions your steering may suddenly feel lighter than usual. This means that the tyres have lifted off the surface of the road and are skating on the surface of the water. This is known as aquaplaning. Reduce speed but don't brake until your steering returns to a normal feel.

246 Mark *one* answer
Your overall stopping distance will be much longer when driving

☐ **A** in the rain   ☐ **B** in fog
☐ **C** at night   ☐ **D** in strong winds

Extra care should be taken in wet weather as, on wet roads, your stopping distance could be double that necessary for dry conditions.

247 Mark *one* answer

You have driven through a flood. What is the first thing you should do?

☐ **A** Stop and check the tyres
☐ **B** Stop and dry the brakes
☐ **C** Check your exhaust
☐ **D** Test your brakes

Before you test your brakes you must check for following traffic. If it is safe, gently apply the brakes to clear any water that may be covering the braking surfaces.

248 Mark *one* answer

You are on a fast, open road in good conditions. For safety, the distance between you and the vehicle in front should be

☐ **A** a two-second time gap
☐ **B** one car length
☐ **C** 2 metres (6 feet 6 inches)
☐ **D** two car lengths

One useful method of checking that you've allowed enough room between you and the vehicle in front is the two-second rule.

To check for a two-second time gap, choose a stationary object ahead, such as a bridge or road sign. When the car in front passes the object say 'Only a fool breaks the two-second rule'. If you reach the object before you finish saying it you're too close.

249 Mark *one* answer

How can you use your vehicle's engine as a brake?

☐ **A** By changing to a lower gear
☐ **B** By selecting reverse gear
☐ **C** By changing to a higher gear
☐ **D** By selecting neutral gear

When driving on downhill stretches of road selecting a lower gear gives increased engine braking. This will prevent excess use of the brakes, which become less effective if they overheat.

250 Mark *one* answer

Anti-lock brakes are most effective when you

☐ **A** keep pumping the foot brake to prevent skidding
☐ **B** brake normally, but grip the steering wheel tightly
☐ **C** brake promptly and firmly until you have slowed down
☐ **D** apply the handbrake to reduce the stopping distance

Releasing the brake before you have slowed right down will disable the system. If you have to brake in an emergency ensure that you keep your foot firmly on the brake pedal until the vehicle has stopped.

251 Mark *one* answer

Your car is fitted with anti-lock brakes. You need to stop in an emergency. You should

☐ **A** brake normally and avoid turning the steering wheel

☐ **B** press the brake pedal promptly and firmly until you have stopped

☐ **C** keep pushing and releasing the foot brake quickly to prevent skidding

☐ **D** apply the handbrake to reduce the stopping distance

Keep pressure on the brake pedal until you have come to a stop. The anti-lock mechanism will activate automatically if it senses the wheels are about to lock.

252 Mark *one* answer

When would an anti-lock braking system start to work?

☐ **A** After the parking brake has been applied

☐ **B** Whenever pressure on the brake pedal is applied

☐ **C** Just as the wheels are about to lock

☐ **D** When the normal braking system fails to operate

The anti-lock braking system has sensors that detect when the wheels are about to lock. It releases the brakes momentarily to allow the wheels to revolve and grip, then automatically reapplies them. This cycle is repeated several times a second to maximise braking performance.

253 Mark *one* answer

Anti-lock brakes will take effect when

☐ **A** you do not brake quickly enough

☐ **B** maximum brake pressure has been applied

☐ **C** you have not seen a hazard ahead

☐ **D** speeding on slippery road surfaces

If your car is fitted with anti-lock brakes they will take effect when you use them very firmly in an emergency. The system will only activate when it senses the wheels are about to lock.

254 Mark *one* answer

You are on a wet motorway with surface spray. You should use

☐ **A** hazard flashers

☐ **B** dipped headlights

☐ **C** rear fog lights

☐ **D** sidelights

When surface spray reduces visibility switch on your dipped headlights. This will help other road users to see you.

255 Mark *one* answer

Your vehicle is fitted with anti-lock brakes. To stop quickly in an emergency you should

- ☐ **A** brake firmly and pump the brake pedal on and off
- ☐ **B** brake rapidly and firmly without releasing the brake pedal
- ☐ **C** brake gently and pump the brake pedal on and off
- ☐ **D** brake rapidly once, and immediately release the brake pedal

Once you have applied the brake keep your foot firmly on the pedal. Releasing the brake and reapplying it will disable the anti-lock brake system.

256 Mark *one* answer

Travelling for long distances in neutral (known as coasting)

- ☐ **A** improves the driver's control
- ☐ **B** makes steering easier
- ☐ **C** reduces the driver's control
- ☐ **D** uses more fuel

Coasting is the term used when the clutch is held down, or the gear lever is in neutral, and the vehicle is allowed to freewheel. This reduces the driver's control of the vehicle. When you coast, the engine can't drive the wheels to pull you through a corner. Coasting also removes the assistance of engine braking that helps to slow the car.

257 Mark *one* answer

How can you tell when you are driving over black ice?

- ☐ **A** It is easier to brake
- ☐ **B** The noise from your tyres sounds louder
- ☐ **C** You will see tyre tracks on the road
- ☐ **D** Your steering feels light

Sometimes you may not be able to see that the road is icy. Black ice makes a road look damp. The signs that you're travelling on black ice can be that
- the steering feels light
- the noise from your tyres suddenly goes quiet.

258 Mark *three* answers

When driving in fog, which THREE of these are correct?

- ☐ **A** Use dipped headlights
- ☐ **B** Position close to the centre line
- ☐ **C** Allow more time for your journey
- ☐ **D** Keep close to the car in front
- ☐ **E** Slow down
- ☐ **F** Use side lights only

Don't venture out if your journey is not necessary. If you have to travel and someone is expecting you at the other end, let them know that you will be taking longer than usual for your journey. This will stop them worrying if you don't turn up on time and will also take the pressure off you, so you don't feel you have to rush.

259 Mark *two* answers
Where would you expect to see these markers?

- ☐ **A** On a motorway sign
- ☐ **B** At the entrance to a narrow bridge
- ☐ **C** On a large goods vehicle
- ☐ **D** On a builder's skip placed on the road

These markers must be fitted to vehicles over 13 metres (42 feet 8 inches) long, large goods vehicles, and rubbish skips placed in the road. They are reflective to make them easier to see in the dark.

260 Mark *one* answer
What is the main hazard shown in this picture?

- ☐ **A** Vehicles turning right
- ☐ **B** Vehicles doing U-turns
- ☐ **C** The cyclist crossing the road
- ☐ **D** Parked cars around the corner

Look at the picture carefully and try to imagine you're there. The cyclist in this picture appears to be trying to cross the road. You must be able to deal with the unexpected, especially when you're approaching a hazardous junction. Look well ahead to give yourself time to deal with any hazards.

261 Mark *one* answer
Which road user has caused a hazard?

- ☐ **A** The parked car (arrowed A)
- ☐ **B** The pedestrian waiting to cross (arrowed B)
- ☐ **C** The moving car (arrowed C)
- ☐ **D** The car turning (arrowed D)

The car arrowed A is parked within the area marked by zigzag lines at the pedestrian crossing. Parking here is illegal. It also
- blocks the view for pedestrians wishing to cross the road
- restricts the view of the crossing for approaching traffic.

262 Mark *one* answer
What should the driver of the car approaching the crossing do?

- ☐ **A** Continue at the same speed
- ☐ **B** Sound the horn
- ☐ **C** Drive through quickly
- ☐ **D** Slow down and get ready to stop

Look well ahead to see if any hazards are developing. This will give you more time to deal with them in the correct way. The man in the picture is clearly intending to cross the road. You should be travelling at a speed that allows you to check your mirror, slow down and stop in good time. You shouldn't have to brake harshly.

263 Mark *three* answers

What THREE things should the driver of the grey car (arrowed) be especially aware of?

- ☐ **A** Pedestrians stepping out between cars
- ☐ **B** Other cars behind the grey car
- ☐ **C** Doors opening on parked cars
- ☐ **D** The bumpy road surface
- ☐ **E** Cars leaving parking spaces
- ☐ **F** Empty parking spaces

You need to be aware that other road users may not have seen you. Always be on the lookout for hazards that may develop suddenly and need you to take avoiding action.

264 Mark *one* answer

You see this sign ahead. You should expect the road to

- ☐ **A** go steeply uphill
- ☐ **B** go steeply downhill
- ☐ **C** bend sharply to the left
- ☐ **D** bend sharply to the right

Adjust your speed in good time and select the correct gear for your speed. Going too fast into the bend could cause you to lose control.

Braking late and harshly while changing direction reduces your vehicle's grip on the road, and is likely to cause a skid.

265 Mark *one* answer

You are approaching this cyclist. You should

- ☐ **A** overtake before the cyclist gets to the junction
- ☐ **B** flash your headlights at the cyclist
- ☐ **C** slow down and allow the cyclist to turn
- ☐ **D** overtake the cyclist on the left-hand side

Keep well back and allow the cyclist room to take up the correct position for the turn. Don't get too close behind or try to squeeze past.

266 Mark *one* answer

Why must you take extra care when turning right at this junction?

- ☐ **A** Road surface is poor
- ☐ **B** Footpaths are narrow
- ☐ **C** Road markings are faint
- ☐ **D** There is reduced visibility

You may have to pull forward slowly until you can see up and down the road. Be aware that the traffic approaching the junction can't see you either. If you don't know that it's clear, don't go.

267 Mark *one* answer
When approaching this bridge you should give way to

☐ **A** bicycles
☐ **B** buses
☐ **C** motorcycles
☐ **D** cars

A double-deck bus or high-sided lorry will have to take up a position in the centre of the road so that it can clear the bridge. There is normally a sign to indicate this.

Look well down the road, through the bridge and be aware you may have to stop and give way to an oncoming large vehicle.

268 Mark *one* answer
What type of vehicle could you expect to meet in the middle of the road?

☐ **A** Lorry
☐ **B** Bicycle
☐ **C** Car
☐ **D** Motorcycle

The highest point of the bridge is in the centre so a large vehicle might have to move to the centre of the road to allow it enough room to pass under the bridge.

269 Mark *one* answer
At this blind junction you must stop

☐ **A** behind the line, then edge forward to see clearly
☐ **B** beyond the line at a point where you can see clearly
☐ **C** only if there is traffic on the main road
☐ **D** only if you are turning to the right

The 'stop' sign has been put here because there is a poor view into the main road. You must stop because it will not be possible to assess the situation on the move, however slowly you are travelling.

270 Mark *one* answer
A driver pulls out of a side road in front of you. You have to brake hard. You should

☐ **A** ignore the error and stay calm
☐ **B** flash your lights to show your annoyance
☐ **C** sound your horn to show your annoyance
☐ **D** overtake as soon as possible

Where there are a number of side roads, be alert. Be especially careful if there are a lot of parked vehicles because they can make it more difficult for drivers emerging to see you. Try to be tolerant if a vehicle does emerge and you have to brake quickly. Don't react aggressively.

271 Mark *one* answer

An elderly person's driving ability could be affected because they may be unable to

- ☐ **A** obtain car insurance
- ☐ **B** understand road signs
- ☐ **C** react very quickly
- ☐ **D** give signals correctly

Be tolerant of older drivers. Poor eyesight and hearing could affect the speed with which they react to a hazard and may cause them to be hesitant.

272 Mark *one* answer

You have just passed these warning lights. What hazard would you expect to see next?

- ☐ **A** A level crossing with no barrier
- ☐ **B** An ambulance station
- ☐ **C** A school crossing patrol
- ☐ **D** An opening bridge

These lights warn that children may be crossing the road to a nearby school. Slow down so that you're ready to stop if necessary.

273 Mark *one* answer

You are planning a long journey. Do you need to plan rest stops?

- ☐ **A** Yes, you should plan to stop every half an hour
- ☐ **B** Yes, regular stops help concentration
- ☐ **C** No, you will be less tired if you get there as soon as possible
- ☐ **D** No, only fuel stops will be needed

Try to plan your journey so that you can take rest stops. It's recommended that you take a break of at least 15 minutes after every two hours of driving. This should help to maintain your concentration.

274 Mark *one* answer

A driver does something that upsets you. You should

- ☐ **A** try not to react
- ☐ **B** let them know how you feel
- ☐ **C** flash your headlights several times
- ☐ **D** sound your horn

There are times when other road users make a misjudgement or mistake. When this happens try not to get annoyed and don't react by showing anger. Sounding your horn, flashing your headlights or shouting won't help the situation. Good anticipation will help to prevent these incidents becoming collisions.

275 Mark *one* answer

The red lights are flashing. What should you do when approaching this level crossing?

- ☐ **A** Go through quickly
- ☐ **B** Go through carefully
- ☐ **C** Stop before the barrier
- ☐ **D** Switch on hazard warning lights

At level crossings the red lights flash before and when the barrier is down. At most crossings an amber light will precede the red lights. You must stop behind the white line unless you have already crossed it when the amber light comes on. NEVER zigzag around half-barriers.

276 Mark *one* answer

You are approaching crossroads. The traffic lights have failed. What should you do?

- ☐ **A** Brake and stop only for large vehicles
- ☐ **B** Brake sharply to a stop before looking
- ☐ **C** Be prepared to brake sharply to a stop
- ☐ **D** Be prepared to stop for any traffic.

When approaching a junction where the traffic lights have failed, you should proceed with caution. Treat the situation as an unmarked junction and be prepared to stop.

277 Mark *one* answer

What should the driver of the red car (arrowed) do?

- ☐ **A** Wave the pedestrians who are waiting to cross
- ☐ **B** Wait for the pedestrian in the road to cross
- ☐ **C** Quickly drive behind the pedestrian in the road
- ☐ **D** Tell the pedestrian in the road she should not have crossed

Some people might take longer to cross the road. They may be older or have a disability. Be patient and don't hurry them by showing your impatience. They might have poor eyesight or not be able to hear traffic approaching. If pedestrians are standing at the side of the road, don't signal or wave them to cross. Other road users may not have seen your signal and this could lead the pedestrians into a hazardous situation.

278 Mark *one* answer
You are following a slower-moving vehicle on a narrow country road. There is a junction just ahead on the right. What should you do?

- ☐ **A** Overtake after checking your mirrors and signalling
- ☐ **B** Stay behind until you are past the junction
- ☐ **C** Accelerate quickly to pass before the junction
- ☐ **D** Slow down and prepare to overtake on the left

You should never overtake as you approach a junction. If a vehicle emerged from the junction while you were overtaking, a dangerous situation could develop very quickly.

279 Mark *one* answer
What should you do as you approach this overhead bridge?

- ☐ **A** Move out to the centre of the road before going through
- ☐ **B** Find another route, this is only for high vehicles
- ☐ **C** Be prepared to give way to large vehicles in the middle of the road
- ☐ **D** Move across to the right-hand side before going through

Oncoming large vehicles may need to move to the middle of the road so that they can pass safely under the bridge. There will not be enough room for you to continue and you should be ready to stop and wait.

280 Mark *one* answer
Why are mirrors often slightly curved (convex)?

- ☐ **A** They give a wider field of vision
- ☐ **B** They totally cover blind spots
- ☐ **C** They make it easier to judge the speed of following traffic
- ☐ **D** They make following traffic look bigger

Although a convex mirror gives a wide view of the scene behind, you should be aware that it will not show you everything behind or to the side of the vehicle. Before you move off you will need to check over your shoulder to look for anything not visible in the mirrors.

281 Mark *one* answer
You see this sign on the rear of a slow-moving lorry that you want to pass. It is travelling in the middle lane of a three-lane motorway. You should

- ☐ **A** cautiously approach the lorry then pass on either side
- ☐ **B** follow the lorry until you can leave the motorway
- ☐ **C** wait on the hard shoulder until the lorry has stopped
- ☐ **D** approach with care and keep to the left of the lorry

This sign is found on slow-moving or stationary works vehicles. If you wish to overtake, do so on the left, as indicated. Be aware that there might be workmen in the area.

282 Mark *one* answer

You think the driver of the vehicle in front has forgotten to cancel their right indicator. You should

☐ **A** flash your lights to alert the driver
☐ **B** sound your horn before overtaking
☐ **C** overtake on the left if there is room
☐ **D** stay behind and not overtake

The driver may be unsure of the location of a junction and turn suddenly. Be cautious and don't attempt to overtake.

283 Mark *one* answer

What is the main hazard the driver of the red car (arrowed) should be aware of?

☐ **A** Glare from the sun may affect the driver's vision
☐ **B** The black car may stop suddenly
☐ **C** The bus may move out into the road
☐ **D** Oncoming vehicles will assume the driver is turning right

If you can do so safely give way to buses signalling to move off at bus stops. Try to anticipate the actions of other road users around you. The driver of the red car should be prepared for the bus pulling out. As you approach a bus stop look to see how many passengers are waiting to board. If the last one has just got on, the bus is likely to move off.

284 Mark *one* answer

This yellow sign on a vehicle indicates this is

☐ **A** a broken-down vehicle
☐ **B** a school bus
☐ **C** an ice cream van
☐ **D** a private ambulance

Buses which carry children to and from school may stop at places other than scheduled bus stops. Be aware that they might pull over at any time to allow children to get on or off. This will normally be when traffic is heavy during rush hour.

285 Mark *two* answers
What TWO main hazards should you be aware of when going along this street?

- ☐ **A** Glare from the sun
- ☐ **B** Car doors opening suddenly
- ☐ **C** Lack of road markings
- ☐ **D** The headlights on parked cars being switched on
- ☐ **E** Large goods vehicles
- ☐ **F** Children running out from between vehicles

On roads where there are many parked vehicles you should take extra care. You might not be able to see children between parked cars and they may run out into the road without looking.

People may open car doors without realising the hazard this can create. You will also need to look well down the road for oncoming traffic.

286 Mark *one* answer
What is the main hazard you should be aware of when following this cyclist?

- ☐ **A** The cyclist may move to the left and dismount
- ☐ **B** The cyclist may swerve out into the road
- ☐ **C** The contents of the cyclist's carrier may fall onto the road
- ☐ **D** The cyclist may wish to turn right at the end of the road

When following a cyclist be aware that they have to deal with the hazards around them. They may wobble or swerve to avoid a pothole in the road or see a potential hazard and change direction suddenly. Don't follow them too closely or rev your engine impatiently.

287 Mark *one* answer
A driver's behaviour has upset you. It may help if you

- ☐ **A** stop and take a break
- ☐ **B** shout abusive language
- ☐ **C** gesture to them with your hand
- ☐ **D** follow their car, flashing your headlights

Tiredness may make you more irritable than you would be normally. You might react differently to situations because of it. If you feel yourself becoming tense, take a break.

288 Mark *one* answer

In areas where there are 'traffic-calming' measures you should

☐ **A** travel at a reduced speed
☐ **B** always travel at the speed limit
☐ **C** position in the centre of the road
☐ **D** only slow down if pedestrians are near

Traffic-calming measures such as road humps, chicanes and narrowings are intended to slow you down. Maintain a reduced speed until you reach the end of these features. They are there to protect pedestrians. Kill your speed!

289 Mark *two* answers

When approaching this hazard why should you slow down?

☐ **A** Because of the bend
☐ **B** Because it's hard to see to the right
☐ **C** Because of approaching traffic
☐ **D** Because of animals crossing
☐ **E** Because of the level crossing

There are two hazards clearly signed in this picture. You should be preparing for the bend by slowing down and selecting the correct gear. You might also have to stop at the level crossing, so be alert and be prepared to stop if necessary.

290 Mark *one* answer

Why are place names painted on the road surface?

☐ **A** To restrict the flow of traffic
☐ **B** To warn you of oncoming traffic
☐ **C** To enable you to change lanes early
☐ **D** To prevent you changing lanes

The names of towns and cities may be painted on the road at busy junctions and complex road systems. Their purpose is to let you move into the correct lane in good time, allowing traffic to flow more freely.

291 Mark *one* answer

Some two-way roads are divided into three lanes. Why are these particularly dangerous?

☐ **A** Traffic in both directions can use the middle lane to overtake
☐ **B** Traffic can travel faster in poor weather conditions
☐ **C** Traffic can overtake on the left
☐ **D** Traffic uses the middle lane for emergencies only

If you intend to overtake you must consider that approaching traffic could be planning the same manoeuvre. When you have considered the situation and have decided it is safe, indicate your intentions early. This will show the approaching traffic that you intend to pull out.

292 Mark *one* answer
You are on a dual carriageway. Ahead you see a vehicle with an amber flashing light. What could this be?

☐ **A** An ambulance
☐ **B** A fire engine
☐ **C** A doctor on call
☐ **D** A disabled person's vehicle

An amber flashing light on a vehicle indicates that it is slow-moving. Battery powered vehicles used by disabled people are limited to 8mph. It's not advisable for them to be used on dual carriageways where the speed limit exceeds 50mph. If they are then an amber flashing light must be used.

293 Mark *one* answer
What does this signal from a police officer mean to oncoming traffic?

☐ **A** Go ahead
☐ **B** Stop
☐ **C** Turn left
☐ **D** Turn right

Police officers may need to direct traffic, for example, at a junction where the traffic lights have broken down. Check your copy of The Highway Code for the signals that they use.

294 Mark *two* answers
Why should you be especially cautious when going past this stationary bus?

☐ **A** There is traffic approaching in the distance
☐ **B** The driver may open the door
☐ **C** It may suddenly move off
☐ **D** People may cross the road in front of it
☐ **E** There are bicycles parked on the pavement

A stationary bus at a bus stop can hide pedestrians just in front of it who might be about to cross the road. Only go past at a speed that will enable you to stop safely if you need to.

295 Mark *three* answers
Overtaking is a major cause of collisions. In which THREE of these situations should you NOT overtake?

☐ **A** If you are turning left shortly afterwards
☐ **B** When you are in a one-way street
☐ **C** When you are approaching a junction
☐ **D** If you are travelling up a long hill
☐ **E** When your view ahead is blocked

You should not overtake unless it is really necessary. Arriving safely is more important than taking risks. Also look out for road signs and markings that show it is illegal or would be unsafe to overtake. In many cases overtaking is unlikely to significantly improve journey times.

296 Mark *three* answers
Which THREE result from drinking alcohol?

☐ **A** Less control
☐ **B** A false sense of confidence
☐ **C** Faster reactions
☐ **D** Poor judgement of speed
☐ **E** Greater awareness of danger

You must understand the serious dangers of mixing alcohol with driving or riding. Alcohol will severely reduce your ability to drive or ride safely. Just one drink could put you over the limit. Don't risk people's lives – DON'T DRINK AND DRIVE OR RIDE!

297 Mark *one* answer
What does the solid white line at the side of the road indicate?

☐ **A** Traffic lights ahead
☐ **B** Edge of the carriageway
☐ **C** Footpath on the left
☐ **D** Cycle path

The continuous white line shows the edge of the carriageway. It can be especially useful when visibility is restricted, for example at night or in bad weather. It is discontinued where it crosses junctions, lay-bys etc.

298 Mark *one* answer
You are driving towards this level crossing. What would be the first warning of an approaching train?

☐ **A** Both half barriers down
☐ **B** A steady amber light
☐ **C** One half barrier down
☐ **D** Twin flashing red lights

The steady amber light will be followed by twin flashing red lights that mean you must stop. An alarm will also sound to alert you to the fact that a train is approaching.

299 Mark *one* answer
You are behind this cyclist. When the traffic lights change, what should you do?

☐ **A** Try to move off before the cyclist
☐ **B** Allow the cyclist time and room
☐ **C** Turn right but give the cyclist room
☐ **D** Tap your horn and drive through first

Hold back and allow the cyclist to move off. In some towns, junctions have special areas marked across the front of the traffic lane. These allow cyclists to wait for the lights to change and move off ahead of other traffic.

300 Mark *one* answer

While driving, you see this sign ahead. You should

- ☐ **A** stop at the sign
- ☐ **B** slow, but continue around the bend
- ☐ **C** slow to a crawl and continue
- ☐ **D** stop and look for open farm gates

Drive around the bend at a steady speed in the correct gear. Be aware that you might have to stop for approaching trains.

301 Mark *one* answer

When the traffic lights change to green the white car should

- ☐ **A** wait for the cyclist to pull away
- ☐ **B** move off quickly and turn in front of the cyclist
- ☐ **C** move close up to the cyclist to beat the lights
- ☐ **D** sound the horn to warn the cyclist

If you are waiting at traffic lights, check all around you before you move away, as cyclists often filter through waiting traffic. Allow the cyclist to move off safely.

302 Mark *one* answer

You intend to turn left at the traffic lights. Just before turning you should

- ☐ **A** check your right mirror
- ☐ **B** move close up to the white car
- ☐ **C** straddle the lanes
- ☐ **D** check for bicycles on your left

Check your nearside for cyclists before moving away. This is especially important if you have been in a stationary queue of traffic and are about to move off, as cyclists often try to filter past on the nearside of stationary vehicles.

303 Mark *one* answer

You should reduce your speed when driving along this road because

- ☐ **A** there is a staggered junction ahead
- ☐ **B** there is a low bridge ahead
- ☐ **C** there is a change in the road surface
- ☐ **D** the road ahead narrows

Traffic could be turning off ahead of you, to the left or right.

Vehicles turning left will be slowing down before the junction and any vehicles turning right may have to stop to allow oncoming traffic to clear. Be prepared for this as you might have to slow down or stop behind them.

304 Mark *one* answer

You are driving at 60mph. As you approach this hazard you should

- ☐ **A** maintain your speed
- ☐ **B** reduce your speed
- ☐ **C** take the next right turn
- ☐ **D** take the next left turn

There could be stationary traffic ahead, waiting to turn right. Other traffic could be emerging and it may take time for them to gather speed.

305 Mark *one* answer

What might you expect to happen in this situation?

- ☐ **A** Traffic will move into the right-hand lane
- ☐ **B** Traffic speed will increase
- ☐ **C** Traffic will move into the left-hand lane
- ☐ **D** Traffic will not need to change position

Be courteous and allow the traffic to merge into the left-hand lane.

306 Mark *one* answer

You are driving on a road with several lanes. You see these signs above the lanes. What do they mean?

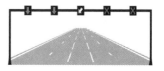

- ☐ **A** The two right lanes are open
- ☐ **B** The two left lanes are open
- ☐ **C** Traffic in the left lanes should stop
- ☐ **D** Traffic in the right lanes should stop

If you see a red cross above your lane it means that there is an obstruction ahead. You will have to move into one of the lanes which is showing the green light. If all the lanes are showing a red cross, then you must stop.

307 Mark *one* answer

You are invited to a pub lunch. You know that you will have to drive in the evening. What is your best course of action?

- ☐ **A** Avoid mixing your alcoholic drinks
- ☐ **B** Not drink any alcohol at all
- ☐ **C** Have some milk before drinking alcohol
- ☐ **D** Eat a hot meal with your alcoholic drinks

Alcohol will stay in the body for several hours and may make you unfit to drive later in the day. Drinking during the day will also affect your performance at work or study.

308 Mark *one* answer

You have been convicted of driving whilst unfit through drink or drugs. You will find this is likely to cause the cost of one of the following to rise considerably. Which one?

- ☐ **A** Road fund licence
- ☐ **B** Insurance premiums
- ☐ **C** Vehicle test certificate
- ☐ **D** Driving licence

You have shown that you are a risk to yourself and others on the road. For this reason insurance companies may charge you a higher premium.

309 Mark *one* answer

What advice should you give to a driver who has had a few alcoholic drinks at a party?

- ☐ **A** Have a strong cup of coffee and then drive home
- ☐ **B** Drive home carefully and slowly
- ☐ **C** Go home by public transport
- ☐ **D** Wait a short while and then drive home

Drinking black coffee or waiting a few hours won't make any difference. Alcohol takes time to leave the body.

A driver who has been drinking should go home by public transport or taxi. They might even be unfit to drive the following morning.

310 Mark *one* answer

You have been taking medicine for a few days which made you feel drowsy. Today you feel better but still need to take the medicine. You should only drive

- ☐ **A** if your journey is necessary
- ☐ **B** at night on quiet roads
- ☐ **C** if someone goes with you
- ☐ **D** after checking with your doctor

Take care – it's not worth taking risks. Always check with your doctor to be really sure. You may not feel drowsy now, but the medicine could have an effect on you later in the day.

311 Mark *one* answer

You are about to return home from holiday when you become ill. A doctor prescribes drugs which are likely to affect your driving. You should

- ☐ **A** drive only if someone is with you
- ☐ **B** avoid driving on motorways
- ☐ **C** not drive yourself
- ☐ **D** never drive at more than 30mph

Find another way to get home even if this proves to be very inconvenient. You must not put other road users, your passengers or yourself at risk.

312 Mark *two* answers
During periods of illness your ability to drive may be impaired. You MUST

☐ **A** see your doctor each time before you drive
☐ **B** only take smaller doses of any medicines
☐ **C** be medically fit to drive
☐ **D** not drive after taking certain medicines
☐ **E** take all your medicines with you when you drive

Be responsible and only drive if you are fit to do so. Some medication can affect your concentration and judgement when dealing with hazards. It may also cause you to become drowsy or even fall asleep. Driving while taking such medication is highly dangerous.

313 Mark *two* answers
You feel drowsy when driving. You should

☐ **A** stop and rest as soon as possible
☐ **B** turn the heater up to keep you warm and comfortable
☐ **C** make sure you have a good supply of fresh air
☐ **D** continue with your journey but drive more slowly
☐ **E** close the car windows to help you concentrate

You will be putting other road users at risk if you continue to drive when drowsy. Pull over and stop in a safe place. If you are driving a long distance, think about finding some accommodation so you can get some sleep before continuing your journey.

314 Mark *two* answers
You are driving along a motorway and become tired. You should

☐ **A** stop at the next service area and rest
☐ **B** leave the motorway at the next exit and rest
☐ **C** increase your speed and turn up the radio volume
☐ **D** close all your windows and set heating to warm
☐ **E** pull up on the hard shoulder and change drivers

If you have planned your journey properly, to include rest stops, you should arrive at your destination in good time.

315 Mark *one* answer
You are taking drugs that are likely to affect your driving. What should you do?

☐ **A** Seek medical advice before driving
☐ **B** Limit your driving to essential journeys
☐ **C** Only drive if accompanied by a full licence-holder
☐ **D** Drive only for short distances

Check with your doctor or pharmacist if you think that the drugs you're taking are likely to make you feel drowsy or impair your judgement.

316 Mark *one* answer

You are about to drive home. You feel very tired and have a severe headache. You should

☐ **A** wait until you are fit and well before driving

☐ **B** drive home, but take a tablet for headaches

☐ **C** drive home if you can stay awake for the journey

☐ **D** wait for a short time, then drive home slowly

All your concentration should be on your driving. Any pain you feel will distract you and you should avoid driving when drowsy. The safest course of action is to wait until you have rested and feel better.

317 Mark *one* answer

If you are feeling tired it is best to stop as soon as you can. Until then you should

☐ **A** increase your speed to find a stopping place quickly

☐ **B** ensure a supply of fresh air

☐ **C** gently tap the steering wheel

☐ **D** keep changing speed to improve concentration

If you're going on a long journey plan your route before you leave. This will help you to be decisive at intersections and junctions, plan rest stops and have an idea of how long the journey will take.

Make sure your vehicle is well-ventilated to stop you becoming drowsy. You need to maintain concentration so that your judgement is not impaired.

318 Mark *three* answers

Driving long distances can be tiring. You can prevent this by

☐ **A** stopping every so often for a walk

☐ **B** opening a window for some fresh air

☐ **C** ensuring plenty of refreshment breaks

☐ **D** completing the journey without stopping

☐ **E** eating a large meal before driving

Long-distance driving can be boring. This, coupled with a stuffy, warm vehicle, can make you feel tired. Make sure you take rest breaks to keep yourself awake and alert. Stop in a safe place before you get to the stage of fighting sleep.

319 Mark *one* answer

You go to a social event and need to drive a short time after. What precaution should you take?

☐ **A** Avoid drinking alcohol on an empty stomach

☐ **B** Drink plenty of coffee after drinking alcohol

☐ **C** Avoid drinking alcohol completely

☐ **D** Drink plenty of milk before drinking alcohol

This is always going to be the safest option. Just one drink could put you over the limit and dangerously impair your judgement and reactions.

320 Mark *one* answer

You take some cough medicine given to you by a friend. What should you do before driving?

☐ **A** Ask your friend if taking the medicine affected their driving
☐ **B** Drink some strong coffee one hour before driving
☐ **C** Check the label to see if the medicine will affect your driving
☐ **D** Drive a short distance to see if the medicine is affecting your driving

Never drive if you have taken drugs, without first checking what the side effects might be. They might affect your judgement and perception, and therefore endanger lives.

321 Mark *one* answer

You take the wrong route and find you are on a one-way street. You should

☐ **A** reverse out of the road
☐ **B** turn round in a side road
☐ **C** continue to the end of the road
☐ **D** reverse into a driveway

Never reverse or turn your vehicle around in a one-way street. This is highly dangerous. Carry on and find another route, checking the direction signs as you drive. If you need to check a map, first stop in a safe place.

322 Mark *three* answers

Which THREE are likely to make you lose concentration while driving?

☐ **A** Looking at road maps
☐ **B** Listening to loud music
☐ **C** Using your windscreen washers
☐ **D** Looking in your wing mirror
☐ **E** Using a mobile phone

Looking at road maps while driving is very dangerous. If you aren't sure of your route stop in a safe place and check the map. You must not allow anything to take your attention away from the road.
 If you need to use a mobile phone, stop in a safe place before doing so.

323 Mark *one* answer

You are driving along this road. The driver on the left is reversing from a driveway. You should

☐ **A** move to the opposite side of the road
☐ **B** drive through as you have priority
☐ **C** sound your horn and be prepared to stop
☐ **D** speed up and drive through quickly

White lights at the rear of a car show that it is about to reverse. Sound your horn to warn of your presence and reduce your speed as a precaution.

324 Mark *one* answer
You have been involved in an argument before starting your journey. This has made you feel angry. You should

☐ **A** start to drive, but open a window
☐ **B** drive slower than normal and turn your radio on
☐ **C** have an alcoholic drink to help you relax before driving
☐ **D** calm down before you start to drive

If you are feeling upset or angry you should wait until you have calmed down before setting out on a journey.

325 Mark *one* answer
You start to feel tired while driving. What should you do?

☐ **A** Increase your speed slightly
☐ **B** Decrease your speed slightly
☐ **C** Find a less busy route
☐ **D** Pull over at a safe place to rest

If you start to feel tired, stop at a safe place for a rest break.

Every year many fatal incidents are caused by drivers falling asleep at the wheel.

326 Mark *one* answer
You are driving on this dual carriageway. Why may you need to slow down?

☐ **A** There is a broken white line in the centre
☐ **B** There are solid white lines either side
☐ **C** There are roadworks ahead of you
☐ **D** There are no footpaths

Look well ahead and read any road signs as you drive. They are there to inform you of what is ahead. In this case you may need to slow right down and change direction.

Make sure you can take whatever action is necessary in plenty of time. Check your mirrors so you know what is happening around you before you change speed or direction.

327 Mark *one* answer
You have just been overtaken by this motor-cyclist who is cutting in sharply. You should

☐ **A** sound the horn   ☐ **B** brake firmly
☐ **C** keep a safe gap   ☐ **D** flash your lights

If another vehicle cuts in too sharply, ease off the accelerator and drop back to allow a safe separation distance. Try not to overreact by braking sharply or swerving, as you could lose control. If vehicles behind you are too close or unprepared, it could lead to a crash.

328 Mark *one* answer
You are about to drive home. You cannot find the glasses you need to wear. You should

- ☐ **A** drive home slowly, keeping to quiet roads
- ☐ **B** borrow a friend's glasses and use those
- ☐ **C** drive home at night, so that the lights will help you
- ☐ **D** find a way of getting home without driving

Don't be tempted to drive if you've lost or forgotten your glasses. You must be able to see clearly when driving.

329 Mark *three* answers
Which THREE of these are likely effects of drinking alcohol?

- ☐ **A** Reduced co-ordination
- ☐ **B** Increased confidence
- ☐ **C** Poor judgement
- ☐ **D** Increased concentration
- ☐ **E** Faster reactions
- ☐ **F** Colour blindness

Alcohol can increase confidence to a point where a driver's behaviour might become 'out of character'. Someone who normally behaves sensibly suddenly takes risks and enjoys it. Never let yourself or your friends get into this situation.

330 Mark *one* answer
How does alcohol affect you?

- ☐ **A** It speeds up your reactions
- ☐ **B** It increases your awareness
- ☐ **C** It improves your co-ordination
- ☐ **D** It reduces your concentration

Concentration and good judgement are needed at all times to be a good, safe driver. Don't put yourself or others at risk by drinking and driving.

331 Mark *one* answer
Your doctor has given you a course of medicine. Why should you ask how it will affect you?

- ☐ **A** Drugs make you a better driver by quickening your reactions
- ☐ **B** You will have to let your insurance company know about the medicine
- ☐ **C** Some types of medicine can cause your reactions to slow down
- ☐ **D** The medicine you take may affect your hearing

Always check the label of any medication container. The contents might affect your driving. If you aren't sure, ask your doctor or pharmacist.

332 Mark *one* answer
You are on a motorway. You feel tired. You should

- ☐ **A** carry on but go slowly
- ☐ **B** leave the motorway at the next exit
- ☐ **C** complete your journey as quickly as possible
- ☐ **D** stop on the hard shoulder

If you do feel tired and there's no service station for many miles, leave the motorway at the next exit. Find a road off the motorway where you can pull up and stop safely.

333 Mark *one* answer
You find that you need glasses to read vehicle number plates at the required distance. When MUST you wear them?

- ☐ **A** Only in bad weather conditions
- ☐ **B** At all times when driving
- ☐ **C** Only when you think it necessary
- ☐ **D** Only in bad light or at night time

Have your eyesight tested before you start your practical training. Then, throughout your driving life, have checks periodically to ensure that your eyes haven't deteriorated.

334 Mark *two* answers
Which TWO things would help to keep you alert during a long journey?

- ☐ **A** Finishing your journey as fast as you can
- ☐ **B** Keeping off the motorways and using country roads
- ☐ **C** Making sure that you get plenty of fresh air
- ☐ **D** Making regular stops for refreshments

Make sure that the vehicle you're driving is well ventilated. A warm, stuffy atmosphere will make you feel drowsy. Open a window and turn down the heating.

335 Mark *one* answer
Which of the following types of glasses should NOT be worn when driving at night?

- ☐ **A** Half-moon
- ☐ **B** Round
- ☐ **C** Bi-focal
- ☐ **D** Tinted

If you are driving at night or in poor visibility, tinted lenses will reduce the efficiency of your vision, by reducing the amount of available light reaching your eyes.

336 Mark *three* answers
Drinking any amount of alcohol is likely to

- ☐ **A** slow down your reactions to hazards
- ☐ **B** increase the speed of your reactions
- ☐ **C** worsen your judgement of speed
- ☐ **D** improve your awareness of danger
- ☐ **E** give a false sense of confidence

If you are going to drive it's always the safest option not to drink at all. Don't be tempted – it's not worth it.

337 Mark *three* answers
What else can seriously affect your concentration, other than alcoholic drinks?

- ☐ **A** Drugs
- ☐ **B** Tiredness
- ☐ **C** Tinted windows
- ☐ **D** Contact lenses
- ☐ **E** Loud music

Even a slight distraction can allow your concentration to drift. Maintain full concentration at all times so you stay in full control of your vehicle.

338 Mark *one* answer
As a driver you find that your eyesight has become very poor. Your optician says they cannot help you. The law says that you should tell

- ☐ **A** the licensing authority
- ☐ **B** your own doctor
- ☐ **C** the local police station
- ☐ **D** another optician

This will have a serious effect on your judgement and concentration. If you cannot meet the eyesight requirements you must tell DVLA (or DVA in Northern Ireland).

339 Mark *one* answer
When should you use hazard warning lights?

- ☐ **A** When you are double-parked on a two-way road
- ☐ **B** When your direction indicators are not working
- ☐ **C** When warning oncoming traffic that you intend to stop
- ☐ **D** When your vehicle has broken down and is causing an obstruction

Hazard warning lights are an important safety feature and should be used if you have broken down and are causing an obstruction. Don't use them as an excuse to park illegally such as when using a cash machine or post box. You may also use them on motorways to warn traffic behind you of danger ahead.

340 Mark *one* answer
You want to turn left at this junction. The view of the main road is restricted. What should you do?

- ☐ **A** Stay well back and wait to see if something comes
- ☐ **B** Build up your speed so that you can emerge quickly
- ☐ **C** Stop and apply the handbrake even if the road is clear
- ☐ **D** Approach slowly and edge out until you can see more clearly

You should slow right down, and stop if necessary, at any junction where the view is restricted. Edge forward until you can see properly. Only then can you decide if it is safe to go.

341 Mark *one* answer
When may you use hazard warning lights?

- ☐ **A** To park alongside another car
- ☐ **B** To park on double yellow lines
- ☐ **C** When you are being towed
- ☐ **D** When you have broken down

Hazard warning lights may be used to warn other road users when you have broken down and are causing an obstruction, or are on a motorway and want to warn following traffic of a hazard ahead. Don't use them when being towed or when parking illegally.

342 Mark *one* answer
Hazard warning lights should be used when vehicles are

- ☐ **A** broken down and causing an obstruction
- ☐ **B** faulty and moving slowly
- ☐ **C** being towed along a road
- ☐ **D** reversing into a side road

Don't use hazard lights as an excuse for illegal parking. If you do use them, don't forget to switch them off when you move away. There must be a warning light on the control panel to show when the hazard lights are in operation.

343 Mark *one* answer
When driving a car fitted with automatic transmission what would you use 'kick down' for?

- ☐ **A** Cruise control
- ☐ **B** Quick acceleration
- ☐ **C** Slow braking
- ☐ **D** Fuel economy

'Kick down' selects a lower gear, enabling the vehicle to accelerate faster.

344 Mark *two* answers
You are driving along this motorway. It is raining. When following this lorry you should

- ☐ **A** allow at least a two-second gap
- ☐ **B** move left and drive on the hard shoulder
- ☐ **C** allow at least a four-second gap
- ☐ **D** be aware of spray reducing your vision
- ☐ **E** move right and stay in the right-hand lane

The usual two-second time gap will increase to four seconds when the roads are wet. If you stay well back you will
- be able to see past the vehicle
- be out of the spray thrown up by the lorry's tyres
- give yourself more time to stop if the need arises
- increase your chances of being seen by the lorry driver.

345 Mark *one* answer

You are driving towards this left-hand bend. What dangers should you be aware of?

☐ **A** A vehicle overtaking you
☐ **B** No white lines in the centre of the road
☐ **C** No sign to warn you of the bend
☐ **D** Pedestrians walking towards you

Pedestrians walking on a road with no pavement should walk against the direction of the traffic. You can't see around this bend: there may be hidden dangers. Always keep this in mind so you give yourself time to react if a hazard does arise.

346 Mark *two* answers

The traffic ahead of you in the left-hand lane is slowing. You should

☐ **A** be wary of cars on your right cutting in
☐ **B** accelerate past the vehicles in the left-hand lane
☐ **C** pull up on the left-hand verge
☐ **D** move across and continue in the right-hand lane
☐ **E** slow down, keeping a safe separation distance

Allow the traffic to merge into the nearside lane. Leave enough room so that your separation distance is not reduced drastically if a vehicle pulls in ahead of you.

347 Mark *two* answers

As a provisional licence holder, you must not drive a motor car

☐ **A** at more than 40mph
☐ **B** on your own
☐ **C** on the motorway
☐ **D** under the age of 18 years at night
☐ **E** with passengers in the rear seats

When you have passed your practical test you will be able to drive on a motorway. It is recommended that you have instruction on motorway driving before you venture out on your own. Ask your instructor about this.

348 Mark *two* answers

You are not sure if your cough medicine will affect you. What TWO things should you do?

☐ **A** Ask your doctor
☐ **B** Check the medicine label
☐ **C** Drive if you feel alright
☐ **D** Ask a friend or relative for advice

If you're taking medicine or drugs prescribed by your doctor, check to ensure that they won't make you drowsy. If you forget to ask at the time of your visit to the surgery, check with your pharmacist.

Some over-the-counter medication can also cause drowsiness. Read the label and don't drive if you are affected.

349 Mark *one* answer
For which of these may you use hazard warning lights?

☐ **A** When driving on a motorway to warn traffic behind of a hazard ahead
☐ **B** When you are double-parked on a two-way road
☐ **C** When your direction indicators are not working
☐ **D** When warning oncoming traffic that you intend to stop

Hazard warning lights are an important safety feature. Use them when driving on a motorway to warn traffic behind you of danger ahead. You should also use them if your vehicle has broken down and is causing an obstruction.

350 Mark *one* answer
You are waiting to emerge at a junction. Your view is restricted by parked vehicles. What can help you to see traffic on the road you are joining?

☐ **A** Looking for traffic behind you
☐ **B** Reflections of traffic in shop windows
☐ **C** Making eye contact with other road users
☐ **D** Checking for traffic in your interior mirror

When your view is restricted into the new road you must still be completely sure it is safe to emerge. Try to look for traffic through the windows of the parked cars or the reflections in shop windows. Keep looking in all directions as you slowly edge forwards until you can see it is safe.

351 Mark *one* answer
After passing your driving test, you suffer from ill health. This affects your driving. You MUST

☐ **A** inform your local police station
☐ **B** avoid using motorways
☐ **C** always drive accompanied
☐ **D** inform the licensing authority

The licensing authority won't automatically take away your licence without investigation. For advice, contact the Driver and Vehicle Licensing Agency (or DVA in Northern Ireland).

352 Mark *one* answer
Why should the junction on the left be kept clear?

☐ **A** To allow vehicles to enter and emerge
☐ **B** To allow the bus to reverse
☐ **C** To allow vehicles to make a U-turn
☐ **D** To allow vehicles to park

You should always try to keep junctions clear. If you are in queuing traffic make sure that when you stop you leave enough space for traffic to flow in and out of the junction.

353 Mark *one* answer
Your motorway journey seems boring and you feel drowsy. What should you do?

☐ **A** Stop on the hard shoulder for a sleep
☐ **B** Open a window and stop as soon as it's safe and legal
☐ **C** Speed up to arrive at your destination sooner
☐ **D** Slow down and let other drivers overtake

Never stop on the hard shoulder to rest. If there is no service station for several miles, leave the motorway at the next exit and find somewhere safe and legal to pull over.

---

354 Mark *one* answer
You are driving on a motorway. The traffic ahead is braking sharply because of an incident. How could you warn traffic behind you?

☐ **A** Briefly use the hazard warning lights
☐ **B** Switch on the hazard warning lights continuously
☐ **C** Briefly use the rear fog lights
☐ **D** Switch on the headlights continuously

The only time you are permitted to use your hazard warning lights while moving is if you are on a motorway or dual carriageway and you need to warn other road users, particularly those behind, of a hazard or obstruction ahead. Only use them long enough to ensure your warning has been seen.

355 Mark *one* answer

Which sign means that there may be people walking along the road?

☐ A   ☐ B

☐ C   ☐ D

Always check the road signs. Triangular signs are warning signs and they'll keep you informed of hazards ahead and help you to anticipate any problems. There are a number of different signs showing pedestrians. Learn the meaning of each one.

356 Mark *one* answer

You are turning left at a junction. Pedestrians have started to cross the road. You should

☐ A go on, giving them plenty of room
☐ B stop and wave at them to cross
☐ C blow your horn and proceed
☐ D give way to them

If you're turning into a side road, pedestrians already crossing the road have priority and you should give way to them. Don't wave them across the road, sound your horn, flash your lights or give any other misleading signal. Other road users may misinterpret your signal and this may lead the pedestrians into a dangerous situation. If a pedestrian is slow or indecisive be patient and wait. Don't hurry them across by revving your engine.

357 Mark *one* answer

You are turning left from a main road into a side road. People are already crossing the road into which you are turning. You should

☐ A continue, as it is your right of way
☐ B signal to them to continue crossing
☐ C wait and allow them to cross
☐ D sound your horn to warn them of your presence

Always check the road into which you are turning. Approaching at the correct speed will allow you enough time to observe and react.

Give way to any pedestrians already crossing the road.

358 Mark *one* answer
You are at a road junction, turning into a minor road. There are pedestrians crossing the minor road. You should

- ☐ **A** stop and wave the pedestrians across
- ☐ **B** sound your horn to let the pedestrians know that you are there
- ☐ **C** give way to the pedestrians who are already crossing
- ☐ **D** carry on; the pedestrians should give way to you

Always look into the road into which you are turning. If there are pedestrians crossing, give way to them, but don't wave or signal to them to cross. Signal your intention to turn as you approach.

359 Mark *one* answer
You are turning left into a side road. What hazards should you be especially aware of?

- ☐ **A** One-way street
- ☐ **B** Pedestrians
- ☐ **C** Traffic congestion
- ☐ **D** Parked vehicles

Make sure that you have reduced your speed and are in the correct gear for the turn. Look into the road before you turn and always give way to any pedestrians who are crossing.

360 Mark *one* answer
You intend to turn right into a side road. Just before turning you should check for motorcyclists who might be

- ☐ **A** overtaking on your left
- ☐ **B** following you closely
- ☐ **C** emerging from the side road
- ☐ **D** overtaking on your right

Never attempt to change direction to the right without first checking your right-hand mirror. A motorcyclist might not have seen your signal and could be hidden by the car behind you. This action should become a matter of routine.

361 Mark *one* answer
A toucan crossing is different from other crossings because

- ☐ **A** moped riders can use it
- ☐ **B** it is controlled by a traffic warden
- ☐ **C** it is controlled by two flashing lights
- ☐ **D** cyclists can use it

Toucan crossings are shared by pedestrians and cyclists and they are shown the green light together. Cyclists are permitted to cycle across.

The signals are push-button operated and there is no flashing amber phase.

362 Mark *one* answer

How will a school crossing patrol signal you to stop?

- ☐ **A** By pointing to children on the opposite pavement
- ☐ **B** By displaying a red light
- ☐ **C** By displaying a stop sign
- ☐ **D** By giving you an arm signal

If a school crossing patrol steps out into the road with a stop sign you must stop. Don't wave anyone across the road and don't get impatient or rev your engine.

363 Mark *one* answer

Where would you see this sign?

- ☐ **A** In the window of a car taking children to school
- ☐ **B** At the side of the road
- ☐ **C** At playground areas
- ☐ **D** On the rear of a school bus or coach

Vehicles that are used to carry children to and from school will be travelling at busy times of the day. If you're following a vehicle with this sign be prepared for it to make frequent stops. It might pick up or set down passengers in places other than normal bus stops.

364 Mark *one* answer

Which sign tells you that pedestrians may be walking in the road as there is no pavement?

☐ A   ☐ B

☐ C   ☐ D

Give pedestrians who are walking at the side of the road plenty of room when you pass them. They may turn around when they hear your engine and unintentionally step into the path of your vehicle.

365 Mark *one* answer

What does this sign mean?

- ☐ **A** No route for pedestrians and cyclists
- ☐ **B** A route for pedestrians only
- ☐ **C** A route for cyclists only
- ☐ **D** A route for pedestrians and cyclists

This sign shows a shared route for pedestrians and cyclists: when it ends, the cyclists will be rejoining the main road.

366 Mark *one* answer
You see a pedestrian with a white stick and red band. This means that the person is

☐ **A** physically disabled
☐ **B** deaf only
☐ **C** blind only
☐ **D** deaf and blind

If someone is deaf as well as blind, they may be carrying a white stick with a red reflective band. You can't see if a pedestrian is deaf. Don't assume everyone can hear you approaching.

367 Mark *one* answer
What action would you take when elderly people are crossing the road?

☐ **A** Wave them across so they know that you have seen them
☐ **B** Be patient and allow them to cross in their own time
☐ **C** Rev the engine to let them know that you are waiting
☐ **D** Tap the horn in case they are hard of hearing

Be aware that older people might take a long time to cross the road. They might also be hard of hearing and not hear you approaching. Don't hurry older people across the road by getting too close to them or revving your engine.

368 Mark *one* answer
You see two elderly pedestrians about to cross the road ahead. You should

☐ **A** expect them to wait for you to pass
☐ **B** speed up to get past them quickly
☐ **C** stop and wave them across the road
☐ **D** be careful, they may misjudge your speed

Older people may have impaired hearing, vision, concentration and judgement. They may also walk slowly and so could take a long time to cross the road.

369 Mark *one* answer
You are coming up to a roundabout. A cyclist is signalling to turn right. What should you do?

☐ **A** Overtake on the right
☐ **B** Give a horn warning
☐ **C** Signal the cyclist to move across
☐ **D** Give the cyclist plenty of room

If you're following a cyclist who's signalling to turn right at a roundabout leave plenty of room. Give them space and time to get into the correct lane.

370 Mark *two* answers
Which TWO should you allow extra room when overtaking?

☐ **A** Motorcycles
☐ **B** Tractors
☐ **C** Bicycles
☐ **D** Road-sweeping vehicles

Don't pass riders too closely as this may cause them to lose balance. Always leave as much room as you would for a car, and don't cut in.

371 Mark *one* answer
Why should you look particularly for motorcyclists and cyclists at junctions?

☐ **A** They may want to turn into the side road
☐ **B** They may slow down to let you turn
☐ **C** They are harder to see
☐ **D** They might not see you turn

Cyclists and motorcyclists are smaller than other vehicles and so are more difficult to see. They can easily become hidden from your view by cars parked near a junction.

372 Mark *one* answer
You are waiting to come out of a side road. Why should you watch carefully for motorcycles?

☐ **A** Motorcycles are usually faster than cars
☐ **B** Police patrols often use motorcycles
☐ **C** Motorcycles are small and hard to see
☐ **D** Motorcycles have right of way

If you're waiting to emerge from a side road watch out for motorcycles: they're small and can be difficult to see. Be especially careful if there are parked vehicles restricting your view, there might be a motorcycle approaching.
IF YOU DON'T KNOW, DON'T GO.

373 Mark *one* answer
In daylight, an approaching motorcyclist is using a dipped headlight. Why?

☐ **A** So that the rider can be seen more easily
☐ **B** To stop the battery overcharging
☐ **C** To improve the rider's vision
☐ **D** The rider is inviting you to proceed

A motorcycle can be lost from sight behind another vehicle. The use of the headlight helps to make it more conspicuous and therefore more easily seen.

374 Mark *one* answer
Motorcyclists should wear bright clothing mainly because

☐ **A** they must do so by law
☐ **B** it helps keep them cool in summer
☐ **C** the colours are popular
☐ **D** drivers often do not see them

Motorcycles are small vehicles and can be difficult to see. If the rider wears bright clothing it can make it easier for other road users to see them approaching, especially at junctions.

375 Mark *one* answer
There is a slow-moving motorcyclist ahead of you. You are unsure what the rider is going to do. You should

☐ **A** pass on the left ☐ **B** pass on the right
☐ **C** stay behind ☐ **D** move closer

If a motorcyclist is travelling slowly it may be that they are looking for a turning or entrance. Be patient and stay behind them in case they need to make a sudden change of direction.

376 Mark *one* answer
Motorcyclists will often look round over their right shoulder just before turning right. This is because

☐ **A** they need to listen for following traffic
☐ **B** motorcycles do not have mirrors
☐ **C** looking around helps them balance as they turn
☐ **D** they need to check for traffic in their blind area

If you see a motorcyclist take a quick glance over their shoulder, this could mean they are about to change direction. Recognising a clue like this helps you to be prepared and take appropriate action, making you safer on the road.

377 Mark *three* answers
At road junctions which of the following are most vulnerable?

☐ **A** Cyclists
☐ **B** Motorcyclists
☐ **C** Pedestrians
☐ **D** Car drivers
☐ **E** Lorry drivers

Pedestrians and riders on two wheels can be harder to see than other road users. Make sure you keep a look-out for them, especially at junctions. Good effective observation, coupled with appropriate action, can save lives.

378 Mark *one* answer
Motorcyclists are particularly vulnerable

☐ **A** when moving off
☐ **B** on dual carriageways
☐ **C** when approaching junctions
☐ **D** on motorways

Another road user failing to see a motorcyclist is a major cause of collisions at junctions. Wherever streams of traffic join or cross there's the potential for this type of incident to occur.

379 Mark *two* answers
You are approaching a roundabout. There are horses just ahead of you. You should

☐ **A** be prepared to stop
☐ **B** treat them like any other vehicle
☐ **C** give them plenty of room
☐ **D** accelerate past as quickly as possible
☐ **E** sound your horn as a warning

Horse riders often keep to the outside of the roundabout even if they are turning right. Give them plenty of room and remember that they may have to cross lanes of traffic.

380 Mark *one* answer

As you approach a pelican crossing the lights change to green. Elderly people are halfway across. You should

- ☐ **A** wave them to cross as quickly as they can
- ☐ **B** rev your engine to make them hurry
- ☐ **C** flash your lights in case they have not heard you
- ☐ **D** wait because they will take longer to cross

Even if the lights turn to green, wait for them to clear the crossing. Allow them to cross the road in their own time, and don't try to hurry them by revving your engine.

381 Mark *one* answer

There are flashing amber lights under a school warning sign. What action should you take?

- ☐ **A** Reduce speed until you are clear of the area
- ☐ **B** Keep up your speed and sound the horn
- ☐ **C** Increase your speed to clear the area quickly
- ☐ **D** Wait at the lights until they change to green

The flashing amber lights are switched on to warn you that children may be crossing near a school. Slow down and take extra care as you may have to stop.

382 Mark *one* answer

These road markings must be kept clear to allow

- ☐ **A** school children to be dropped off
- ☐ **B** for teachers to park
- ☐ **C** school children to be picked up
- ☐ **D** a clear view of the crossing area

The markings are there to show that the area must be kept clear to allow an unrestricted view for

- • approaching drivers and riders
- • children wanting to cross the road.

383 Mark *one* answer

Where would you see this sign?

- ☐ **A** Near a school crossing
- ☐ **B** At a playground entrance
- ☐ **C** On a school bus
- ☐ **D** At a 'pedestrians only' area

Watch out for children crossing the road from the other side of the bus.

384 Mark *one* answer

You are following two cyclists. They approach a roundabout in the left-hand lane. In which direction should you expect the cyclists to go?

☐ **A** Left
☐ **B** Right
☐ **C** Any direction
☐ **D** Straight ahead

Cyclists approaching a roundabout in the left-hand lane may be turning right but may not have been able to get into the correct lane due to the heavy traffic. They may also feel safer keeping to the left all the way round the roundabout. Be aware of them and give them plenty of room.

385 Mark *one* answer

You are travelling behind a moped. You want to turn left just ahead. You should

☐ **A** overtake the moped before the junction
☐ **B** pull alongside the moped and stay level until just before the junction
☐ **C** sound your horn as a warning and pull in front of the moped
☐ **D** stay behind until the moped has passed the junction

Passing the moped and turning into the junction could mean that you cut across the front of the rider. This might force them to slow down, stop or even lose control. Slow down and stay behind the moped until it has passed the junction and you can then turn safely.

386 Mark *one* answer

You see a horse rider as you approach a roundabout. They are signalling right but keeping well to the left. You should

☐ **A** proceed as normal
☐ **B** keep close to them
☐ **C** cut in front of them
☐ **D** stay well back

Allow the horse rider to enter and exit the roundabout in their own time. They may feel safer keeping to the left all the way around the roundabout. Don't get up close behind or alongside them. This is very likely to upset the horse and create a dangerous situation.

387 Mark *one* answer

How would you react to drivers who appear to be inexperienced?

☐ **A** Sound your horn to warn them of your presence
☐ **B** Be patient and prepare for them to react more slowly
☐ **C** Flash your headlights to indicate that it is safe for them to proceed
☐ **D** Overtake them as soon as possible

Learners might not have confidence when they first start to drive. Allow them plenty of room and don't react adversely to their hesitation. We all learn from experience, but new drivers will have had less practice in dealing with all the situations that might occur.

388 Mark *one* answer
You are following a learner driver who stalls at a junction. You should

- **A** be patient as you expect them to make mistakes
- **B** stay very close behind and flash your headlights
- **C** start to rev your engine if they take too long to restart
- **D** immediately steer around them and drive on

Learning is a process of practice and experience. Try to understand this and tolerate those who are at the beginning of this process.

389 Mark *one* answer
You are on a country road. What should you expect to see coming towards you on YOUR side of the road?

- **A** Motorcycles
- **B** Bicycles
- **C** Pedestrians
- **D** Horse riders

On a quiet country road always be aware that there may be a hazard just around the next bend, such as a slow-moving vehicle or pedestrians. Pedestrians are advised to walk on the right-hand side of the road if there is no pavement, so they may be walking towards you on your side of the road.

390 Mark *one* answer
You are turning left into a side road. Pedestrians are crossing the road near the junction. You must

- **A** wave them on
- **B** sound your horn
- **C** switch on your hazard lights
- **D** wait for them to cross

Check that it's clear before you turn into a junction. If there are pedestrians crossing they have priority, so let them cross in their own time.

391 Mark *one* answer
You are following a car driven by an elderly driver. You should

- **A** expect the driver to drive badly
- **B** flash your lights and overtake
- **C** be aware that the driver's reactions may not be as fast as yours
- **D** stay very close behind but be careful

You must show consideration to other road users. The reactions of older drivers may be slower and they might need more time to deal with a situation. Be tolerant and don't lose patience or show your annoyance.

392 Mark *one* answer
You are following a cyclist. You wish to turn left just ahead. You should

- ☐ **A** overtake the cyclist before the junction
- ☐ **B** pull alongside the cyclist and stay level until after the junction
- ☐ **C** hold back until the cyclist has passed the junction
- ☐ **D** go around the cyclist on the junction

Make allowances for cyclists. Allow them plenty of room. Don't try to overtake and then immediately turn left. Be patient and stay behind them until they have passed the junction.

393 Mark *one* answer
A horse rider is in the left-hand lane approaching a roundabout. You should expect the rider to

- ☐ **A** go in any direction
- ☐ **B** turn right
- ☐ **C** turn left
- ☐ **D** go ahead

Horses and their riders will move more slowly than other road users. They might not have time to cut across heavy traffic to take up positions in the offside lane. For this reason a horse and rider may approach a roundabout in the left-hand lane, even though they're turning right.

394 Mark *one* answer
Powered vehicles used by disabled people are small and hard to see. How do they give early warning when on a dual carriageway?

- ☐ **A** They will have a flashing red light
- ☐ **B** They will have a flashing green light
- ☐ **C** They will have a flashing blue light
- ☐ **D** They will have a flashing amber light.

Powered vehicles used by disabled people are small, low, hard to see and travel very slowly. On a dual carriageway a flashing amber light will warn other road users.

395 Mark *one* answer
You should never attempt to overtake a cyclist

- ☐ **A** just before you turn left
- ☐ **B** on a left-hand bend
- ☐ **C** on a one-way street
- ☐ **D** on a dual carriageway

If you want to turn left and there's a cyclist in front of you, hold back. Wait until the cyclist has passed the junction and then turn left behind them.

396 Mark *one* answer
Ahead of you there is a moving vehicle with a flashing amber beacon. This means it is

- ☐ **A** slow moving
- ☐ **B** broken down
- ☐ **C** a doctor's car
- ☐ **D** a school crossing patrol

As you approach the vehicle, assess the situation. Due to its slow progress you will need to judge whether it is safe to overtake.

397 Mark *one* answer
What does this sign mean?

- ☐ **A** Contraflow pedal cycle lane
- ☐ **B** With-flow pedal cycle lane
- ☐ **C** Pedal cycles and buses only
- ☐ **D** No pedal cycles or buses

The picture of a cycle will also usually be painted on the road, sometimes with a different coloured surface. Leave these clear for cyclists and don't pass too closely when you overtake.

398 Mark *one* answer
You notice horse riders in front. What should you do FIRST?

- ☐ **A** Pull out to the middle of the road
- ☐ **B** Slow down and be ready to stop
- ☐ **C** Accelerate around them
- ☐ **D** Signal right

Be particularly careful when approaching horse riders – slow down and be prepared to stop. Always pass wide and slowly and look out for signals given by horse riders. Horses are unpredictable: always treat them as potential hazards and take great care when passing them.

399 Mark *one* answer
You must not stop on these road markings because you may obstruct

- ☐ **A** children's view of the crossing area
- ☐ **B** teachers' access to the school
- ☐ **C** delivery vehicles' access to the school
- ☐ **D** emergency vehicles' access to the school

These markings are found on the road outside schools. DO NOT stop (even to set down or pick up children) or park on them. The markings are to make sure that drivers, riders, children and other pedestrians have a clear view.

400 Mark *one* answer
The left-hand pavement is closed due to street repairs. What should you do?

- ☐ **A** Watch out for pedestrians walking in the road
- ☐ **B** Use your right-hand mirror more often
- ☐ **C** Speed up to get past the roadworks quicker
- ☐ **D** Position close to the left-hand kerb

Where street repairs have closed off pavements, proceed carefully and slowly as pedestrians might have to walk in the road.

401 Mark *one* answer
You are following a motorcyclist on an uneven road. You should

- ☐ **A** allow less room so you can be seen in their mirrors
- ☐ **B** overtake immediately
- ☐ **C** allow extra room in case they swerve to avoid potholes
- ☐ **D** allow the same room as normal because road surfaces do not affect motorcyclists

Potholes and bumps in the road can unbalance a motorcyclist. For this reason the rider might swerve to avoid an uneven road surface. Watch out at places where this is likely to occur.

402 Mark *one* answer
What does this sign tell you?

- ☐ **A** No cycling
- ☐ **B** Cycle route ahead
- ☐ **C** Cycle parking only
- ☐ **D** End of cycle route

With people's concern today for the environment, cycle routes are being created in our towns and cities. These are usually defined by road markings and signs. Respect the presence of cyclists on the road and give them plenty of room if you need to pass.

403 Mark *one* answer
You are approaching this roundabout and see the cyclist signal right. Why is the cyclist keeping to the left?

- ☐ **A** It is a quicker route for the cyclist
- ☐ **B** The cyclist is going to turn left instead
- ☐ **C** The cyclist thinks The Highway Code does not apply to bicycles
- ☐ **D** The cyclist is slower and more vulnerable

Cycling in today's heavy traffic can be hazardous. Some cyclists may not feel happy about crossing the path of traffic to take up a position in an outside lane. Be aware of this and understand that, although in the left-hand lane, the cyclist might be turning right.

404 Mark *one* answer
You are approaching this crossing. You should

- ☐ **A** prepare to slow down and stop
- ☐ **B** stop and wave the pedestrians across
- ☐ **C** speed up and pass by quickly
- ☐ **D** continue unless the pedestrians step out

Be courteous and prepare to stop. Do not wave people across as this could be dangerous if another vehicle is approaching the crossing.

405 Mark *one* answer

You see a pedestrian with a dog. The dog has a yellow or burgundy coat. This especially warns you that the pedestrian is

☐ **A** elderly
☐ **B** dog training
☐ **C** colour blind
☐ **D** deaf

Take extra care as the pedestrian may not be aware of vehicles approaching.

406 Mark *one* answer

At toucan crossings

☐ **A** you only stop if someone is waiting to cross
☐ **B** cyclists are not permitted
☐ **C** there is a continuously flashing amber beacon
☐ **D** pedestrians and cyclists may cross

There are some crossings where cycle routes lead the cyclists to cross at the same place as pedestrians. These are called toucan crossings. Always look out for cyclists, as they're likely to be approaching faster than pedestrians.

407 Mark *one* answer

Some junctions controlled by traffic lights have a marked area between two stop lines. What is this for?

☐ **A** To allow taxis to position in front of other traffic
☐ **B** To allow people with disabilities to cross the road
☐ **C** To allow cyclists and pedestrians to cross the road together
☐ **D** To allow cyclists to position in front of other traffic

These are known as advanced stop lines. When the lights are red (or about to become red) you should stop at the first white line. However if you have crossed that line as the lights change you must stop at the second line even if it means you are in the area reserved for cyclists.

408 Mark *one* answer

At some traffic lights there are advance stop lines and a marked area. What are these for?

☐ **A** To allow cyclists to position in front of other traffic
☐ **B** To let pedestrians cross when the lights change
☐ **C** To prevent traffic from jumping the lights
☐ **D** To let passengers get off a bus which is queuing

You should always stop at the first white line. Avoid going into the marked area which is reserved for cyclists only. However, if you have crossed the first white line at the time the signal changes to red you must stop at the second line even if you are in the marked area.

409 Mark *one* answer

When you are overtaking a cyclist you should leave as much room as you would give to a car. What is the main reason for this?

- ☐ **A** The cyclist might speed up
- ☐ **B** The cyclist might get off the bike
- ☐ **C** The cyclist might swerve
- ☐ **D** The cyclist might have to make a left turn

Before overtaking assess the situation. Look well ahead to see if the cyclist will need to change direction. Be especially aware of the cyclist approaching parked vehicles as they will need to alter course. Do not pass too closely or cut in sharply.

410 Mark *three* answers

Which THREE should you do when passing sheep on a road?

- ☐ **A** Allow plenty of room
- ☐ **B** Go very slowly
- ☐ **C** Pass quickly but quietly
- ☐ **D** Be ready to stop
- ☐ **E** Briefly sound your horn

Slow down and be ready to stop if you see animals in the road ahead. Animals are easily frightened by noise and vehicles passing too close to them. Stop if signalled to do so by the person in charge.

411 Mark *one* answer

At night you see a pedestrian wearing reflective clothing and carrying a bright red light. What does this mean?

- ☐ **A** You are approaching roadworks
- ☐ **B** You are approaching an organised walk
- ☐ **C** You are approaching a slow-moving vehicle
- ☐ **D** You are approaching a traffic danger spot

The people on the walk should be keeping to the left, but don't assume this. Pass slowly, make sure you have time to do so safely. Be aware that the pedestrians have their backs to you and may not know that you're there.

412 Mark *one* answer

You have just passed your test. How can you reduce your risk of being involved in a collision?

- ☐ **A** By always staying close to the vehicle in front
- ☐ **B** By never going over 40mph
- ☐ **C** By staying only in the left-hand lane on all roads
- ☐ **D** By taking further training

New drivers and riders are often involved in a collision or incident early in their driving career. Due to a lack of experience they may not react to hazards as quickly as more experienced road users. Approved training courses are offered by driver and rider training schools. The Pass Plus scheme has been created by DSA for new drivers who would like to improve their basic skills and safely widen their driving experience.

413 Mark *one* answer
You want to reverse into a side road. You are not sure that the area behind your car is clear. What should you do?

☐ **A** Look through the rear window only
☐ **B** Get out and check
☐ **C** Check the mirrors only
☐ **D** Carry on, assuming it is clear

If you cannot be sure whether there is anything behind you, it is always safest to check before reversing. There may be a small child or a low obstruction close behind your car. The shape and size of your vehicle can restrict visibility.

414 Mark *one* answer
You are about to reverse into a side road. A pedestrian wishes to cross behind you. You should

☐ **A** wave to the pedestrian to stop
☐ **B** give way to the pedestrian
☐ **C** wave to the pedestrian to cross
☐ **D** reverse before the pedestrian starts to cross

If you need to reverse into a side road try to find a place that's free from traffic and pedestrians. Look all around before and during the manoeuvre. Stop and give way to any pedestrians who want to cross behind you. Avoid waving them across, sounding the horn, flashing your lights or giving any misleading signals that could lead them into a dangerous situation.

415 Mark *one* answer
Who is especially in danger of not being seen as you reverse your car?

☐ **A** Motorcyclists
☐ **B** Car drivers
☐ **C** Cyclists
☐ **D** Children

As you look through the rear of your vehicle you may not be able to see a small child. Be aware of this before you reverse. If there are children about, get out and check if it is clear before reversing.

416 Mark *one* answer
You are reversing around a corner when you notice a pedestrian walking behind you. What should you do?

☐ **A** Slow down and wave the pedestrian across
☐ **B** Continue reversing and steer round the pedestrian
☐ **C** Stop and give way
☐ **D** Continue reversing and sound your horn

Wait until the pedestrian has passed, then look around again before you start to reverse. Don't forget that you may not be able to see a small child directly behind your vehicle. Be aware of the possibility of hidden dangers.

417 Mark *one* answer

You want to turn right from a junction but your view is restricted by parked vehicles. What should you do?

- ☐ **A** Move out quickly, but be prepared to stop
- ☐ **B** Sound your horn and pull out if there is no reply
- ☐ **C** Stop, then move slowly forward until you have a clear view
- ☐ **D** Stop, get out and look along the main road to check

If you want to turn right from a junction and your view is restricted, STOP. Ease forward until you can see – there might be something approaching.
IF YOU DON'T KNOW, DON'T GO.

418 Mark *one* answer

You are at the front of a queue of traffic waiting to turn right into a side road. Why is it important to check your right mirror just before turning?

- ☐ **A** To look for pedestrians about to cross
- ☐ **B** To check for overtaking vehicles
- ☐ **C** To make sure the side road is clear
- ☐ **D** To check for emerging traffic

There could be a motorcyclist riding along the outside of the queue. Always check your mirror before turning as situations behind you can change in the time you have been waiting to turn.

419 Mark *one* answer

What must a driver do at a pelican crossing when the amber light is flashing?

- ☐ **A** Signal the pedestrian to cross
- ☐ **B** Always wait for the green light before proceeding
- ☐ **C** Give way to any pedestrians on the crossing
- ☐ **D** Wait for the red-and-amber light before proceeding

The flashing amber light allows pedestrians already on the crossing to get to the other side before a green light shows to the traffic. Be aware that some pedestrians, such as elderly people and young children, need longer to cross. Let them do this at their own pace.

420 Mark *two* answers

You have stopped at a pelican crossing. A disabled person is crossing slowly in front of you. The lights have now changed to green. You should

- ☐ **A** allow the person to cross
- ☐ **B** drive in front of the person
- ☐ **C** drive behind the person
- ☐ **D** sound your horn
- ☐ **E** be patient
- ☐ **F** edge forward slowly

At a pelican crossing the green light means you may proceed as long as the crossing is clear. If someone hasn't finished crossing, be patient and wait for them.

421 Mark *one* answer

You are driving past a line of parked cars. You notice a ball bouncing out into the road ahead. What should you do?

- ☐ **A** Continue driving at the same speed and sound your horn
- ☐ **B** Continue driving at the same speed and flash your headlights
- ☐ **C** Slow down and be prepared to stop for children
- ☐ **D** Stop and wave the children across to fetch their ball

Beware of children playing in the street and running out into the road. If a ball bounces out from the pavement, slow down and stop. Don't encourage anyone to retrieve it. Other road users may not see your signal and you might lead a child into a dangerous situation.

422 Mark *one* answer

You want to turn right from a main road into a side road. Just before turning you should

- ☐ **A** cancel your right-turn signal
- ☐ **B** select first gear
- ☐ **C** check for traffic overtaking on your right
- ☐ **D** stop and set the handbrake

Motorcyclists often overtake queues of vehicles. Make one last check in your mirror and your blind spot to avoid turning across their path.

423 Mark *one* answer

You are driving in slow-moving queues of traffic. Just before changing lane you should

- ☐ **A** sound the horn
- ☐ **B** look for motorcyclists filtering through the traffic
- ☐ **C** give a 'slowing down' arm signal
- ☐ **D** change down to first gear

In this situation motorcyclists could be passing you on either side. Always check before you change lanes or change direction.

424 Mark *one* answer

You are driving in town. There is a bus at the bus stop on the other side of the road. Why should you be careful?

- ☐ **A** The bus may have broken down
- ☐ **B** Pedestrians may come from behind the bus
- ☐ **C** The bus may move off suddenly
- ☐ **D** The bus may remain stationary

If you see a bus ahead watch out for pedestrians. They may not be able to see you if they're crossing from behind the bus.

425 Mark *one* answer
How should you overtake horse riders?

☐ **A** Drive up close and overtake as soon as possible
☐ **B** Speed is not important but allow plenty of room
☐ **C** Use your horn just once to warn them
☐ **D** Drive slowly and leave plenty of room

When you're on country roads be aware of particular dangers. Be prepared for farm animals, horses, pedestrians, farm vehicles and wild animals. Always be prepared to slow down or stop.

426 Mark *one* answer
You are driving on a main road. You intend to turn right into a side road. Just before turning you should

☐ **A** adjust your interior mirror
☐ **B** flash your headlamps
☐ **C** steer over to the left
☐ **D** check for traffic overtaking on your right

A last check in the offside mirror and blind spot will allow you sight of any cyclist or motorcyclist overtaking as you wait to turn.

427 Mark *one* answer
Why should you allow extra room when overtaking a motorcyclist on a windy day?

☐ **A** The rider may turn off suddenly to get out of the wind
☐ **B** The rider may be blown across in front of you
☐ **C** The rider may stop suddenly
☐ **D** The rider may be travelling faster than normal

If you're driving in high winds, be aware that the conditions might force a motorcyclist or cyclist to swerve or wobble. Take this into consideration if you're following or wish to overtake a two-wheeled vehicle.

428 Mark *one* answer
Where in particular should you look out for motorcyclists?

☐ **A** In a filling station
☐ **B** At a road junction
☐ **C** Near a service area
☐ **D** When entering a car park

Always look out for motorcyclists, and cyclists, particularly at junctions. They are smaller and usually more difficult to see than other vehicles.

429 Mark *one* answer

Where should you take particular care to look out for motorcyclists and cyclists?

☐ **A** On dual carriageways
☐ **B** At junctions
☐ **C** At zebra crossings
☐ **D** On one-way streets

Motorcyclists and cyclists are often more difficult to see on the road. This is especially the case at junctions. You may not be able to see a motorcyclist approaching a junction if your view is blocked by other traffic. A motorcycle may be travelling as fast as a car, sometimes faster. Make sure that you judge speeds correctly before you emerge.

430 Mark *one* answer

The road outside this school is marked with yellow zigzag lines. What do these lines mean?

☐ **A** You may park on the lines when dropping off school children
☐ **B** You may park on the lines when picking school children up
☐ **C** You must not wait or park your vehicle here at all
☐ **D** You must stay with your vehicle if you park here

Parking here would block the view of the school entrance and would endanger the lives of children on their way to and from school.

431 Mark *one* answer

You are driving past parked cars. You notice a bicycle wheel sticking out between them. What should you do?

☐ **A** Accelerate past quickly and sound your horn
☐ **B** Slow down and wave the cyclist across
☐ **C** Brake sharply and flash your headlights
☐ **D** Slow down and be prepared to stop for a cyclist

Scan the road as you drive. Try to anticipate hazards by being aware of the places where they are likely to occur. You'll then be able to react in good time, if necessary.

432 Mark *one* answer

You are dazzled at night by a vehicle behind you. You should

☐ **A** set your mirror to anti-dazzle
☐ **B** set your mirror to dazzle the other driver
☐ **C** brake sharply to a stop
☐ **D** switch your rear lights on and off

The interior mirror of most vehicles can be set to the anti-dazzle position. You will still be able to see the lights of the traffic behind you, but the dazzle will be greatly reduced.

433 Mark *one* answer

You are driving towards a zebra crossing. A person in a wheelchair is waiting to cross. What should you do?

- ☐ **A** Continue on your way
- ☐ **B** Wave to the person to cross
- ☐ **C** Wave to the person to wait
- ☐ **D** Be prepared to stop

You should slow down and be prepared to stop as you would with an able-bodied person. Don't wave them across as other traffic may not stop.

434 Mark *one* answer

Yellow zigzag lines on the road outside schools mean

- ☐ **A** sound your horn to alert other road users
- ☐ **B** stop to allow children to cross
- ☐ **C** you should not park or stop on these lines
- ☐ **D** you must not drive over these lines

Where there are yellow zigzag markings, you should not park, wait or stop, even to pick up or drop off children. A vehicle parked on the zigzag lines would obstruct children's view of the road and other drivers view of the pavement. Where there is an upright sign there is mandatory prohibition of stopping during the times shown.

435 Mark *one* answer

What do these road markings outside a school mean?

- ☐ **A** You may park here if you are a teacher
- ☐ **B** Sound your horn before parking
- ☐ **C** When parking, use your hazard warning lights
- ☐ **D** You should not wait or park your vehicle here

These markings are used outside schools so that children can see and be seen clearly when crossing the road. Parking here would block people's view of the school entrance. This could endanger the lives of children on their way to and from school.

436 Mark *one* answer

You are about to overtake a slow-moving motorcyclist. Which one of these signs would make you take special care?

☐ A  ☐ B

☐ C ☐ D

In windy weather, watch out for motorcyclists and also cyclists as they can be blown sideways into your path. When you pass them, leave plenty of room and check their position in your mirror before pulling back in.

437 Mark *one* answer

You are waiting to emerge left from a minor road. A large vehicle is approaching from the right. You have time to turn, but you should wait. Why?

☐ A The large vehicle can easily hide an overtaking vehicle
☐ B The large vehicle can turn suddenly
☐ C The large vehicle is difficult to steer in a straight line
☐ D The large vehicle can easily hide vehicles from the left

Large vehicles can hide other vehicles that are overtaking, especially motorcycles which may be filtering past queuing traffic. You need to be aware of the possibility of hidden vehicles and not assume that it is safe to emerge.

438 Mark *one* answer

You are following a long vehicle. It approaches a crossroads and signals left, but moves out to the right. You should

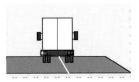

☐ A get closer in order to pass it quickly
☐ B stay well back and give it room
☐ C assume the signal is wrong and it is really turning right
☐ D overtake as it starts to slow down

A lorry may swing out to the right as it approaches a left turn. This is to allow the rear wheels to clear the kerb as it turns. Don't try to filter through if you see a gap on the nearside.

439 Mark *one* answer

You are following a long vehicle approaching a crossroads. The driver signals right but moves close to the left-hand kerb. What should you do?

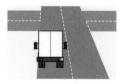

☐ **A** Warn the driver of the wrong signal
☐ **B** Wait behind the long vehicle
☐ **C** Report the driver to the police
☐ **D** Overtake on the right-hand side

When a long vehicle is going to turn right it may need to keep close to the left-hand kerb. This is to prevent the rear end of the trailer cutting the corner. You need to be aware of how long vehicles behave in such situations. Don't overtake the lorry because it could turn as you're alongside. Stay behind and wait for it to turn.

440 Mark *one* answer

You are approaching a mini-roundabout. The long vehicle in front is signalling left but positioned over to the right. You should

☐ **A** sound your horn
☐ **B** overtake on the left
☐ **C** follow the same course as the lorry
☐ **D** keep well back

At mini-roundabouts there isn't much room for a long vehicle to manoeuvre. It will have to swing out wide so that it can complete the turn safely. Keep well back and don't try to move up alongside it.

441 Mark *one* answer

Before overtaking a large vehicle you should keep well back. Why is this?

☐ **A** To give acceleration space to overtake quickly on blind bends
☐ **B** To get the best view of the road ahead
☐ **C** To leave a gap in case the vehicle stops and rolls back
☐ **D** To offer other drivers a safe gap if they want to overtake you

When following a large vehicle keep well back. If you're too close you won't be able to see the road ahead and the driver of the long vehicle might not be able to see you in their mirrors.

442 Mark *two* answers
You are travelling behind a bus that pulls up at a bus stop. What should you do?

☐ **A** Accelerate past the bus sounding your horn
☐ **B** Watch carefully for pedestrians
☐ **C** Be ready to give way to the bus
☐ **D** Pull in closely behind the bus

There might be pedestrians crossing from in front of the bus. Look out for them if you intend to pass. Consider staying back and waiting.

How many people are waiting to get on the bus? Check the queue if you can. The bus might move off straight away if there is no one waiting to get on.

If a bus is signalling to pull out, give it priority as long as it is safe to do so.

443 Mark *one* answer
You are following a large lorry on a wet road. Spray makes it difficult to see. You should

☐ **A** drop back until you can see better
☐ **B** put your headlights on full beam
☐ **C** keep close to the lorry, away from the spray
☐ **D** speed up and overtake quickly

Large vehicles may throw up a lot of spray when the roads are wet. This will make it difficult for you to see ahead. Dropping back further will
• move you out of the spray and allow you to see further
• increase your separation distance. It takes longer to stop when the roads are wet and you need to allow more room.

Don't
• follow the vehicle in front too closely
• overtake, unless you can see and are sure that the way ahead is clear.

444 Mark *one* answer
You are following a large articulated vehicle. It is going to turn left into a narrow road. What action should you take?

☐ **A** Move out and overtake on the right
☐ **B** Pass on the left as the vehicle moves out
☐ **C** Be prepared to stop behind
☐ **D** Overtake quickly before the lorry moves out

Lorries are larger and longer than other vehicles and this can affect their position when approaching junctions. When turning left they may move out to the right so that they don't cut in and mount the kerb with the rear wheels.

445 Mark *one* answer
You keep well back while waiting to overtake a large vehicle. A car fills the gap. You should

☐ **A** sound your horn
☐ **B** drop back further
☐ **C** flash your headlights
☐ **D** start to overtake

It's very frustrating when your separation distance is shortened by another vehicle. React positively, stay calm and drop further back.

446 Mark *one* answer
You are following a long lorry. The driver signals to turn left into a narrow road. What should you do?

☐ **A** Overtake on the left before the lorry reaches the junction
☐ **B** Overtake on the right as soon as the lorry slows down
☐ **C** Do not overtake unless you can see there is no oncoming traffic
☐ **D** Do not overtake, stay well back and be prepared to stop.

When turning into narrow roads articulated and long vehicles will need more room. Initially they will need to swing out in the opposite direction to which they intend to turn. They could mask another vehicle turning out of the same junction. DON'T be tempted to overtake them or pass on the inside.

447 Mark *one* answer
When you approach a bus signalling to move off from a bus stop you should

☐ **A** get past before it moves
☐ **B** allow it to pull away, if it is safe to do so
☐ **C** flash your headlights as you approach
☐ **D** signal left and wave the bus on

Try to give way to buses if you can do so safely, especially when they signal to pull away from bus stops. Look out for people who've stepped off the bus, or are running to catch it, and may try to cross the road without looking. Don't try to accelerate past before it moves away or flash your lights as other road users may be misled by this signal.

448 Mark *one* answer
You wish to overtake a long, slow-moving vehicle on a busy road. You should

- ☐ **A** follow it closely and keep moving out to see the road ahead
- ☐ **B** flash your headlights for the oncoming traffic to give way
- ☐ **C** stay behind until the driver waves you past
- ☐ **D** keep well back until you can see that it is clear

If you want to overtake a long vehicle, stay well back so that you can get a better view of the road ahead. The closer you get the less you will be able to see of the road ahead. Be patient, overtaking calls for sound judgement. DON'T take a gamble, only overtake when you are certain that you can complete the manoeuvre safely.

449 Mark *one* answer
Which of these is LEAST likely to be affected by crosswinds?

- ☐ **A** Cyclists
- ☐ **B** Motorcyclists
- ☐ **C** High-sided vehicles
- ☐ **D** Cars

Although cars are the least likely to be affected, crosswinds can take anyone by surprise. This is most likely to happen after overtaking a large vehicle, when passing gaps between hedges or buildings, and on exposed sections of road.

450 Mark *one* answer
What should you do as you approach this lorry?

- ☐ **A** Slow down and be prepared to wait
- ☐ **B** Make the lorry wait for you
- ☐ **C** Flash your lights at the lorry
- ☐ **D** Move to the right-hand side of the road

When turning, long vehicles need much more room on the road than other vehicles. At junctions they may take up the whole of the road space, so be patient and allow them the room they need.

451 Mark *one* answer
You are following a large vehicle approaching crossroads. The driver signals to turn left. What should you do?

- ☐ **A** Overtake if you can leave plenty of room
- ☐ **B** Overtake only if there are no oncoming vehicles
- ☐ **C** Do not overtake until the vehicle begins to turn.
- ☐ **D** Do not overtake when at or approaching a junction.

Hold back and wait until the vehicle has turned before proceeding. Do not overtake because the vehicle turning left could hide a vehicle emerging from the same junction.

452 Mark *one* answer

Powered vehicles, such as wheelchairs or scooters, used by disabled people have a maximum speed of

☐ **A** 8mph
☐ **B** 12mph
☐ **C** 16mph
☐ **D** 20mph

These are small battery powered vehicles and include wheelchairs and mobility scooters. Some are designed for use on the pavement only and have an upper speed limit of 4mph (6km/h). Others can go on the road as well and have a speed limit of 8mph (12km/h). They are now very common and are generally used by the elderly, disabled or infirm. Take great care as they are extremely vulnerable because of their low speed and small size.

453 Mark *one* answer

Why is it more difficult to overtake a large vehicle than a car?

☐ **A** It takes longer to pass one
☐ **B** They may suddenly pull up
☐ **C** Their brakes are not as good
☐ **D** They climb hills more slowly

Depending on relevant speed, it will usually take you longer to pass a lorry than other vehicles. Some hazards to watch for include oncoming traffic, junctions ahead, bends or dips which could restrict your view, and signs or road markings that prohibit overtaking. Make sure you can see that it's safe to complete the manoeuvre before you start to overtake.

454 Mark *one* answer

In front of you is a class 3 powered vehicle (powered wheelchair) driven by a disabled person. These vehicles have a maximum speed of

☐ **A** 8mph (12km/h)
☐ **B** 18mph (29km/h)
☐ **C** 28mph (45km/h)
☐ **D** 38mph (61km/h)

These vehicles are battery powered and very vulnerable due to their slow speed, small size and low height. Some are designed for pavement and road use and have a maximum speed of 8mph (12km/h). Others are for pavement use only and are restricted to 4mph (6km/h). Take extra care and be patient if you are following one. Allow plenty of room when overtaking and do not go past unless you can do so safely.

455 Mark *one* answer

It is very windy. You are behind a motorcyclist who is overtaking a high-sided vehicle. What should you do?

☐ **A** Overtake the motorcyclist immediately
☐ **B** Keep well back
☐ **C** Stay level with the motorcyclist
☐ **D** Keep close to the motorcyclist

Motorcyclists are affected more by windy weather than other vehicles. In windy conditions, high-sided vehicles cause air turbulence. You should keep well back as the motorcyclist could be blown off course.

456 Mark *one* answer

It is very windy. You are about to overtake a motorcyclist. You should

☐ **A** overtake slowly
☐ **B** allow extra room
☐ **C** sound your horn
☐ **D** keep close as you pass

Crosswinds can blow a motorcyclist or cyclist across the lane. Passing too close could also cause a draught, unbalancing the rider.

---

457 Mark *two* answers

You are driving in town. Ahead of you a bus is at a bus stop. Which TWO of the following should you do?

☐ **A** Be prepared to give way if the bus suddenly moves off
☐ **B** Continue at the same speed but sound your horn as a warning
☐ **C** Watch carefully for the sudden appearance of pedestrians
☐ **D** Pass the bus as quickly as you possibly can

As you approach, look out for any signal the driver might make. If you pass the vehicle watch out for pedestrians attempting to cross the road from the other side of the bus. They will be hidden from view until the last moment.

458 Mark *one* answer

You are driving along this road. What should you be prepared to do?

☐ **A** Sound your horn and continue
☐ **B** Slow down and give way
☐ **C** Report the driver to the police
☐ **D** Squeeze through the gap

Sometimes large vehicles may need more space than other road users. If a vehicle needs more time and space to turn be prepared to stop and wait.

---

459 Mark *one* answer

As a driver why should you be more careful where trams operate?

☐ **A** Because they do not have a horn
☐ **B** Because they do not stop for cars
☐ **C** Because they do not have lights
☐ **D** Because they cannot steer to avoid you

You should take extra care when you first encounter trams. You will have to get used to dealing with a different traffic system.
    Be aware that they can accelerate and travel very quickly and that they cannot change direction to avoid obstructions.

460 Mark *one* answer
You are towing a caravan. Which is the safest type of rear-view mirror to use?

☐ **A** Interior wide-angle mirror
☐ **B** Extended-arm side mirrors
☐ **C** Ordinary door mirrors
☐ **D** Ordinary interior mirror

Towing a large trailer or caravan can greatly reduce your view of the road behind. You need to use the correct equipment to make sure you can see clearly behind and down both sides of the caravan or trailer.

461 Mark *two* answers
You are driving in heavy traffic on a wet road. Spray makes it difficult to be seen. You should use your

☐ **A** full beam headlights
☐ **B** rear fog lights if visibility is less than 100 metres (328 feet)
☐ **C** rear fog lights if visibility is more than 100 metres (328 feet)
☐ **D** dipped headlights
☐ **E** sidelights only

You must ensure that you can be seen by others on the road. Use your dipped headlights during the day if the visibility is bad. If you use your rear fog lights, don't forget to turn them off when the visibility improves.

462 Mark *one* answer
It is a very windy day and you are about to overtake a cyclist. What should you do?

☐ **A** Overtake very closely
☐ **B** Keep close as you pass
☐ **C** Sound your horn repeatedly
☐ **D** Allow extra room

Cyclists, and motorcyclists, are very vulnerable in crosswinds. They can easily be blown well off course and veer into your path. Always allow plenty of room when overtaking them. Passing too close could cause a draught and unbalance the rider.

463 Mark *three* answers
In which THREE of these situations may you overtake another vehicle on the left?

☐ **A** When you are in a one-way street
☐ **B** When approaching a motorway slip road where you will be turning off
☐ **C** When the vehicle in front is signalling to turn right
☐ **D** When a slower vehicle is travelling in the right-hand lane of a dual carriageway
☐ **E** In slow-moving traffic queues when traffic in the right-hand lane is moving more slowly

At certain times of the day, traffic might be heavy. If traffic is moving slowly in queues and vehicles in the right-hand lane are moving more slowly, you may overtake on the left. Don't keep changing lanes to try and beat the queue.

464 Mark *one* answer
You are travelling in very heavy rain. Your overall stopping distance is likely to be

☐ **A** doubled
☐ **B** halved
☐ **C** up to ten times greater
☐ **D** no different

As well as visibility being reduced, the road will be extremely wet. This will reduce the grip the tyres have on the road and increase the distance it takes to stop. Double your separation distance.

465 Mark *two* answers
Which TWO of the following are correct? When overtaking at night you should

☐ **A** wait until a bend so that you can see the oncoming headlights
☐ **B** sound your horn twice before moving out
☐ **C** be careful because you can see less
☐ **D** beware of bends in the road ahead
☐ **E** put headlights on full beam

Only overtake the vehicle in front if it's really necessary. At night the risks are increased due to the poor visibility. Don't overtake if there's a possibility of
• road junctions
• bends ahead
• the brow of a bridge or hill, except on a dual carriageway
• pedestrian crossings
• double white lines ahead
• vehicles changing direction
• any other potential hazard.

466 Mark *one* answer
When may you wait in a box junction?

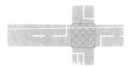

- ☐ **A** When you are stationary in a queue of traffic
- ☐ **B** When approaching a pelican crossing
- ☐ **C** When approaching a zebra crossing
- ☐ **D** When oncoming traffic prevents you turning right

The purpose of a box junction is to keep the junction clear by preventing vehicles from stopping in the path of crossing traffic.

You must not enter a box junction unless your exit is clear. But, you may enter the box and wait if you want to turn right and are only prevented from doing so by oncoming traffic.

467 Mark *one* answer
Which of these plates normally appear with this road sign?

- ☐ **A** Humps for ½ mile
- ☐ **B** Hump Bridge
- ☐ **C** Low Bridge
- ☐ **D** Soft Verge

Road humps are used to slow down the traffic. They are found in places where there are often pedestrians, such as
- in shopping areas   • near schools
- in residential areas.

Watch out for people close to the kerb or crossing the road.

468 Mark *one* answer
Traffic-calming measures are used to

- ☐ **A** stop road rage
- ☐ **B** help overtaking
- ☐ **C** slow traffic down
- ☐ **D** help parking

Traffic-calming measures are used to make the roads safer for vulnerable road users, such as cyclists, pedestrians and children. These can be designed as chicanes, road humps or other obstacles that encourage drivers and riders to slow down.

469 Mark *one* answer
You are on a motorway in fog. The left-hand edge of the motorway can be identified by reflective studs. What colour are they?

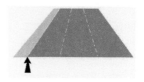

- ☐ **A** Green
- ☐ **B** Amber
- ☐ **C** Red
- ☐ **D** White

Be especially careful if you're on a motorway in fog. Reflective studs are used to help you in poor visibility. Different colours are used so that you'll know which lane you are in. These are
- red on the left-hand side of the road
- white between lanes
- amber on the right-hand edge of the carriageway
- green between the carriageway and slip roads.

470 Mark *two* answers
A rumble device is designed to

☐ **A** give directions
☐ **B** prevent cattle escaping
☐ **C** alert you to low tyre pressure
☐ **D** alert you to a hazard
☐ **E** encourage you to reduce speed

A rumble device usually consists of raised markings or strips across the road. It gives an audible, visual and tactile warning of a hazard. These strips are found in places where traffic has constantly ignored warning or restriction signs. They are there for a good reason. Slow down and be ready to deal with a hazard.

471 Mark *one* answer
You have to make a journey in foggy conditions. You should

☐ **A** follow other vehicles' tail lights closely
☐ **B** avoid using dipped headlights
☐ **C** leave plenty of time for your journey
☐ **D** keep two seconds behind other vehicles

If you're planning to make a journey when it's foggy, listen to the weather reports on the radio or television. Don't travel if visibility is very poor or your trip isn't necessary.

If you do travel, leave plenty of time for your journey. If someone is expecting you at the other end, let them know that you'll be taking longer than normal to arrive.

472 Mark *one* answer
You are overtaking a car at night. You must be sure that

☐ **A** you flash your headlights before overtaking
☐ **B** you select a higher gear
☐ **C** you have switched your lights to full beam before overtaking
☐ **D** you do not dazzle other road users

To prevent your lights from dazzling the driver of the car in front, wait until you've overtaken before switching to full beam.

473 Mark *one* answer
You are on a road which has speed humps. A driver in front is travelling slower than you. You should

☐ **A** sound your horn
☐ **B** overtake as soon as you can
☐ **C** flash your headlights
☐ **D** slow down and stay behind

Be patient and stay behind the car in front. Normally you should not overtake other vehicles in traffic-calmed areas. If you overtake here your speed may exceed that which is safe along that road, defeating the purpose of the traffic-calming measures.

474 Mark *one* answer

You see these markings on the road. Why are they there?

- ☐ **A** To show a safe distance between vehicles
- ☐ **B** To keep the area clear of traffic
- ☐ **C** To make you aware of your speed
- ☐ **D** To warn you to change direction

These lines may be painted on the road on the approach to a roundabout, village or a particular hazard. The lines are raised and painted yellow and their purpose is to make you aware of your speed. Reduce your speed in good time so that you avoid having to brake harshly over the last few metres before reaching the junction.

475 Mark *three* answers

Areas reserved for trams may have

- ☐ **A** metal studs around them
- ☐ **B** white line markings
- ☐ **C** zigzag markings
- ☐ **D** a different coloured surface
- ☐ **E** yellow hatch markings
- ☐ **F** a different surface texture

Trams can run on roads used by other vehicles and pedestrians. The part of the road used by the trams is known as the reserved area and this should be kept clear. It has a coloured surface and is usually edged with white road markings. It might also have different surface texture.

476 Mark *one* answer

You see a vehicle coming towards you on a single-track road. You should

- ☐ **A** go back to the main road
- ☐ **B** do an emergency stop
- ☐ **C** stop at a passing place
- ☐ **D** put on your hazard warning lights

You must take extra care when on single track roads. You may not be able to see around bends due to high hedges or fences. Proceed with caution and expect to meet oncoming vehicles around the next bend. If you do, pull into or opposite a passing place.

477 Mark *one* answer

The road is wet. Why might a motorcyclist steer round drain covers on a bend?

- ☐ **A** To avoid puncturing the tyres on the edge of the drain covers
- ☐ **B** To prevent the motorcycle sliding on the metal drain covers
- ☐ **C** To help judge the bend using the drain covers as marker points
- ☐ **D** To avoid splashing pedestrians on the pavement

Other drivers or riders may have to change course due to the size or characteristics of their vehicle. Understanding this will help you to anticipate their actions. Motorcyclists and cyclists will be checking the road ahead for uneven or slippery surfaces, especially in wet weather. They may need to move across their lane to avoid surface hazards such as potholes and drain covers.

478 Mark *one* answer
After this hazard you should test your brakes. Why is this?

- ☐ **A** You will be on a slippery road
- ☐ **B** Your brakes will be soaking wet
- ☐ **C** You will be going down a long hill
- ☐ **D** You will have just crossed a long bridge

A ford is a crossing over a stream that's shallow enough to go through. After you've gone through a ford or deep puddle the water will affect your brakes. To dry them out apply a light brake pressure while moving slowly. Don't travel at normal speeds until you are sure your brakes are working properly again.

479 Mark *one* answer
Why should you always reduce your speed when travelling in fog?

- ☐ **A** The brakes do not work as well
- ☐ **B** You will be dazzled by other headlights
- ☐ **C** The engine will take longer to warm up
- ☐ **D** It is more difficult to see events ahead

You won't be able to see as far ahead in fog as you can on a clear day. You will need to reduce your speed so that, if a hazard looms out of the fog, you have the time and space to take avoiding action.

Travelling in fog is hazardous. If you can, try and delay your journey until it has cleared.

480 Mark *two* answers
Hills can affect the performance of your vehicle. Which TWO apply when driving up steep hills?

- ☐ **A** Higher gears will pull better
- ☐ **B** You will slow down sooner
- ☐ **C** Overtaking will be easier
- ☐ **D** The engine will work harder
- ☐ **E** The steering will feel heavier

The engine will need more power to pull the vehicle up the hill. When approaching a steep hill you should select a lower gear to help maintain your speed. You should do this without hesitation, so that you don't lose too much speed before engaging the lower gear.

481 Mark *one* answer
You are driving on the motorway in windy conditions. When passing high-sided vehicles you should

- ☐ **A** increase your speed
- ☐ **B** be wary of a sudden gust
- ☐ **C** drive alongside very closely
- ☐ **D** expect normal conditions

The draught caused by other vehicles could be strong enough to push you out of your lane. Keep both hands on the steering wheel to maintain full control.

482 Mark *one* answer
To correct a rear-wheel skid you should

☐ **A** not steer at all
☐ **B** steer away from it
☐ **C** steer into it
☐ **D** apply your handbrake

Prevention is better than cure, so it's important that you take every precaution to avoid a skid from starting.

If you feel the rear wheels of your vehicle beginning to skid, try to steer in the same direction to recover control. Don't brake suddenly – this will only make the situation worse.

483 Mark *one* answer
You are driving in fog. Why should you keep well back from the vehicle in front?

☐ **A** In case it changes direction suddenly
☐ **B** In case its fog lights dazzle you
☐ **C** In case it stops suddenly
☐ **D** In case its brake lights dazzle you

If you're following another road user in fog stay well back. The driver in front won't be able to see hazards until they're close and might brake suddenly. Another reason why it is important to maintain a good separation distance in fog is that the road surface is likely to be wet and slippery.

484 Mark *one* answer
You should switch your rear fog lights on when visibility drops below

☐ **A** your overall stopping distance
☐ **B** ten car lengths
☐ **C** 200 metres (656 feet)
☐ **D** 100 metres (328 feet)

If visibility falls below 100 metres (328 feet) in fog, switching on your rear fog lights will help following road users to see you. Don't forget to turn them off once visibility improves: their brightness might be mistaken for brake lights and they could dazzle other drivers.

485 Mark *one* answer
Whilst driving, the fog clears and you can see more clearly. You must remember to

☐ **A** switch off the fog lights
☐ **B** reduce your speed
☐ **C** switch off the demister
☐ **D** close any open windows

Bright rear fog lights might be mistaken for brake lights and could be misleading for the traffic behind.

486 Mark *one* answer
You have to park on the road in fog. You should

☐ **A** leave sidelights on
☐ **B** leave dipped headlights and fog lights on
☐ **C** leave dipped headlights on
☐ **D** leave main beam headlights on

If you have to park your vehicle in foggy conditions it's important that it can be seen by other road users. Try to find a place to park off the road. If this isn't possible leave it facing in the same direction as the traffic. Make sure that your lights are clean and that you leave your sidelights on.

487 Mark *one* answer
On a foggy day you unavoidably have to park your car on the road. You should

☐ **A** leave your headlights on
☐ **B** leave your fog lights on
☐ **C** leave your sidelights on
☐ **D** leave your hazard lights on

Ensure that your vehicle can be seen by other traffic. If possible, park your car off the road in a car park or driveway to avoid the extra risk to other road users.

488 Mark *one* answer
You are travelling at night. You are dazzled by headlights coming towards you. You should

☐ **A** pull down your sun visor
☐ **B** slow down or stop
☐ **C** switch on your main beam headlights
☐ **D** put your hand over your eyes

You will have additional hazards to deal with at night. Visibility may be very limited and the lights of oncoming vehicles can often dazzle you. When this happens don't close your eyes, swerve or flash your headlights, as this will also distract other drivers. It may help to focus on the left kerb, verge or lane line.

489 Mark *one* answer
Front fog lights may be used ONLY if

☐ **A** visibility is seriously reduced
☐ **B** they are fitted above the bumper
☐ **C** they are not as bright as the headlights
☐ **D** an audible warning device is used

Your vehicle should have a warning light on the dashboard which illuminates when the fog lights are being used. You need to be familiar with the layout of your dashboard so you are aware if they have been switched on in error, or you have forgotten to switch them off.

490 Mark *one* answer
Front fog lights may be used ONLY if

- ☐ **A** your headlights are not working
- ☐ **B** they are operated with rear fog lights
- ☐ **C** they were fitted by the vehicle manufacturer
- ☐ **D** visibility is seriously reduced

It is illegal to use fog lights unless visibility is seriously reduced, which is generally when you cannot see for more than 100 metres (328 feet). Check that they have been switched off when conditions improve.

491 Mark *one* answer
You are driving with your front fog lights switched on. Earlier fog has now cleared. What should you do?

- ☐ **A** Leave them on if other drivers have their lights on
- ☐ **B** Switch them off as long as visibility remains good
- ☐ **C** Flash them to warn oncoming traffic that it is foggy
- ☐ **D** Drive with them on instead of your headlights

Switch off your fog lights if the weather improves, but be prepared to use them again if visibility reduces to less than 100 metres (328 feet).

492 Mark *one* answer
Front fog lights should be used ONLY when

- ☐ **A** travelling in very light rain
- ☐ **B** visibility is seriously reduced
- ☐ **C** daylight is fading
- ☐ **D** driving after midnight

Fog lights will help others see you, but remember, they must only be used if visibility is seriously reduced to less than 100 metres (328 feet).

493 Mark *three* answers
You forget to switch off your rear fog lights when the fog has cleared. This may

- ☐ **A** dazzle other road users
- ☐ **B** reduce battery life
- ☐ **C** cause brake lights to be less clear
- ☐ **D** be breaking the law
- ☐ **E** seriously affect engine power

Don't forget to switch off your fog lights when the weather improves. You could be prosecuted for driving with them on in good visibility. The high intensity of the rear fog lights can look like brake lights, and on a high speed road this can cause other road users to brake unnecessarily.

494 Mark *one* answer

You have been driving in thick fog which has now cleared. You must switch OFF your rear fog lights because

☐ **A** they use a lot of power from the battery
☐ **B** they make your brake lights less clear
☐ **C** they will cause dazzle in your rear view mirrors
☐ **D** they may not be properly adjusted

It is essential that the traffic behind is given a clear warning when you brake. In good visibility, your rear fog lights can make it hard for others to see your brake lights. Make sure you switch off your fog lights when the visibility improves.

495 Mark *one* answer

Front fog lights should be used

☐ **A** when visibility is reduced to 100 metres (328 feet)
☐ **B** as a warning to oncoming traffic
☐ **C** when driving during the hours of darkness
☐ **D** in any conditions and at any time

When visibility is seriously reduced, switch on your fog lights if you have them fitted. It is essential not only that you can see ahead, but also that other road users are able to see you.

496 Mark *one* answer

Using rear fog lights in clear daylight will

☐ **A** be useful when towing a trailer
☐ **B** give extra protection
☐ **C** dazzle other drivers
☐ **D** make following drivers keep back

Rear fog lights shine brighter than normal rear lights so that they show up in reduced visibility. When the weather is clear they could dazzle the driver behind, so switch them off.

497 Mark *one* answer

Using front fog lights in clear daylight will

☐ **A** flatten the battery
☐ **B** dazzle other drivers
☐ **C** improve your visibility
☐ **D** increase your awareness

Fog lights can be brighter than normal dipped headlights. If the weather has improved turn them off to avoid dazzling other road users.

498 Mark *one* answer

You may use front fog lights with headlights ONLY when visibility is reduced to less than

☐ **A** 100 metres (328 feet)
☐ **B** 200 metres (656 feet)
☐ **C** 300 metres (984 feet)
☐ **D** 400 metres (1,312 feet)

It is an offence to use fog lights if the visibility is better than 100 metres (328 feet). Switch front fog lights off if the fog clears to avoid dazzling other road users, but be aware that the fog may be patchy.

499 Mark *one* answer

Chains can be fitted to your wheels to help prevent

☐ **A** damage to the road surface
☐ **B** wear to the tyres
☐ **C** skidding in deep snow
☐ **D** the brakes locking

Snow chains can be fitted to your tyres during snowy conditions. They can help you to move off from rest or to keep moving in deep snow. You will still need to adjust your driving according to the road conditions at the time.

500 Mark *one* answer
How can you use the engine of your vehicle to control your speed?

☐ **A** By changing to a lower gear
☐ **B** By selecting reverse gear
☐ **C** By changing to a higher gear
☐ **D** By selecting neutral

You should brake and slow down before selecting a lower gear. The gear can then be used to keep the speed low and help you control the vehicle. This is particularly helpful on long downhill stretches, where brake fade can occur if the brakes overheat.

501 Mark *one* answer
Why could keeping the clutch down or selecting neutral for long periods of time be dangerous?

☐ **A** Fuel spillage will occur
☐ **B** Engine damage may be caused
☐ **C** You will have less steering and braking control
☐ **D** It will wear tyres out more quickly

Letting your vehicle roll or coast in neutral reduces your control over steering and braking. This can be dangerous on downhill slopes where your vehicle could pick up speed very quickly.

502 Mark *one* answer
You are driving on an icy road. What distance should you drive from the car in front?

☐ **A** four times the normal distance
☐ **B** six times the normal distance
☐ **C** eight times the normal distance
☐ **D** ten times the normal distance

Don't travel in icy or snowy weather unless your journey is necessary.
   Drive extremely carefully when roads are or may be icy. Stopping distances can be ten times greater than on dry roads.

503 Mark *one* answer
You are on a well-lit motorway at night. You must

☐ **A** use only your sidelights
☐ **B** always use your headlights
☐ **C** always use rear fog lights
☐ **D** use headlights only in bad weather

If you're driving on a motorway at night or in poor visibility, you must always use your headlights, even if the road is well-lit. The other road users in front must be able to see you in their mirrors.

504 Mark *one* answer

You are on a motorway at night with other vehicles just ahead of you. Which lights should you have on?

☐ **A** Front fog lights
☐ **B** Main beam headlights
☐ **C** Sidelights only
☐ **D** Dipped headlights

If you're driving behind other traffic at night on the motorway, leave a two-second time gap and use dipped headlights. Full beam will dazzle the other drivers. Your headlights' beam should fall short of the vehicle in front.

505 Mark *three* answers

Which THREE of the following will affect your stopping distance?

☐ **A** How fast you are going
☐ **B** The tyres on your vehicle
☐ **C** The time of day
☐ **D** The weather
☐ **E** The street lighting

There are several factors that can affect the distance it takes to stop your vehicle.
   Adjust your driving to take account of how the weather conditions could affect your tyres' grip on the road.

506 Mark *one* answer

You are on a motorway at night. You MUST have your headlights switched on unless

☐ **A** there are vehicles close in front of you
☐ **B** you are travelling below 50mph
☐ **C** the motorway is lit
☐ **D** your vehicle is broken down on the hard shoulder

Always use your headlights at night on a motorway unless you have stopped on the hard shoulder. If you break down and have to stop on the hard shoulder, switch off the headlights but leave the sidelights on so that other road users can see your vehicle.

507 Mark *one* answer

You will feel the effects of engine braking when you

☐ **A** only use the handbrake
☐ **B** only use neutral
☐ **C** change to a lower gear
☐ **D** change to a higher gear

When going downhill, prolonged use of the brakes can cause them to overheat and lose their effectiveness. Changing to a lower gear will assist your braking.

508 Mark *one* answer

Daytime visibility is poor but not seriously reduced. You should switch on

☐ **A** headlights and fog lights
☐ **B** front fog lights
☐ **C** dipped headlights
☐ **D** rear fog lights

Only use your fog lights when visibility is seriously reduced. Use dipped headlights in poor conditions.

509 Mark *one* answer
Why are vehicles fitted with rear fog lights?

- ☐ **A** To be seen when driving at high speed
- ☐ **B** To use if broken down in a dangerous position
- ☐ **C** To make them more visible in thick fog
- ☐ **D** To warn drivers following closely to drop back

Rear fog lights make it easier to spot a vehicle ahead in foggy conditions. Avoid the temptation to use other vehicles' lights as a guide, as they may give you a false sense of security.

510 Mark *one* answer
While you are driving in fog, it becomes necessary to use front fog lights. You should

- ☐ **A** only turn them on in heavy traffic conditions
- ☐ **B** remember not to use them on motorways
- ☐ **C** only use them on dual carriageways
- ☐ **D** remember to switch them off as visibility improves

It is an offence to have your fog lights on in conditions other than seriously reduced visibility, i.e. less than 100 metres (328 feet).

511 Mark *one* answer
When snow is falling heavily you should

- ☐ **A** only drive with your hazard lights on
- ☐ **B** not drive unless you have a mobile phone
- ☐ **C** only drive when your journey is short
- ☐ **D** not drive unless it is essential

Consider if the increased risk is worth it. If the weather conditions are bad and your journey isn't essential, then stay at home.

512 Mark *one* answer
You are driving down a long steep hill. You suddenly notice your brakes are not working as well as normal. What is the usual cause of this?

- ☐ **A** The brakes overheating
- ☐ **B** Air in the brake fluid
- ☐ **C** Oil on the brakes
- ☐ **D** Badly adjusted brakes

This is more likely to happen on vehicles fitted with drum brakes but can apply to disc brakes as well. Using a lower gear will assist the braking and help you to keep control of your vehicle.

513 Mark *two* answers
You have to make a journey in fog. What are the TWO most important things you should do before you set out?

- ☐ **A** Top up the radiator with anti-freeze
- ☐ **B** Make sure that you have a warning triangle in the vehicle
- ☐ **C** Check that your lights are working
- ☐ **D** Check the battery
- ☐ **E** Make sure that the windows are clean

Don't drive in fog unless you really have to. Adjust your driving to the conditions. You should always be able to pull up within the distance you can see ahead.

514 Mark *one* answer
You have just driven out of fog. Visibility is now good. You MUST

- ☐ **A** switch off all your fog lights
- ☐ **B** keep your rear fog lights on
- ☐ **C** keep your front fog lights on
- ☐ **D** leave fog lights on in case fog returns

You MUST turn off your fog lights if visibility is over 100 metres (328 feet). However, be prepared for the fact that the fog may be patchy.

515 Mark *one* answer
You may drive with front fog lights switched on

- ☐ **A** when visibility is less than 100 metres (328 feet)
- ☐ **B** at any time to be noticed
- ☐ **C** instead of headlights on high speed roads
- ☐ **D** when dazzled by the lights of oncoming vehicles

Only use front fog lights if the distance you are able to see is less than 100 metres (328 feet). Turn off your fog lights as the visibility improves.

516 Mark *two* answers
Why is it dangerous to leave rear fog lights on when they are not needed?

- ☐ **A** Brake lights are less clear
- ☐ **B** Following drivers can be dazzled
- ☐ **C** Electrical systems could be overloaded
- ☐ **D** Direction indicators may not work properly
- ☐ **E** The battery could fail

If your rear fog lights are left on when it isn't foggy, the glare they cause makes it difficult for road users behind to know whether you are braking or you have just forgotten to turn off your rear fog lights. This can be a particular problem on wet roads and on motorways. If you leave your rear fog lights on at night, road users behind you are likely to be dazzled and this could put them at risk.

517 Mark *one* answer

Holding the clutch pedal down or rolling in neutral for too long while driving will

- ☐ **A** use more fuel
- ☐ **B** cause the engine to overheat
- ☐ **C** reduce your control
- ☐ **D** improve tyre wear

Holding the clutch down or staying in neutral for too long will cause your vehicle to freewheel. This is known as 'coasting' and it is dangerous as it reduces your control of the vehicle.

518 Mark *one* answer

You are driving down a steep hill. Why could keeping the clutch down or rolling in neutral for too long be dangerous?

- ☐ **A** Fuel consumption will be higher
- ☐ **B** Your vehicle will pick up speed
- ☐ **C** It will damage the engine
- ☐ **D** It will wear tyres out more quickly

Driving in neutral or with the clutch down for long periods is known as 'coasting'. There will be no engine braking and your vehicle will pick up speed on downhill slopes. Coasting can be very dangerous because it reduces steering and braking control.

519 Mark *two* answers

What are TWO main reasons why coasting downhill is wrong?

- ☐ **A** Fuel consumption will be higher
- ☐ **B** The vehicle will get faster
- ☐ **C** It puts more wear and tear on the tyres
- ☐ **D** You have less braking and steering control
- ☐ **E** It damages the engine

Coasting is when you allow the vehicle to freewheel in neutral or with the clutch pedal depressed. Doing this gives you less control over the vehicle. It's especially important not to let your vehicle coast when approaching hazards such as junctions and bends and when travelling downhill.

520 Mark *four* answers

Which FOUR of the following may apply when dealing with this hazard?

- ☐ **A** It could be more difficult in winter
- ☐ **B** Use a low gear and drive slowly
- ☐ **C** Use a high gear to prevent wheel-spin
- ☐ **D** Test your brakes afterwards
- ☐ **E** Always switch on fog lamps
- ☐ **F** There may be a depth gauge

During the winter the stream is likely to flood. It is also possible that in extremely cold weather it could ice over. Assess the situation carefully before you drive through. If you drive a vehicle with low suspension you may have to find a different route.

521 Mark *one* answer

Why is travelling in neutral for long distances (known as 'coasting') wrong?

- ☐ **A** It will cause the car to skid
- ☐ **B** It will make the engine stall
- ☐ **C** The engine will run faster
- ☐ **D** There is no engine braking

Try to look ahead and read the road. Plan your approach to junctions and select the correct gear in good time. This will give you the control you need to deal with any hazards that occur.

You'll coast a little every time you change gear. This can't be avoided, but it should be kept to a minimum.

522 Mark *one* answer

When MUST you use dipped headlights during the day?

- ☐ **A** All the time
- ☐ **B** Along narrow streets
- ☐ **C** In poor visibility
- ☐ **D** When parking

You MUST use dipped headlights and/or fog lights in fog when visibility is seriously reduced to 100 metres (328 feet) or less.

You should use dipped headlights, but NOT fog lights, when visibility is poor, such as in heavy rain.

523 Mark *one* answer

You are braking on a wet road. Your vehicle begins to skid. It does not have anti-lock brakes. What is the FIRST thing you should do?

- ☐ **A** Quickly pull up the handbrake
- ☐ **B** Release the footbrake
- ☐ **C** Push harder on the brake pedal
- ☐ **D** Gently use the accelerator

If the skid has been caused by braking too hard for the conditions, release the brake. You may then need to reapply and release the brake again. You may need to do this a number of times. This will allow the wheels to turn and so limit the skid. Skids are much easier to get into than they are to get out of. Prevention is better than cure. Stay alert to the road and weather conditions. Drive so that you can stop within the distance you can see to be clear.

524 Mark *two* answers

Using rear fog lights on a clear dry night will

- ☐ **A** reduce glare from the road surface
- ☐ **B** make your brake lights less visible
- ☐ **C** give a better view of the road ahead
- ☐ **D** dazzle following drivers
- ☐ **E** help your indicators to be seen more clearly

You should not use rear fog lights unless visibility is seriously reduced. A warning light will show on the dashboard to indicate when your rear fog lights are on. You should know the meaning of all the lights on your dashboard and check them before you move off and as you drive.

525 Mark *one* answer

When joining a motorway you must always

- ☐ **A** use the hard shoulder
- ☐ **B** stop at the end of the acceleration lane
- ☐ **C** come to a stop before joining the motorway
- ☐ **D** give way to traffic already on the motorway

You should give way to traffic already on the motorway. Where possible they may move over to let you in but don't force your way into the traffic stream. The traffic may be travelling at high speed so you should match your speed to fit in.

526 Mark *one* answer

What is the national speed limit for cars and motorcycles in the centre lane of a three-lane motorway?

- ☐ **A** 40mph
- ☐ **B** 50mph
- ☐ **C** 60mph
- ☐ **D** 70mph

Unless shown otherwise, the speed limit on a motorway applies to all the lanes. Look out for any signs of speed limit changes due to roadworks or traffic flow control.

527 Mark *one* answer

What is the national speed limit on motorways for cars and motorcycles?

- ☐ **A** 30mph
- ☐ **B** 50mph
- ☐ **C** 60mph
- ☐ **D** 70mph

Travelling at the national speed limit doesn't allow you to hog the right-hand lane. Always use the left-hand lane whenever possible. When leaving a motorway get into the left-hand lane well before your exit. Reduce your speed on the slip road and look out for sharp bends or curves and traffic queuing at roundabouts.

528 Mark *one* answer

The left-hand lane on a three-lane motorway is for use by

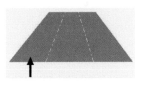

- ☐ **A** any vehicle
- ☐ **B** large vehicles only
- ☐ **C** emergency vehicles only
- ☐ **D** slow vehicles only

On a motorway all traffic should use the left-hand lane unless overtaking. Use the centre or right-hand lanes if you need to overtake. If you're overtaking a number of slower vehicles move back to the left-hand lane when you're safely past. Check your mirrors frequently and don't stay in the middle or right-hand lane if the left-hand lane is free.

529 Mark *one* answer
Which of these IS NOT allowed to travel in the right-hand lane of a three-lane motorway?

☐ **A** A small delivery van
☐ **B** A motorcycle
☐ **C** A vehicle towing a trailer
☐ **D** A motorcycle and side-car

A vehicle with a trailer is restricted to 60mph. For this reason it isn't allowed in the right-hand lane as it might hold up the faster-moving traffic that wishes to overtake in that lane.

530 Mark *one* answer
You break down on a motorway. You need to call for help. Why may it be better to use an emergency roadside telephone rather than a mobile phone?

☐ **A** It connects you to a local garage
☐ **B** Using a mobile phone will distract other drivers
☐ **C** It allows easy location by the emergency services
☐ **D** Mobile phones do not work on motorways

On a motorway it is best to use a roadside emergency telephone so that the emergency services are able to locate you easily. The nearest telephone is shown by an arrow on marker posts at the edge of the hard shoulder. If you use a mobile, they will need to know your exact location. Before you call, find out the number on the nearest marker post. This number will identify your exact location.

531 Mark *one* answer
After a breakdown you need to rejoin the main carriageway of a motorway from the hard shoulder. You should

☐ **A** move out onto the carriageway then build up your speed
☐ **B** move out onto the carriageway using your hazard lights
☐ **C** gain speed on the hard shoulder before moving out onto the carriageway
☐ **D** wait on the hard shoulder until someone flashes their headlights at you

Wait for a safe gap in the traffic before you move out. Indicate your intention and use the hard shoulder to gain speed but don't force your way into the traffic.

532 Mark *one* answer
A crawler lane on a motorway is found

☐ **A** on a steep gradient
☐ **B** before a service area
☐ **C** before a junction
☐ **D** along the hard shoulder

Slow-moving, large vehicles might slow down the progress of other traffic. On a steep gradient this extra lane is provided for these slow-moving vehicles to allow the faster-moving traffic to flow more easily.

533 Mark *one* answer
What do these motorway signs show?

- ☐ **A** They are countdown markers to a bridge
- ☐ **B** They are distance markers to the next telephone
- ☐ **C** They are countdown markers to the next exit
- ☐ **D** They warn of a police control ahead

The exit from a motorway is indicated by countdown markers. These are positioned 90 metres (100 yards) apart, the first being 270 metres (300 yards) from the start of the slip road. Move into the left-hand lane well before you reach the start of the slip road.

534 Mark *one* answer
On a motorway the amber reflective studs can be found between

- ☐ **A** the hard shoulder and the carriageway
- ☐ **B** the acceleration lane and the carriageway
- ☐ **C** the central reservation and the carriageway
- ☐ **D** each pair of the lanes

On motorways reflective studs are located into the road to help you in the dark and in conditions of poor visibility. Amber-coloured studs are found on the right-hand edge of the main carriageway, next to the central reservation.

535 Mark *one* answer
What colour are the reflective studs between the lanes on a motorway?

- ☐ **A** Green
- ☐ **B** Amber
- ☐ **C** White
- ☐ **D** Red

White studs are found between the lanes on motorways. The light from your headlights is reflected back and this is especially useful in bad weather, when visibility is restricted.

536 Mark *one* answer
What colour are the reflective studs between a motorway and its slip road?

- ☐ **A** Amber
- ☐ **B** White
- ☐ **C** Green
- ☐ **D** Red

The studs between the carriageway and the hard shoulder are normally red. These change to green where there is a slip road. They will help you identify slip roads when visibility is poor or when it is dark.

537 Mark *one* answer

You have broken down on a motorway. To find the nearest emergency telephone you should always walk

- ☐ **A** with the traffic flow
- ☐ **B** facing oncoming traffic
- ☐ **C** in the direction shown on the marker posts
- ☐ **D** in the direction of the nearest exit

Along the hard shoulder there are marker posts at 100-metre intervals. These will direct you to the nearest emergency telephone.

538 Mark *one* answer

You are joining a motorway. Why is it important to make full use of the slip road?

- ☐ **A** Because there is space available to turn round if you need to
- ☐ **B** To allow you direct access to the overtaking lanes
- ☐ **C** To build up a speed similar to traffic on the motorway
- ☐ **D** Because you can continue on the hard shoulder

Try to join the motorway without affecting the progress of the traffic already travelling on it. Always give way to traffic already on the motorway. At busy times you may have to slow down to merge into slow-moving traffic.

539 Mark *one* answer

How should you use the emergency telephone on a motorway?

- ☐ **A** Stay close to the carriageway
- ☐ **B** Face the oncoming traffic
- ☐ **C** Keep your back to the traffic
- ☐ **D** Stand on the hard shoulder

Traffic is passing you at speed. If the draught from a large lorry catches you by surprise it could blow you off balance and even onto the carriageway. By facing the oncoming traffic you can see approaching lorries and so be prepared for their draught. You are also in a position to see other hazards approaching.

540 Mark *one* answer

You are on a motorway. What colour are the reflective studs on the left of the carriageway?

- ☐ **A** Green
- ☐ **B** Red
- ☐ **C** White
- ☐ **D** Amber

Red studs are placed between the edge of the carriageway and the hard shoulder. Where slip roads leave or join the motorway the studs are green.

541 Mark *one* answer
On a three-lane motorway which lane should you normally use?

☐ **A** Left
☐ **B** Right
☐ **C** Centre
☐ **D** Either the right or centre

On a three-lane motorway you should travel in the left-hand lane unless you're overtaking. This applies regardless of the speed at which you're travelling.

542 Mark *one* answer
When going through a contraflow system on a motorway you should

☐ **A** ensure that you do not exceed 30mph
☐ **B** keep a good distance from the vehicle ahead
☐ **C** switch lanes to keep the traffic flowing
☐ **D** stay close to the vehicle ahead to reduce queues

There's likely to be a speed restriction in force. Keep to this. Don't
• switch lanes
• get too close to traffic in front of you.
Be aware there will be no permanent barrier between you and the oncoming traffic.

543 Mark *one* answer
You are on a three-lane motorway. There are red reflective studs on your left and white ones to your right. Where are you?

☐ **A** In the right-hand lane
☐ **B** In the middle lane
☐ **C** On the hard shoulder
☐ **D** In the left-hand lane

The colours of the reflective studs on the motorway and their locations are
• red – between the hard shoulder and the carriageway
• white – lane markings
• amber – between the edge of the carriageway and the central reservation
• green – along slip road exits and entrances
• bright green/yellow – roadworks and contraflow systems.

544 Mark *one* answer
You are approaching roadworks on a motorway. What should you do?

☐ **A** Speed up to clear the area quickly
☐ **B** Always use the hard shoulder
☐ **C** Obey all speed limits
☐ **D** Stay very close to the vehicle in front

Collisions can often happen at roadworks. Be aware of the speed limits, slow down in good time and keep your distance from the vehicle in front.

545 Mark *four* answers
Which FOUR of these must NOT use motorways?

☐ **A** Learner car drivers
☐ **B** Motorcycles over 50cc
☐ **C** Double-deck buses
☐ **D** Farm tractors
☐ **E** Horse riders
☐ **F** Cyclists

In addition, motorways MUST NOT be used by pedestrians, motorcycles under 50cc, certain slow-moving vehicles without permission, and invalid carriages weighing less than 254kg (560lbs).

546 Mark *four* answers
Which FOUR of these must NOT use motorways?

☐ **A** Learner car drivers
☐ **B** Motorcycles over 50cc
☐ **C** Double-deck buses
☐ **D** Farm tractors
☐ **E** Learner motorcyclists
☐ **F** Cyclists

Learner car drivers and motorcyclists are not allowed on the motorway until they have passed their practical test.

Motorways have rules that you need to know before you venture out for the first time. When you've passed your practical test it's a good idea to have some lessons on motorways. Check with your instructor about this.

547 Mark *one* answer
Immediately after joining a motorway you should normally

☐ **A** try to overtake
☐ **B** re-adjust your mirrors
☐ **C** position your vehicle in the centre lane
☐ **D** keep in the left-hand lane

Stay in the left-hand lane long enough to get used to the higher speeds of motorway traffic.

548 Mark *one* answer
What is the right-hand lane used for on a three-lane motorway?

☐ **A** Emergency vehicles only
☐ **B** Overtaking
☐ **C** Vehicles towing trailers
☐ **D** Coaches only

You should keep to the left and only use the right-hand lane if you're passing slower-moving traffic.

549 Mark *one* answer
What should you use the hard shoulder of a motorway for?

- ☐ **A** Stopping in an emergency
- ☐ **B** Leaving the motorway
- ☐ **C** Stopping when you are tired
- ☐ **D** Joining the motorway

Don't use the hard shoulder for stopping unless it is an emergency. If you want to stop for any other reason go to the next exit or service station.

550 Mark *one* answer
You are in the right-hand lane on a motorway. You see these overhead signs. This means

- ☐ **A** move to the left and reduce your speed to 50mph
- ☐ **B** there are roadworks 50 metres (55 yards) ahead
- ☐ **C** use the hard shoulder until you have passed the hazard
- ☐ **D** leave the motorway at the next exit

You MUST obey this sign. There might not be any visible signs of a problem ahead. However, there might be queuing traffic or another hazard which you cannot yet see.

551 Mark *one* answer
You are allowed to stop on a motorway when you

- ☐ **A** need to walk and get fresh air
- ☐ **B** wish to pick up hitchhikers
- ☐ **C** are told to do so by flashing red lights
- ☐ **D** need to use a mobile telephone

You MUST stop if there are red lights flashing above every lane on the motorway. However, if any of the other lanes do not show flashing red lights or red cross you may move into that lane and continue if it is safe to do so.

552 Mark *one* answer
You are travelling along the left-hand lane of a three-lane motorway. Traffic is joining from a slip road. You should

- ☐ **A** race the other vehicles
- ☐ **B** move to another lane
- ☐ **C** maintain a steady speed
- ☐ **D** switch on your hazard flashers

You should move to another lane if it is safe to do so. This can greatly assist the flow of traffic joining the motorway, especially at peak times.

553 Mark *one* answer

A basic rule when on motorways is

- ☐ **A** use the lane that has least traffic
- ☐ **B** keep to the left-hand lane unless overtaking
- ☐ **C** overtake on the side that is clearest
- ☐ **D** try to keep above 50mph to prevent congestion

You should normally travel in the left-hand lane unless you are overtaking a slower-moving vehicle. When you are past that vehicle move back into the left-hand lane as soon as it's safe to do so. Don't cut across in front of the vehicle that you're overtaking.

554 Mark *one* answer

On motorways you should never overtake on the left unless

- ☐ **A** you can see well ahead that the hard shoulder is clear
- ☐ **B** the traffic in the right-hand lane is signalling right
- ☐ **C** you warn drivers behind by signalling left
- ☐ **D** there is a queue of slow-moving traffic to your right that is moving more slowly than you are

Only overtake on the left if traffic is moving slowly in queues and the traffic on your right is moving more slowly than the traffic in your lane.

555 Mark *one* answer ▉NI

Motorway emergency telephones are usually linked to the police. In some areas they are now linked to

- ☐ **A** the Highways Agency Control Centre
- ☐ **B** the Driver Vehicle Licensing Agency
- ☐ **C** the Driving Standards Agency
- ☐ **D** the local Vehicle Registration Office

In some areas motorway telephones are now linked to a Highways Agency Control Centre, instead of the police. Highways Agency Traffic Officers work in partnership with the police and assist at motorway emergencies and incidents. They are recognised by a high-visibility orange and yellow jacket and high-visibility vehicle with yellow and black chequered markings.

556 Mark *one* answer

An Emergency Refuge Area is an area

- ☐ **A** on a motorway for use in cases of emergency or breakdown
- ☐ **B** for use if you think you will be involved in a road rage incident
- ☐ **C** on a motorway for a police patrol to park and watch traffic
- ☐ **D** for construction and road workers to store emergency equipment

Emergency Refuge Areas may be found at the side of the hard shoulder about 500 metres apart. If you break down you should use them rather than the hard shoulder if you are able. When re-joining the motorway you must remember to take extra care especially when the hard shoulder is being used as a running lane within an Active Traffic Management area. Try to match your speed to that of traffic in the lane you are joining.

557 Mark *one* answer

What is an Emergency Refuge Area on a motorway for?

- ☐ **A** An area to park in when you want to use a mobile phone
- ☐ **B** To use in cases of emergency or breakdown
- ☐ **C** For an emergency recovery vehicle to park in a contraflow system
- ☐ **D** To drive in when there is queuing traffic ahead

In cases of breakdown or emergency try to get your vehicle into an Emergency Refuge Area. This is safer than just stopping on the hard shoulder as it gives you greater distance from the main carriageway. If you are able to re-join the motorway you must take extra care, especially when the hard shoulder is being used as a running lane.

558 Mark *one* answer NI

Highways Agency Traffic Officers

- ☐ **A** will not be able to assist at a breakdown or emergency
- ☐ **B** are not able to stop and direct anyone on a motorway
- ☐ **C** will tow a broken down vehicle and it's passengers home
- ☐ **D** are able to stop and direct anyone on a motorway

Highways Agency Traffic Officers (HATOs) are able to stop and direct traffic on most motorways and some 'A' class roads. They work in partnership with the police at motorway incidents and provide a highly-trained and visible service. Their role is to help keep traffic moving and make your journey as safe and reliable as possible. They are recognised by an orange and yellow jacket and their vehicle has yellow and black markings.

559 Mark *one* answer NI

You are on a motorway. A red cross is displayed above the hard shoulder. What does this mean?

- ☐ **A** Pull up in this lane to answer your mobile phone
- ☐ **B** Use this lane as a running lane
- ☐ **C** This lane can be used if you need a rest
- ☐ **D** You should not travel in this lane

Active Traffic Management schemes are being introduced on motorways. Within these areas at certain times the hard shoulder will be used as a running lane. A red cross above the hard shoulder shows that this lane should NOT be used, except for emergencies and breakdowns.

560 Mark *one* answer

You are on a motorway in an Active Traffic Management (ATM) area. A mandatory speed limit is displayed above the hard shoulder. What does this mean?

- ☐ **A** You should not travel in this lane
- ☐ **B** The hard shoulder can be used as a running lane
- ☐ **C** You can park on the hard shoulder if you feel tired
- ☐ **D** You can pull up in this lane to answer a mobile phone

A mandatory speed limit sign above the hard shoulder shows that it can be used as a running lane between junctions. You must stay within the speed limit. Look out for vehicles that may have broken down and could be blocking the hard shoulder.

561 Mark *one* answer NI

The aim of an Active Traffic Management scheme on a motorway is to

- ☐ **A** prevent overtaking
- ☐ **B** reduce rest stops
- ☐ **C** prevent tailgating
- ☐ **D** reduce congestion

Active Traffic Management schemes are intended to reduce congestion and make journey times more reliable. In these areas the hard shoulder may be used as a running lane to ease congestion at peak times or in the event of an incident. It may appear that you could travel faster for a short distance, but keeping traffic flow at a constant speed may improve your journey time.

562 Mark *one* answer NI

You are in an Active Traffic Management area on a motorway. When the Actively Managed mode is operating

- ☐ **A** speed limits are only advisory
- ☐ **B** the national speed limit will apply
- ☐ **C** the speed limit is always 30mph
- ☐ **D** all speed limit signals are set

When an Active Traffic Management (ATM) scheme is operating on a motorway you MUST follow the mandatory instructions shown on the gantries above each lane. This includes the hard shoulder.

563 Mark *one* answer   NI
You are travelling on a motorway. A red cross is shown above the hard shoulder. What does this mean?

- ☐ **A** Use this lane as a rest area
- ☐ **B** Use this as a normal running lane
- ☐ **C** Do not use this lane to travel in
- ☐ **D** National speed limit applies in this lane

When a red cross is shown above the hard shoulder it should only be used for breakdowns or emergencies. Within Active Traffic Management (ATM) areas the hard shoulder may sometimes be used as a running lane. Speed limit signs directly above the hard shoulder will show that it's open.

564 Mark *one* answer
Why can it be an advantage for traffic speed to stay constant over a longer distance?

- ☐ **A** You will do more stop-start driving
- ☐ **B** You will use far more fuel
- ☐ **C** You will be able to use more direct routes
- ☐ **D** Your overall journey time will normally improve

When traffic travels at a constant speed over a longer distance, journey times normally improve. You may feel that you could travel faster for short periods but this won't generally improve your overall journey time. Signs will show the maximum speed at which you should travel.

565 Mark *one* answer   NI
You should not normally travel on the hard shoulder of a motorway. When can you use it?

- ☐ **A** When taking the next exit
- ☐ **B** When traffic is stopped
- ☐ **C** When signs direct you to
- ☐ **D** When traffic is slow moving

Normally you should only use the hard shoulder for emergencies and breakdowns, and at roadworks when signs direct you to do so. Active Traffic Management (ATM) areas are being introduced to ease traffic congestion. In these areas the hard shoulder may be used as a running lane when speed limit signs are shown directly above.

566 Mark *one* answer
For what reason may you use the right-hand lane of a motorway?

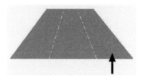

- ☐ **A** For keeping out of the way of lorries
- ☐ **B** For travelling at more than 70mph
- ☐ **C** For turning right
- ☐ **D** For overtaking other vehicles

The right-hand lane of the motorway is for overtaking.

Sometimes you may be directed into a right-hand lane as a result of roadworks or a traffic incident. This will be indicated by signs or officers directing the traffic.

567 Mark *one* answer
On a motorway what is used to reduce traffic bunching?

☐ **A** Variable speed limits
☐ **B** Contraflow systems
☐ **C** National speed limits
☐ **D** Lane closures

Congestion can be reduced by keeping traffic at a constant speed. At busy times maximum speed limits are displayed on overhead gantries. These can be varied quickly depending on the amount of traffic. By keeping to a constant speed on busy sections of motorway overall journey times are normally improved.

568 Mark *three* answers
When should you stop on a motorway?

☐ **A** If you have to read a map
☐ **B** When you are tired and need a rest
☐ **C** If red lights show above every lane
☐ **D** When told to by the police
☐ **E** If your mobile phone rings
☐ **F** When signalled by a Highways Agency Traffic Officer

There are some occasions when you may have to stop on the carriageway of a motorway. These include when being signalled by the police or a Highways Agency Traffic Officer, when flashing red lights show above every lane and in traffic jams.

569 Mark *one* answer
When may you stop on a motorway?

☐ **A** If you have to read a map
☐ **B** When you are tired and need a rest
☐ **C** If your mobile phone rings
☐ **D** In an emergency or breakdown

You should not normally stop on a motorway but there may be occasions when you need to do so. If you are unfortunate enough to break down make every effort to pull up on the hard shoulder.

570 Mark *one* answer NI
You are travelling on a motorway. Unless signs show a lower speed limit you must NOT exceed

☐ **A** 50mph
☐ **B** 60mph
☐ **C** 70mph
☐ **D** 80mph

The national speed limit for a car or motorcycle on the motorway is 70mph. Lower speed limits may be in force, for example at roadworks, so look out for the signs. Variable speed limits operate in some areas to control very busy stretches of motorway. The speed limit may change depending on the volume of traffic.

571 Mark *one* answer

Motorway emergency telephones are usually linked to the police. In some areas they are now linked to

- ☐ **A** the local ambulance service
- ☐ **B** an Highways Agency control centre
- ☐ **C** the local fire brigade
- ☐ **D** a breakdown service control centre

The controller will ask you
- the make and colour of your vehicle
- whether you are a member of an emergency breakdown service
- the number shown on the emergency telephone casing
- whether you are travelling alone.

572 Mark *one* answer

You are on a motorway. There are red flashing lights above every lane. You must

- ☐ **A** pull onto the hard shoulder
- ☐ **B** slow down and watch for further signals
- ☐ **C** leave at the next exit
- ☐ **D** stop and wait

Red flashing lights above every lane mean you must not go on any further. You'll also see a red cross illuminated. Stop and wait. Don't
- change lanes
- continue
- pull onto the hard shoulder (unless in an emergency).

573 Mark *one* answer NI

You are on a three-lane motorway. A red cross is shown above the hard shoulder and mandatory speed limits above all other lanes. This means

- ☐ **A** the hard shoulder can be used as a rest area if you feel tired
- ☐ **B** the hard shoulder is for emergency or breakdown use only
- ☐ **C** the hard shoulder can be used as a normal running lane
- ☐ **D** the hard shoulder has a speed limit of 50mph

A red cross above the hard shoulder shows it is closed as a running lane and should only be used for emergencies or breakdowns. At busy times within an Active Traffic Management (ATM) area the hard shoulder may be used as a running lane. This will be shown by a mandatory speed limit on the gantry above.

574 Mark *one* answer — NI
You are on a three-lane motorway and see this sign. It means you can use

☐ **A** any lane except the hard shoulder
☐ **B** the hard shoulder only
☐ **C** the three right-hand lanes only
☐ **D** all the lanes including the hard shoulder

Mandatory speed limit signs, above all lanes including the hard shoulder, show that you are in an Active Traffic Management (ATM) area. In this case you can use the hard shoulder as a running lane. You must stay within the speed limit shown. Look out for any vehicles that may have broken down and be blocking the hard shoulder.

575 Mark *one* answer
You are travelling on a motorway. You decide you need a rest. You should

☐ **A** stop on the hard shoulder
☐ **B** pull in at the nearest service area
☐ **C** pull up on a slip road
☐ **D** park on the central reservation

If you feel tired stop at the nearest service area. If it's too far away leave the motorway at the next exit and find a safe place to stop. You must not stop on the carriageway or hard shoulder of a motorway except in an emergency, in a traffic queue, when signalled to do so by a police or enforcement officer, or by traffic signals. Plan your journey so that you have regular rest stops.

576 Mark *one* answer
You are on a motorway. You become tired and decide you need to rest. What should you do?

☐ **A** Stop on the hard shoulder
☐ **B** Pull up on a slip road
☐ **C** Park on the central reservation
☐ **D** Leave at the next exit

Ideally you should plan your journey so that you have regular rest stops. If you do become tired leave at the next exit, or pull in at a service area if this is sooner.

577 Mark *one* answer
You are towing a trailer on a motorway. What is your maximum speed limit?

☐ **A** 40mph
☐ **B** 50mph
☐ **C** 60mph
☐ **D** 70mph

Don't forget that you're towing a trailer. If you're towing a small, light, trailer it won't reduce your vehicle's performance by very much. However, strong winds or buffeting from large vehicles might cause the trailer to snake from side to side. Be aware of your speed and don't exceed the lower limit imposed.

578 Mark *one* answer
The left-hand lane of a motorway should be used for

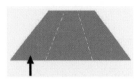

- ☐ **A** breakdowns and emergencies only
- ☐ **B** overtaking slower traffic in the other lanes
- ☐ **C** slow vehicles only
- ☐ **D** normal driving

You should keep to the left-hand lane whenever possible. Only use the other lanes for overtaking or when directed by signals. Using other lanes when the left-hand lane is empty can frustrate drivers behind you.

579 Mark *one* answer
You are driving on a motorway. You have to slow down quickly due to a hazard. You should

- ☐ **A** switch on your hazard lights
- ☐ **B** switch on your headlights
- ☐ **C** sound your horn
- ☐ **D** flash your headlights

Using your hazard lights, as well as brake lights, will give following traffic an extra warning of the problem ahead. Only use them for long enough to ensure that your warning has been seen.

580 Mark *one* answer
You get a puncture on the motorway. You manage to get your vehicle onto the hard shoulder. You should

- ☐ **A** change the wheel yourself immediately
- ☐ **B** use the emergency telephone and call for assistance
- ☐ **C** try to wave down another vehicle for help
- ☐ **D** only change the wheel if you have a passenger to help you

Due to the danger from passing traffic you should park as far to the left as you can and leave the vehicle by the nearside door.
Do not attempt even simple repairs. Instead walk to an emergency telephone on your side of the road and phone for assistance. While waiting for assistance to arrive wait near your car, keeping well away from the carriageway and hard shoulder.

581 Mark *one* answer
You are driving on a motorway. By mistake, you go past the exit that you wanted to take. You should

- ☐ **A** carefully reverse on the hard shoulder
- ☐ **B** carry on to the next exit
- ☐ **C** carefully reverse in the left-hand lane
- ☐ **D** make a U-turn at the next gap in the central reservation

It is against the law to reverse, cross the central reservation or drive against the traffic flow on a motorway. If you have missed your exit ask yourself if your concentration is fading. It could be that you need to take a rest break before completing your journey.

582 Mark *one* answer

You are driving at 70mph on a three-lane motorway. There is no traffic ahead. Which lane should you use?

☐ **A** Any lane
☐ **B** Middle lane
☐ **C** Right lane
☐ **D** Left lane

If the left-hand lane is free you should use it, regardless of the speed you're travelling.

583 Mark *one* answer

Your vehicle has broken down on a motorway. You are not able to stop on the hard shoulder. What should you do?

☐ **A** Switch on your hazard warning lights
☐ **B** Stop following traffic and ask for help
☐ **C** Attempt to repair your vehicle quickly
☐ **D** Stand behind your vehicle to warn others

If you can't get your vehicle onto the hard shoulder, use your hazard warning lights to warn others. Leave your vehicle only when you can safely get clear of the carriageway. Do not try to repair the vehicle or attempt to place any warning device on the carriageway.

584 Mark *one* answer

Why is it particularly important to carry out a check on your vehicle before making a long motorway journey?

☐ **A** You will have to do more harsh braking on motorways
☐ **B** Motorway service stations do not deal with breakdowns
☐ **C** The road surface will wear down the tyres faster
☐ **D** Continuous high speeds may increase the risk of your vehicle breaking down

Before you start your journey make sure that your vehicle can cope with the demands of high-speed driving. You should check a number of things, the main ones being oil, water and tyres. You also need to plan rest stops if you're going a long way.

585 Mark *one* answer

You are driving on a motorway. The car ahead shows its hazard lights for a short time. This tells you that

☐ **A** the driver wants you to overtake
☐ **B** the other car is going to change lanes
☐ **C** traffic ahead is slowing or stopping suddenly
☐ **D** there is a police speed check ahead

If the vehicle in front shows its hazard lights there may be an incident or queuing traffic ahead. As well as keeping a safe distance, look beyond it to help you get an early warning of any hazards and a picture of the situation ahead.

586 Mark *one* answer

You are intending to leave the motorway at the next exit. Before you reach the exit you should normally position your vehicle

- ☐ **A** in the middle lane
- ☐ **B** in the left-hand lane
- ☐ **C** on the hard shoulder
- ☐ **D** in any lane

You'll see the first advance direction sign one mile from the exit. If you're travelling at 60mph in the right-hand lane you'll only have about 50 seconds before you reach the countdown markers. There will be another sign at the half-mile point. Move in to the left-hand lane in good time. Don't cut across traffic at the last moment and don't risk missing your exit.

587 Mark *one* answer

As a provisional licence holder you should not drive a car

- ☐ **A** over 30mph
- ☐ **B** at night
- ☐ **C** on the motorway
- ☐ **D** with passengers in rear seats

When you've passed your practical test ask your instructor to take you for a lesson on the motorway. You'll need to get used to the speed of traffic and how to deal with multiple lanes. The Pass Plus scheme has been created for new drivers, and includes motorway driving. Ask your ADI for details.

588 Mark *one* answer

Your vehicle breaks down on the hard shoulder of a motorway. You decide to use your mobile phone to call for help. You should

- ☐ **A** stand at the rear of the vehicle while making the call
- ☐ **B** try to repair the vehicle yourself
- ☐ **C** get out of the vehicle by the right-hand door
- ☐ **D** check your location from the marker posts on the left

The emergency services need to know your exact location so they can reach you as quickly as possible. Look for a number on the nearest marker post beside the hard shoulder. Give this number when you call the emergency services as it will help them to locate you. Be ready to describe where you are, for example, by reference to the last junction or service station you passed.

589 Mark *one* answer NI

You are on a three-lane motorway towing a trailer. You may use the right-hand lane when

- ☐ **A** there are lane closures
- ☐ **B** there is slow-moving traffic
- ☐ **C** you can maintain a high speed
- ☐ **D** large vehicles are in the left and centre lanes

If you are towing a caravan or trailer you must not use the right-hand lane on a motorway with three or more lanes, except in certain circumstances, such as lane closures.

590 Mark *one* answer
You are on a motorway. There is a contraflow system ahead. What would you expect to find?

☐ **A** Temporary traffic lights
☐ **B** Lower speed limits
☐ **C** Wider lanes than normal
☐ **D** Speed humps

When approaching a contraflow system reduce speed in good time and obey all speed limits. You may be travelling in a narrower lane than normal with no permanent barrier between you and the oncoming traffic. Be aware that the hard shoulder may be used for traffic and the road ahead could be obstructed by slow-moving or broken-down vehicles.

591 Mark *one* answer
On a motorway you may only stop on the hard shoulder

☐ **A** in an emergency
☐ **B** if you feel tired and need to rest
☐ **C** if you miss the exit that you wanted
☐ **D** to pick up a hitchhiker

You should only stop on the hard shoulder in a genuine emergency. DON'T stop on it to have a rest or picnic, pick up hitchhikers, answer a mobile phone or check a map. If you miss your intended exit carry on to the next, never reverse along the hard shoulder.

592 Mark *one* answer
What is the meaning of this sign?

☐ **A** Local speed limit applies
☐ **B** No waiting on the carriageway
☐ **C** National speed limit applies
☐ **D** No entry to vehicular traffic

This sign doesn't tell you the speed limit in figures. You should know the speed limit for the type of road that you're on. Study your copy of The Highway Code.

593 Mark *one* answer
What is the national speed limit for cars and motorcycles on a dual carriageway?

☐ **A** 30mph
☐ **B** 50mph
☐ **C** 60mph
☐ **D** 70mph

Ensure that you know the speed limit for the road that you're on. The speed limit on a dual carriageway or motorway is 70mph for cars and motorcycles, unless there are signs to indicate otherwise. The speed limits for different types of vehicles are listed in The Highway Code.

594 Mark *one* answer
There are no speed limit signs on the road. How is a 30mph limit indicated?

☐ **A** By hazard warning lines
☐ **B** By street lighting
☐ **C** By pedestrian islands
☐ **D** By double or single yellow lines

There is usually a 30mph speed limit where there are street lights unless there are signs showing another limit.

595 Mark *one* answer
Where you see street lights but no speed limit signs the limit is usually

☐ **A** 30mph   ☐ **B** 40mph
☐ **C** 50mph   ☐ **D** 60mph

The presence of street lights generally shows that there is a 30mph speed limit, unless signs tell you otherwise.

596 Mark *one* answer
What does this sign mean?

☐ **A** Minimum speed 30mph
☐ **B** End of maximum speed
☐ **C** End of minimum speed
☐ **D** Maximum speed 30mph

A red slash through this sign indicates that the restriction has ended. In this case the restriction was a minimum speed limit of 30mph.

597 Mark *one* answer

There is a tractor ahead of you. You wish to overtake but you are NOT sure if it is safe to do so. You should

- ☐ **A** follow another overtaking vehicle through
- ☐ **B** sound your horn to the slow vehicle to pull over
- ☐ **C** speed through but flash your lights to oncoming traffic
- ☐ **D** not overtake if you are in doubt

Never overtake if you're not sure whether it's safe. Can you see far enough down the road to ensure that you can complete the manoeuvre safely? If the answer is no, DON'T GO.

598 Mark *three* answers

Which three of the following are most likely to take an unusual course at roundabouts?

- ☐ **A** Horse riders
- ☐ **B** Milk floats
- ☐ **C** Delivery vans
- ☐ **D** Long vehicles
- ☐ **E** Estate cars
- ☐ **F** Cyclists

Long vehicles might have to take a slightly different position when approaching the roundabout or going around it. This is to stop the rear of the vehicle cutting in and mounting the kerb.

Horse riders and cyclists might stay in the left-hand lane although they are turning right. Be aware of this and allow them room.

599 Mark *one* answer

On a clearway you must not stop

- ☐ **A** at any time
- ☐ **B** when it is busy
- ☐ **C** in the rush hour
- ☐ **D** during daylight hours

Clearways are in place so that traffic can flow without the obstruction of parked vehicles. Just one parked vehicle will cause an obstruction for all other traffic. You MUST NOT stop where a clearway is in force, not even to pick up or set down passengers.

600 Mark *one* answer

What is the meaning of this sign?

- ☐ **A** No entry
- ☐ **B** Waiting restrictions
- ☐ **C** National speed limit
- ☐ **D** School crossing patrol

This sign indicates that there are waiting restrictions. It is normally accompanied by details of when restrictions are in force.

Details of most signs which are in common use are shown in The Highway Code and a more comprehensive selection is available in Know Your Traffic Signs.

601 Mark *one* answer
You can park on the right-hand side of a road at night

☐ **A** in a one-way street
☐ **B** with your sidelights on
☐ **C** more than 10 metres (32 feet) from a junction
☐ **D** under a lamp-post

Red rear reflectors show up when headlights shine on them. These are useful when you are parked at night but will only reflect if you park in the same direction as the traffic flow. Normally you should park on the left, but if you're in a one-way street you may also park on the right-hand side.

602 Mark *one* answer
On a three-lane dual carriageway the right-hand lane can be used for

☐ **A** overtaking only, never turning right
☐ **B** overtaking or turning right
☐ **C** fast-moving traffic only
☐ **D** turning right only, never overtaking

You should normally use the left-hand lane on any dual carriageway unless you are overtaking or turning right.

When overtaking on a dual carriageway, look for vehicles ahead that are turning right. They're likely to be slowing or stopped. You need to see them in good time so that you can take appropriate action.

603 Mark *one* answer
You are approaching a busy junction. There are several lanes with road markings. At the last moment you realise that you are in the wrong lane. You should

☐ **A** continue in that lane
☐ **B** force your way across
☐ **C** stop until the area has cleared
☐ **D** use clear arm signals to cut across

There are times where road markings can be obscured by queuing traffic, or you might be unsure which lane you need to be in.

If you realise that you're in the wrong lane, don't cut across lanes or bully other drivers to let you in. Follow the lane you're in and find somewhere safe to turn around if you need to.

604 Mark *one* answer
Where may you overtake on a one-way street?

☐ **A** Only on the left-hand side
☐ **B** Overtaking is not allowed
☐ **C** Only on the right-hand side
☐ **D** Either on the right or the left

You can overtake other traffic on either side when travelling in a one-way street. Make full use of your mirrors and ensure that it's clear all around before you attempt to overtake. Look for signs and road markings and use the most suitable lane for your destination.

605 Mark *one* answer
When going straight ahead at a roundabout you should

- ☐ **A** indicate left before leaving the roundabout
- ☐ **B** not indicate at any time
- ☐ **C** indicate right when approaching the roundabout
- ☐ **D** indicate left when approaching the roundabout

When you want to go straight on at a roundabout, don't signal as you approach it, but indicate left just after you pass the exit before the one you wish to take.

606 Mark *one* answer
Which vehicle might have to use a different course to normal at roundabouts?

- ☐ **A** Sports car
- ☐ **B** Van
- ☐ **C** Estate car
- ☐ **D** Long vehicle

A long vehicle may have to straddle lanes either on or approaching a roundabout so that the rear wheels don't cut in over the kerb.

If you're following a long vehicle, stay well back and give it plenty of room.

607 Mark *one* answer
You may only enter a box junction when

- ☐ **A** there are less than two vehicles in front of you
- ☐ **B** the traffic lights show green
- ☐ **C** your exit road is clear
- ☐ **D** you need to turn left

Yellow box junctions are marked on the road to prevent the road becoming blocked. Don't enter one unless your exit road is clear. You may only wait in the yellow box if your exit road is clear but oncoming traffic is preventing you from completing the turn.

608 Mark *one* answer
You may wait in a yellow box junction when

- ☐ **A** oncoming traffic is preventing you from turning right
- ☐ **B** you are in a queue of traffic turning left
- ☐ **C** you are in a queue of traffic to go ahead
- ☐ **D** you are on a roundabout

The purpose of this road marking is to keep the junction clear of queuing traffic. You may only wait in the marked area when you're turning right and your exit lane is clear but you can't complete the turn because of oncoming traffic.

609 Mark *three* answers
You MUST stop when signalled to do so by which THREE of these?

☐ **A** A police officer
☐ **B** A pedestrian
☐ **C** A school crossing patrol
☐ **D** A bus driver
☐ **E** A red traffic light

Looking well ahead and 'reading' the road will help you to anticipate hazards. This will enable you to stop safely at traffic lights or if ordered to do so by an authorised person.

610 Mark *one* answer
Someone is waiting to cross at a zebra crossing. They are standing on the pavement. You should normally

☐ **A** go on quickly before they step onto the crossing
☐ **B** stop before you reach the zigzag lines and let them cross
☐ **C** stop, let them cross, wait patiently
☐ **D** ignore them as they are still on the pavement

By standing on the pavement, the pedestrian is showing an intention to cross. If you are looking well down the road you will give yourself enough time to slow down and stop safely. Don't forget to check your mirrors before slowing down.

611 Mark *one* answer
At toucan crossings, apart from pedestrians you should be aware of

☐ **A** emergency vehicles emerging
☐ **B** buses pulling out
☐ **C** trams crossing in front
☐ **D** cyclists riding across

The use of cycles is being encouraged and more toucan crossings are being installed. These crossings enable pedestrians and cyclists to cross the path of other traffic. Watch out as cyclists will approach the crossing faster than pedestrians.

612 Mark *two* answers
Who can use a toucan crossing?

☐ **A** Trains
☐ **B** Cyclists
☐ **C** Buses
☐ **D** Pedestrians
☐ **E** Trams

Toucan crossings are similar to pelican crossings but there is no flashing amber phase. Cyclists share the crossing with pedestrians and are allowed to cycle across when the green cycle symbol is shown.

613 Mark *one* answer
At a pelican crossing, what does a flashing amber light mean?

☐ **A** You must not move off until the lights stop flashing
☐ **B** You must give way to pedestrians still on the crossing
☐ **C** You can move off, even if pedestrians are still on the crossing
☐ **D** You must stop because the lights are about to change to red

If there is no-one on the crossing when the amber light is flashing, you may proceed over the crossing. You don't need to wait for the green light to show.

614 Mark *one* answer
You are waiting at a pelican crossing. The red light changes to flashing amber. This means you must

☐ **A** wait for pedestrians on the crossing to clear
☐ **B** move off immediately without any hesitation
☐ **C** wait for the green light before moving off
☐ **D** get ready and go when the continuous amber light shows

This light allows time for the pedestrians already on the crossing to get to the other side in their own time, without being rushed. Don't rev your engine or start to move off while they are still crossing.

615 Mark *one* answer
When can you park on the left opposite these road markings?

☐ **A** If the line nearest to you is broken
☐ **B** When there are no yellow lines
☐ **C** To pick up or set down passengers
☐ **D** During daylight hours only

You MUST NOT park or stop on a road marked with double white lines (even where one of the lines is broken) except to pick up or set down passengers.

616 Mark *one* answer
You are intending to turn right at a crossroads. An oncoming driver is also turning right. It will normally be safer to

☐ **A** keep the other vehicle to your RIGHT and turn behind it (offside to offside)
☐ **B** keep the other vehicle to your LEFT and turn in front of it (nearside to nearside)
☐ **C** carry on and turn at the next junction instead
☐ **D** hold back and wait for the other driver to turn first

At some junctions the layout may make it difficult to turn offside to offside. If this is the case, be prepared to pass nearside to nearside, but take extra care as your view ahead will be obscured by the vehicle turning in front of you.

617 Mark *one* answer
You are on a road that has no traffic signs. There are street lights. What is the speed limit?

- ☐ **A** 20mph
- ☐ **B** 30mph
- ☐ **C** 40mph
- ☐ **D** 60mph

If you aren't sure of the speed limit a good indication is the presence of street lights. If there is street lighting the speed limit will be 30mph unless otherwise indicated.

618 Mark *three* answers
You are going along a street with parked vehicles on the left-hand side. For which THREE reasons should you keep your speed down?

- ☐ **A** So that oncoming traffic can see you more clearly
- ☐ **B** You may set off car alarms
- ☐ **C** Vehicles may be pulling out
- ☐ **D** Drivers' doors may open
- ☐ **E** Children may run out from between the vehicles

Travel slowly and carefully where there are parked vehicles in a built-up area.
Beware of
- vehicles pulling out, especially bicycles and other motorcycles
- pedestrians, especially children, who may run out from between cars
- drivers opening their doors.

619 Mark *one* answer
You meet an obstruction on your side of the road. You should

- ☐ **A** carry on, you have priority
- ☐ **B** give way to oncoming traffic
- ☐ **C** wave oncoming vehicles through
- ☐ **D** accelerate to get past first

Take care if you have to pass a parked vehicle on your side of the road. Give way to oncoming traffic if there isn't enough room for you both to continue safely.

620 Mark *two* answers
You are on a two-lane dual carriageway. For which TWO of the following would you use the right-hand lane?

- ☐ **A** Turning right
- ☐ **B** Normal progress
- ☐ **C** Staying at the minimum allowed speed
- ☐ **D** Constant high speed
- ☐ **E** Overtaking slower traffic
- ☐ **F** Mending punctures

Normally you should travel in the left-hand lane and only use the right-hand lane for overtaking or turning right. Move back into the left lane as soon as it's safe but don't cut in across the path of the vehicle you've just passed.

621 Mark *one* answer
Who has priority at an unmarked crossroads?

☐ **A** The larger vehicle
☐ **B** No one has priority
☐ **C** The faster vehicle
☐ **D** The smaller vehicle

Practise good observation in all directions before you emerge or make a turn. Proceed only when you're sure it's safe to do so.

622 Mark *one* answer   **NI**
What is the nearest you may park to a junction?

☐ **A** 10 metres (32 feet)
☐ **B** 12 metres (39 feet)
☐ **C** 15 metres (49 feet)
☐ **D** 20 metres (66 feet)

Don't park within 10 metres (32 feet) of a junction (unless in an authorised parking place). This is to allow drivers emerging from, or turning into, the junction a clear view of the road they are joining. It also allows them to see hazards such as pedestrians or cyclists at the junction.

623 Mark *three* answers   **NI**
In which THREE places must you NOT park?

☐ **A** Near the brow of a hill
☐ **B** At or near a bus stop
☐ **C** Where there is no pavement
☐ **D** Within 10 metres (32 feet) of a junction
☐ **E** On a 40mph road

Other traffic will have to pull out to pass you. They may have to use the other side of the road, and if you park near the brow of a hill, they may not be able to see oncoming traffic. It's important not to park at or near a bus stop as this could inconvenience passengers, and may put them at risk as they get on or off the bus. Parking near a junction could restrict the view for emerging vehicles.

624 Mark *one* answer
You are waiting at a level crossing. A train has passed but the lights keep flashing. You must

☐ **A** carry on waiting
☐ **B** phone the signal operator
☐ **C** edge over the stop line and look for trains
☐ **D** park and investigate

If the lights at a level crossing continue to flash after a train has passed, you should still wait as there might be another train coming. Time seems to pass slowly when you're held up in a queue. Be patient and wait until the lights stop flashing.

625 Mark *one* answer
At a crossroads there are no signs or road markings. Two vehicles approach. Which has priority?

- ☐ **A** Neither of the vehicles
- ☐ **B** The vehicle travelling the fastest
- ☐ **C** Oncoming vehicles turning right
- ☐ **D** Vehicles approaching from the right

At a crossroads where there are no 'give way' signs or road markings be very careful. No vehicle has priority, even if the sizes of the roads are different.

626 Mark *one* answer
What does this sign tell you?

- ☐ **A** That it is a no-through road
- ☐ **B** End of traffic-calming zone
- ☐ **C** Free parking zone ends
- ☐ **D** No waiting zone ends

The blue and red circular sign on its own means that waiting restrictions are in force. This sign shows that you are leaving the controlled zone and waiting restrictions no longer apply.

627 Mark *one* answer
You are entering an area of roadworks. There is a temporary speed limit displayed. You should

- ☐ **A** not exceed the speed limit
- ☐ **B** obey the limit only during rush hour
- ☐ **C** ignore the displayed limit
- ☐ **D** obey the limit except at night

Where there are extra hazards such as roadworks, it's often necessary to slow traffic down by imposing a temporary speed limit. These speed limits aren't advisory, they must be obeyed.

628 Mark *two* answers
In which TWO places should you NOT park?

- ☐ **A** Near a school entrance
- ☐ **B** Near a police station
- ☐ **C** In a side road
- ☐ **D** At a bus stop
- ☐ **E** In a one-way street

It may be tempting to park where you shouldn't while you run a quick errand. Careless parking is a selfish act and could endanger other road users.

629 Mark *one* answer

You are travelling on a well-lit road at night in a built-up area. By using dipped headlights you will be able to

- ☐ **A** see further along the road
- ☐ **B** go at a much faster speed
- ☐ **C** switch to main beam quickly
- ☐ **D** be easily seen by others

You may be difficult to see when you're travelling at night, even on a well-lit road. If you use dipped headlights rather than sidelights other road users will see you more easily.

630 Mark *one* answer

The dual carriageway you are turning right onto has a very narrow central reservation. What should you do?

- ☐ **A** Proceed to the central reservation and wait
- ☐ **B** Wait until the road is clear in both directions
- ☐ **C** Stop in the first lane so that other vehicles give way
- ☐ **D** Emerge slightly to show your intentions

When the central reservation is narrow you should treat a dual carriageway as one road. Wait until the road is clear in both directions before emerging to turn right. If you try to treat it as two separate roads and wait in the middle, you are likely to cause an obstruction and possibly a collision.

631 Mark *one* answer

What is the national speed limit on a single carriageway road for cars and motorcycles?

- ☐ **A** 30mph
- ☐ **B** 50mph
- ☐ **C** 60mph
- ☐ **D** 70mph

Exceeding the speed limit is dangerous and can result in you receiving penalty points on your licence. It isn't worth it. You should know the speed limit for the road that you're on by observing the road signs. Different speed limits apply if you are towing a trailer.

632 Mark *one* answer

You park at night on a road with a 40mph speed limit. You should park

- ☐ **A** facing the traffic
- ☐ **B** with parking lights on
- ☐ **C** with dipped headlights on
- ☐ **D** near a street light

You MUST use parking lights when parking at night on a road or lay-by with a speed limit greater than 30mph. You MUST also park in the direction of the traffic flow and not close to a junction.

633 Mark *one* answer

You will see these red and white markers when approaching

- ☐ **A** the end of a motorway
- ☐ **B** a concealed level crossing
- ☐ **C** a concealed speed limit sign
- ☐ **D** the end of a dual carriageway

If there is a bend just before the level crossing you may not be able to see the level crossing barriers or waiting traffic. These signs give you an early warning that you may find these hazards just around the bend.

634 Mark *one* answer   NI

You are travelling on a motorway. You MUST stop when signalled to do so by which of these?

- ☐ **A** Flashing amber lights above your lane
- ☐ **B** A Highways Agency Traffic Officer
- ☐ **C** Pedestrians on the hard shoulder
- ☐ **D** A driver who has broken down

You will find Highways Agency Traffic Officers on many of Britain's motorways. They work in partnership with the police, helping to keep traffic moving and to make your journey as safe as possible. It is an offence not to comply with the directions given by a Traffic Officer.

635 Mark *one* answer

At a busy unmarked crossroads, which of the following has priority?

- ☐ **A** Vehicles going straight ahead
- ☐ **B** Vehicles turning right
- ☐ **C** None of the vehicles
- ☐ **D** The vehicles that arrived first

If there are no road signs or markings do not assume that you have priority. Remember that other drivers may assume they have the right to go. No type of vehicle has priority but it's courteous to give way to large vehicles. Also look out in particular for cyclists and motorcyclists.

636 Mark *one* answer

You are going straight ahead at a roundabout. How should you signal?

- ☐ **A** Signal right on the approach and then left to leave the roundabout
- ☐ **B** Signal left after you leave the roundabout and enter the new road
- ☐ **C** Signal right on the approach to the roundabout and keep the signal on
- ☐ **D** Signal left just after you pass the exit before the one you will take

To go straight ahead at a roundabout you should normally approach in the left-hand lane. You will not normally need to signal, but look out for the road markings. At some roundabouts the left lane on approach is marked as 'left turn only', so make sure you use the correct lane to go ahead. Signal before you leave as other road users need to know your intentions.

637 Mark *one* answer
You may drive over a footpath

- ☐ **A** to overtake slow-moving traffic
- ☐ **B** when the pavement is very wide
- ☐ **C** if no pedestrians are near
- ☐ **D** to get into a property

It is against the law to drive on or over a footpath, except to gain access to a property. If you need to cross a pavement, watch for pedestrians in both directions.

638 Mark *one* answer
A single carriageway road has this sign. What is the maximum permitted speed for a car towing a trailer?

- ☐ **A** 30mph
- ☐ **B** 40mph
- ☐ **C** 50mph
- ☐ **D** 60mph

When towing trailers, speed limits are also lower on dual carriageways and motorways. These speed limits apply to vehicles pulling all sorts of trailers including caravans, horse boxes etc.

639 Mark *one* answer
You are towing a small caravan on a dual carriageway. You must not exceed

- ☐ **A** 50mph
- ☐ **B** 40mph
- ☐ **C** 70mph
- ☐ **D** 60mph

The speed limit is reduced for vehicles towing caravans and trailers, to lessen the risk of the outfit becoming unstable. Due to the increased weight and size of the vehicle and caravan combination, you should plan well ahead. Be extra-careful in windy weather, as strong winds could cause a caravan or large trailer to snake from side to side.

640 Mark *one* answer
You want to park and you see this sign. On the days and times shown you should

- ☐ **A** park in a bay and not pay
- ☐ **B** park on yellow lines and pay
- ☐ **C** park on yellow lines and not pay
- ☐ **D** park in a bay and pay

Parking restrictions apply in a variety of places and situations. Make sure you know the rules and understand where and when restrictions apply. Controlled parking areas will be indicated by signs and road markings. Parking in the wrong place could cause an obstruction and danger to other traffic. It can also result in a fine.

641 Mark *one* answer
You are driving along a road that has a cycle lane. The lane is marked by a solid white line. This means that during its period of operation

☐ **A** the lane may be used for parking your car
☐ **B** you may drive in that lane at any time
☐ **C** the lane may be used when necessary
☐ **D** you must not drive in that lane

Leave the lane free for cyclists. At other times, when the lane is not in operation, you should still be aware that there may be cyclists about. Give them room and don't pass too closely.

642 Mark *one* answer
A cycle lane is marked by a solid white line. You must not drive or park in it

☐ **A** at any time
☐ **B** during the rush hour
☐ **C** if a cyclist is using it
☐ **D** during its period of operation

The cycle lanes are there for a reason. Keep them free and allow cyclists to use them.

It is illegal to drive or park in a cycle lane, marked by a solid white line, during its hours of operation. Parking in a cycle lane will obstruct cyclists and they may move into the path of traffic on the main carriageway as they ride around the obstruction. This could be hazardous for both the cyclist and other road users.

643 Mark *one* answer
While driving, you intend to turn left into a minor road. On the approach you should

☐ **A** keep just left of the middle of the road
☐ **B** keep in the middle of the road
☐ **C** swing out wide just before turning
☐ **D** keep well to the left of the road

Don't swing out into the centre of the road in order to make the turn. This could endanger oncoming traffic and may cause other road users to misunderstand your intentions.

644 Mark *one* answer
You are waiting at a level crossing. The red warning lights continue to flash after a train has passed by. What should you do?

☐ **A** Get out and investigate
☐ **B** Telephone the signal operator
☐ **C** Continue to wait
☐ **D** Drive across carefully

At a level crossing flashing red lights mean you must stop. If the train passes but the lights keep flashing, wait. There may be another train coming.

645 Mark *one* answer
You are driving over a level crossing. The warning lights come on and a bell rings. What should you do?

- ☐ **A** Get everyone out of the vehicle immediately
- ☐ **B** Stop and reverse back to clear the crossing
- ☐ **C** Keep going and clear the crossing
- ☐ **D** Stop immediately and use your hazard warning lights

Keep going, don't stop on the crossing. If the amber warning lights come on as you're approaching the crossing, you MUST stop unless it is unsafe to do so. Red flashing lights together with an audible signal mean you MUST stop.

646 Mark *one* answer
You are on a busy main road and find that you are travelling in the wrong direction. What should you do?

- ☐ **A** Turn into a side road on the right and reverse into the main road
- ☐ **B** Make a U-turn in the main road
- ☐ **C** Make a 'three-point' turn in the main road
- ☐ **D** Turn round in a side road

Don't turn round in a busy street or reverse from a side road into a main road. Find a quiet side road and choose a place where you won't obstruct an entrance or exit. Look out for pedestrians and cyclists as well as other traffic.

647 Mark *one* answer
You may remove your seat belt when carrying out a manoeuvre that involves

- ☐ **A** reversing
- ☐ **B** a hill start
- ☐ **C** an emergency stop
- ☐ **D** driving slowly

Don't forget to put your seat belt back on when you've finished reversing.

648 Mark *one* answer
You must not reverse

- ☐ **A** for longer than necessary
- ☐ **B** for more than a car's length
- ☐ **C** into a side road
- ☐ **D** in a built-up area

You may decide to turn your vehicle around by reversing into an opening or side road. When you reverse, always look behind and all around and watch for pedestrians. Don't reverse from a side road into a main road. You MUST NOT reverse further than is necessary.

649 Mark *one* answer
When you are NOT sure that it is safe to reverse your vehicle you should

- ☐ **A** use your horn
- ☐ **B** rev your engine
- ☐ **C** get out and check
- ☐ **D** reverse slowly

If you can't see all around your vehicle get out and have a look. You could also ask someone reliable outside the vehicle to guide you. A small child could easily be hidden directly behind you. Don't take risks.

650 Mark *one* answer

When may you reverse from a side road into a main road?

- ☐ **A** Only if both roads are clear of traffic
- ☐ **B** Not at any time
- ☐ **C** At any time
- ☐ **D** Only if the main road is clear of traffic

Don't reverse into a main road from a side road. The main road is likely to be busy and the traffic on it moving quickly. Cut down the risks by reversing into a quiet side road.

651 Mark *one* answer

You want to turn right at a box junction. There is oncoming traffic. You should

- ☐ **A** wait in the box junction if your exit is clear
- ☐ **B** wait before the junction until it is clear of all traffic
- ☐ **C** drive on, you cannot turn right at a box junction
- ☐ **D** drive slowly into the box junction when signalled by oncoming traffic

You can move into the box junction to wait as long as your exit is clear. The oncoming traffic will stop when the traffic lights change, allowing you to proceed.

652 Mark *one* answer

You are reversing your vehicle into a side road. When would the greatest hazard to passing traffic occur?

- ☐ **A** After you've completed the manoeuvre
- ☐ **B** Just before you actually begin to manoeuvre
- ☐ **C** After you've entered the side road
- ☐ **D** When the front of your vehicle swings out

Always check road and traffic conditions in all directions before reversing into a side road. Keep a good look-out throughout the manoeuvre. Act on what you see and wait if necessary.

653 Mark *one* answer

Where is the safest place to park your vehicle at night?

- ☐ **A** In a garage
- ☐ **B** On a busy road
- ☐ **C** In a quiet car park
- ☐ **D** Near a red route

If you have a garage, use it. Your vehicle is less likely to be a victim of car crime if it's in a garage. Also in winter the windows will be free from ice and snow.

654 Mark *one* answer
You are driving on an urban clearway. You may stop only to

☐ **A** set down and pick up passengers
☐ **B** use a mobile telephone
☐ **C** ask for directions
☐ **D** load or unload goods

Urban clearways may be in built-up areas and their times of operation will be clearly signed. You should stop only for as long as is reasonable to pick up or set down passengers. You should ensure that you are not causing an obstruction for other traffic.

655 Mark *one* answer
You are looking for somewhere to park your vehicle. The area is full EXCEPT for spaces marked 'disabled use'. You can

☐ **A** use these spaces when elsewhere is full
☐ **B** park if you stay with your vehicle
☐ **C** use these spaces, disabled or not
☐ **D** not park there unless permitted

It is illegal to park in a parking space reserved for disabled users.

These spaces are provided for people with limited mobility, who may need extra space to get in and out of their vehicle.

656 Mark *one* answer
Your vehicle is parked on the road at night. When must you use sidelights?

☐ **A** Where there are continuous white lines in the middle of the road
☐ **B** Where the speed limit exceeds 30mph
☐ **C** Where you are facing oncoming traffic
☐ **D** Where you are near a bus stop

When parking at night, park in the direction of the traffic. This will enable other road users to see the reflectors on the rear of your vehicle. You MUST use your sidelights when parking on a road, or in a lay-by on a road, where the speed limit is over 30mph.

657 Mark *one* answer
You are on a road that is only wide enough for one vehicle. There is a car coming towards you. What should you do?

☐ **A** Pull into a passing place on your right
☐ **B** Force the other driver to reverse
☐ **C** Pull into a passing place if your vehicle is wider
☐ **D** Pull into a passing place on your left

Pull into the nearest passing place on the left if you meet another vehicle in a narrow road. If the nearest passing place is on the right, wait opposite it.

658 Mark *one* answer
You are driving at night with full beam headlights on. A vehicle is overtaking you. You should dip your lights

☐ **A** some time after the vehicle has passed you
☐ **B** before the vehicle starts to pass you
☐ **C** only if the other driver dips their headlights
☐ **D** as soon as the vehicle passes you

On full beam your lights could dazzle the driver in front. Make sure that your light beam falls short of the vehicle in front.

659 Mark *one* answer
When may you drive a motor car in this bus lane?

☐ **A** Outside its hours of operation
☐ **B** To get to the front of a traffic queue
☐ **C** You may not use it at any time
☐ **D** To overtake slow-moving traffic

Some bus lanes only operate during peak hours and other vehicles may use them outside these hours. Make sure you check the sign for the hours of operation before driving in a bus lane.

660 Mark *one* answer
Signals are normally given by direction indicators and

☐ **A** brake lights
☐ **B** side lights
☐ **C** fog lights
☐ **D** interior lights

Your brake lights will give an indication to traffic behind that you're slowing down. Good anticipation will allow you time to check your mirrors before slowing.

661 Mark *one* answer
You are parked in a busy high street. What is the safest way to turn your vehicle around so you can go the opposite way?

☐ **A** Find a quiet side road to turn round in
☐ **B** Drive into a side road and reverse into the main road
☐ **C** Get someone to stop the traffic
☐ **D** Do a U-turn

Make sure you carry out the manoeuvre without causing a hazard to other vehicles. Choose a place to turn which is safe and convenient for you and for other road users.

662 Mark *one* answer
To help keep your vehicle secure at night, where should you park?

☐ **A** Near a police station
☐ **B** In a quiet road
☐ **C** On a red route
☐ **D** In a well-lit area

Whenever possible park in an area which will be well lit at night.

663 Mark *one* answer
You are in the right-hand lane of a dual carriageway. You see signs showing that the right-hand lane is closed 800 yards ahead. You should

- ☐ **A** keep in that lane until you reach the queue
- ☐ **B** move to the left immediately
- ☐ **C** wait and see which lane is moving faster
- ☐ **D** move to the left in good time

Keep a look-out for traffic signs. If you're directed to change lanes, do so in good time. Don't
- push your way into traffic in another lane
- leave changing lanes until the last moment.

664 Mark *two* answers
You are driving on a road that has a cycle lane. The lane is marked by a broken white line. This means that

- ☐ **A** you should not drive in the lane unless it is unavoidable
- ☐ **B** you should not park in the lane unless it is unavoidable
- ☐ **C** cyclists can travel in both directions in that lane
- ☐ **D** the lane must be used by motorcyclists in heavy traffic

Where signs or road markings show lanes are for cyclists only, leave them free. Do not drive or park in a cycle lane unless it is unavoidable.

665 Mark *one* answer
What MUST you have to park in a disabled space?

- ☐ **A** A Blue Badge
- ☐ **B** A wheelchair
- ☐ **C** An advanced driver certificate
- ☐ **D** An adapted vehicle

Don't park in a space reserved for disabled people unless you or your passenger are a disabled badge holder. The badge must be displayed in your vehicle in the bottom left-hand corner of the windscreen.

666 Mark *three* answers
On which THREE occasions MUST you stop your vehicle?

- ☐ **A** When in an incident where damage or injury is caused
- ☐ **B** At a red traffic light
- ☐ **C** When signalled to do so by a police or traffic officer
- ☐ **D** At a junction with double broken white lines
- ☐ **E** At a pelican crossing when the amber light is flashing and no pedestrians are crossing

Situations when you MUST stop include the following. When signalled to do so by a police or traffic officer, traffic warden, school crossing patrol or red traffic light. You must also stop if you are involved in an incident which causes damage or injury to any other person, vehicle, animal or property.

667 Mark *one* answer
You MUST obey signs giving orders. These signs are mostly in

- ☐ **A** green rectangles
- ☐ **B** red triangles
- ☐ **C** blue rectangles
- ☐ **D** red circles

There are three basic types of traffic sign, those that warn, inform or give orders. Generally, triangular signs warn, rectangular ones give information or directions, and circular signs usually give orders. An exception is the eight-sided 'STOP' sign.

668 Mark *one* answer
Traffic signs giving orders are generally which shape?

Road signs in the shape of a circle give orders. Those with a red circle are mostly prohibitive. The 'stop' sign is octagonal to give it greater prominence. Signs giving orders MUST always be obeyed.

669 Mark *one* answer
Which type of sign tells you NOT to do something?

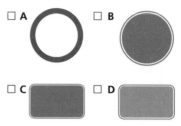

Signs in the shape of a circle give orders. A sign with a red circle means that you aren't allowed to do something. Study Know Your Traffic Signs to ensure that you understand what the different traffic signs mean.

670 Mark *one* answer
What does this sign mean?

- ☐ **A** Maximum speed limit with traffic calming
- ☐ **B** Minimum speed limit with traffic calming
- ☐ **C** '20 cars only' parking zone
- ☐ **D** Only 20 cars allowed at any one time

If you're in places where there are likely to be pedestrians such as outside schools, near parks, residential areas and shopping areas, you should be extra-cautious and keep your speed down.

Many local authorities have taken measures to slow traffic down by creating traffic-calming measures such as speed humps. They are there for a reason; slow down.

671 Mark *one* answer
Which sign means no motor vehicles are allowed?

☐ A 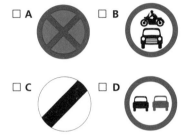   ☐ B

☐ C   ☐ D

You would generally see this sign at the approach to a pedestrian-only zone.

672 Mark *one* answer
Which of these signs means no motor vehicles?

☐ A 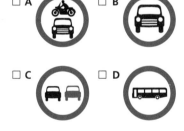   ☐ B

☐ C   ☐ D

If you are driving a motor vehicle or riding a motorcycle you MUST NOT travel past this sign. This area has been designated for use by pedestrians.

673 Mark *one* answer
What does this sign mean?

☐ **A** New speed limit 20mph
☐ **B** No vehicles over 30 tonnes
☐ **C** Minimum speed limit 30mph
☐ **D** End of 20mph zone

Where you see this sign the 20mph restriction ends. Check all around for possible hazards and only increase your speed if it's safe to do so.

674 Mark *one* answer
What does this sign mean?

☐ **A** No overtaking
☐ **B** No motor vehicles
☐ **C** Clearway (no stopping)
☐ **D** Cars and motorcycles only

A sign will indicate which types of vehicles are prohibited from certain roads. Make sure that you know which signs apply to the vehicle you're using.

675 Mark *one* answer
What does this sign mean?

- ☐ **A** No parking
- ☐ **B** No road markings
- ☐ **C** No through road
- ☐ **D** No entry

'No entry' signs are used in places such as one-way streets to prevent vehicles driving against the traffic. To ignore one would be dangerous, both for yourself and other road users, as well as being against the law.

676 Mark *one* answer
What does this sign mean?

- ☐ **A** Bend to the right
- ☐ **B** Road on the right closed
- ☐ **C** No traffic from the right
- ☐ **D** No right turn

The 'no right turn' sign may be used to warn road users that there is a 'no entry' prohibition on a road to the right ahead.

677 Mark *one* answer
Which sign means 'no entry'?

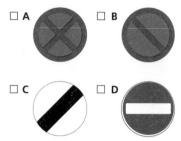

Look out for traffic signs. Disobeying or not seeing a sign could be dangerous. It may also be an offence for which you could be prosecuted.

678 Mark *one* answer
What does this sign mean?

- ☐ **A** Route for trams only
- ☐ **B** Route for buses only
- ☐ **C** Parking for buses only
- ☐ **D** Parking for trams only

Avoid blocking tram routes. Trams are fixed on their route and can't manoeuvre around other vehicles and pedestrians. Modern trams travel quickly and are quiet so you might not hear them approaching.

679 Mark *one* answer
Which type of vehicle does this sign apply to?

- ☐ **A** Wide vehicles
- ☐ **B** Long vehicles
- ☐ **C** High vehicles
- ☐ **D** Heavy vehicles

The triangular shapes above and below the dimensions indicate a height restriction that applies to the road ahead.

680 Mark *one* answer
Which sign means NO motor vehicles allowed?

This sign is used to enable pedestrians to walk free from traffic. It's often found in shopping areas.

681 Mark *one* answer
What does this sign mean?

- ☐ **A** You have priority
- ☐ **B** No motor vehicles
- ☐ **C** Two-way traffic
- ☐ **D** No overtaking

Road signs that prohibit overtaking are placed in locations where passing the vehicle in front is dangerous. If you see this sign don't attempt to overtake. The sign is there for a reason and you must obey it.

682 Mark *one* answer
What does this sign mean?

- ☐ **A** Keep in one lane
- ☐ **B** Give way to oncoming traffic
- ☐ **C** Do not overtake
- ☐ **D** Form two lanes

If you're behind a slow-moving vehicle be patient. Wait until the restriction no longer applies and you can overtake safely.

683 Mark *one* answer
Which sign means no overtaking?

☐ A   ☐ B

☐ C   ☐ D

This sign indicates that overtaking here is not allowed and you could face prosecution if you ignore this prohibition.

684 Mark *one* answer
What does this sign mean?

☐ **A** Waiting restrictions apply
☐ **B** Waiting permitted
☐ **C** National speed limit applies
☐ **D** Clearway (no stopping)

There will be a plate or additional sign to tell you when the restrictions apply.

685 Mark *one* answer
What does this sign mean?

☐ **A** End of restricted speed area
☐ **B** End of restricted parking area
☐ **C** End of clearway
☐ **D** End of cycle route

Even though you have left the restricted area, make sure that you park where you won't endanger other road users or cause an obstruction.

686 Mark *one* answer
Which sign means 'no stopping'?

☐ A   ☐ B

☐ C   ☐ D

Stopping where this clearway restriction applies is likely to cause congestion. Allow the traffic to flow by obeying the signs.

687 Mark *one* answer
What does this sign mean?

- ☐ **A** Roundabout
- ☐ **B** Crossroads
- ☐ **C** No stopping
- ☐ **D** No entry

This sign is in place to ensure a clear route for traffic. Don't stop except in an emergency.

689 Mark *one* answer
What does this sign mean?

- ☐ **A** Distance to parking place ahead
- ☐ **B** Distance to public telephone ahead
- ☐ **C** Distance to public house ahead
- ☐ **D** Distance to passing place ahead

If you intend to stop and rest, this sign allows you time to reduce speed and pull over safely.

688 Mark *one* answer
You see this sign ahead. It means

- ☐ **A** national speed limit applies
- ☐ **B** waiting restrictions apply
- ☐ **C** no stopping
- ☐ **D** no entry

Clearways are stretches of road where you aren't allowed to stop unless in an emergency. You'll see this sign. Stopping where these restrictions apply may be dangerous and likely to cause an obstruction. Restrictions might apply for several miles and this may be indicated on the sign.

690 Mark *one* answer
What does this sign mean?

- ☐ **A** Vehicles may not park on the verge or footway
- ☐ **B** Vehicles may park on the left-hand side of the road only
- ☐ **C** Vehicles may park fully on the verge or footway
- ☐ **D** Vehicles may park on the right-hand side of the road only

In order to keep roads free from parked cars, there are some areas where you're allowed to park on the verge. Only do this where you see the sign. Parking on verges or footways anywhere else could lead to a fine.

691 Mark *one* answer
What does this traffic sign mean?

☐ **A** No overtaking allowed
☐ **B** Give priority to oncoming traffic
☐ **C** Two-way traffic
☐ **D** One-way traffic only

Priority signs are normally shown where the road is narrow and there isn't enough room for two vehicles to pass. These can be at narrow bridges, road works and where there's a width restriction.

Make sure that you know who has priority, don't force your way through. Show courtesy and consideration to other road users.

692 Mark *one* answer
What is the meaning of this traffic sign?

☐ **A** End of two-way road
☐ **B** Give priority to vehicles coming towards you
☐ **C** You have priority over vehicles coming towards you
☐ **D** Bus lane ahead

Don't force your way through. Show courtesy and consideration to other road users. Although you have priority, make sure oncoming traffic is going to give way before you continue.

693 Mark *one* answer
What does this sign mean?

☐ **A** No overtaking
☐ **B** You are entering a one-way street
☐ **C** Two-way traffic ahead
☐ **D** You have priority over vehicles from the opposite direction

Don't force your way through if oncoming vehicles fail to give way. If necessary, slow down and give way to avoid confrontation or a collision.

694 Mark *one* answer
What shape is a STOP sign at a junction?

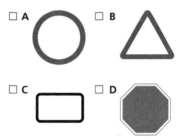

☐ **A**   ☐ **B**

☐ **C**   ☐ **D**

To make it easy to recognise, the 'stop' sign is the only sign of this shape. You must stop and take effective observation before proceeding.

695 Mark *one* answer

At a junction you see this sign partly covered by snow. What does it mean?

☐ **A** Crossroads
☐ **B** Give way
☐ **C** Stop
☐ **D** Turn right

The STOP sign is the only road sign that is octagonal. This is so that it can be recognised and obeyed even if it is obscured, for example by snow.

---

696 Mark *one* answer

What does this sign mean?

☐ **A** Service area 30 miles ahead
☐ **B** Maximum speed 30mph
☐ **C** Minimum speed 30mph
☐ **D** Lay-by 30 miles ahead

This sign is shown where slow-moving vehicles would impede the flow of traffic, for example in tunnels. However, if you need to slow down or even stop to avoid an incident or potential collision, you should do so.

697 Mark *one* answer

What does this sign mean?

☐ **A** Give way to oncoming vehicles
☐ **B** Approaching traffic passes you on both sides
☐ **C** Turn off at the next available junction
☐ **D** Pass either side to get to the same destination

These signs are often seen in one-way streets that have more than one lane. When you see this sign, use the route that's the most convenient and doesn't require a late change of direction.

---

698 Mark *one* answer

What does this sign mean?

☐ **A** Route for trams
☐ **B** Give way to trams
☐ **C** Route for buses
☐ **D** Give way to buses

Take extra care when you encounter trams. Look out for road markings and signs that alert you to them. Modern trams are very quiet and you may not hear them approaching.

699 Mark *one* answer
What does a circular traffic sign with a blue background do?

☐ **A** Give warning of a motorway ahead
☐ **B** Give directions to a car park
☐ **C** Give motorway information
☐ **D** Give an instruction

Signs with blue circles give a positive instruction. These are often found in urban areas and include signs for mini-roundabouts and directional arrows.

700 Mark *one* answer
Where would you see a contraflow bus and cycle lane?

☐ **A** On a dual carriageway
☐ **B** On a roundabout
☐ **C** On an urban motorway
☐ **D** On a one-way street

In a contraflow lane the traffic permitted to use it travels in the opposite direction to traffic in the other lanes on the road.

701 Mark *one* answer
What does this sign mean?

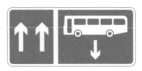

☐ **A** Bus station on the right
☐ **B** Contraflow bus lane
☐ **C** With-flow bus lane
☐ **D** Give way to buses

There will also be markings on the road surface to indicate the bus lane. You must not use this lane for parking or overtaking.

702 Mark *one* answer
What does a sign with a brown background show?

☐ **A** Tourist directions
☐ **B** Primary roads
☐ **C** Motorway routes
☐ **D** Minor routes

Signs with a brown background give directions to places of interest. They will often be seen on a motorway directing you along the easiest route to the attraction.

703 Mark *one* answer
This sign means

- ☐ **A** tourist attraction
- ☐ **B** beware of trains
- ☐ **C** level crossing
- ☐ **D** beware of trams

These signs indicate places of interest and are designed to guide you by the easiest route. They are particularly useful if you are unfamiliar with the area.

704 Mark *one* answer
What are triangular signs for?

- ☐ **A** To give warnings
- ☐ **B** To give information
- ☐ **C** To give orders
- ☐ **D** To give directions

This type of sign will warn you of hazards ahead.
    Make sure you look at each sign that you pass on the road, so that you do not miss any vital instructions or information.

705 Mark *one* answer
What does this sign mean?

- ☐ **A** Turn left ahead
- ☐ **B** T-junction
- ☐ **C** No through road
- ☐ **D** Give way

This type of sign will warn you of hazards ahead. Make sure you look at each sign and road markings that you pass, so that you do not miss any vital instructions or information. This particular sign shows there is a T-junction with priority over vehicles from the right.

706 Mark *one* answer
What does this sign mean?

- ☐ **A** Multi-exit roundabout
- ☐ **B** Risk of ice
- ☐ **C** Six roads converge
- ☐ **D** Place of historical interest

It will take up to ten times longer to stop when it's icy. Where there is a risk of icy conditions you need to be aware of this and take extra care. If you think the road may be icy, don't brake or steer harshly as your tyres could lose their grip on the road.

707 Mark *one* answer
What does this sign mean?

☐ **A** Crossroads
☐ **B** Level crossing with gate
☐ **C** Level crossing without gate
☐ **D** Ahead only

The priority through the junction is shown by the broader line. You need to be aware of the hazard posed by traffic crossing or pulling out onto a major road.

708 Mark *one* answer
What does this sign mean?

☐ **A** Ring road
☐ **B** Mini-roundabout
☐ **C** No vehicles
☐ **D** Roundabout

As you approach a roundabout look well ahead and check all signs. Decide which exit you wish to take and move into the correct position as you approach the roundabout, signalling as required.

709 Mark *four* answers
Which FOUR of these would be indicated by a triangular road sign?

☐ **A** Road narrows
☐ **B** Ahead only
☐ **C** Low bridge
☐ **D** Minimum speed
☐ **E** Children crossing
☐ **F** T-junction

Warning signs are there to make you aware of potential hazards on the road ahead. Act on the signs so you are prepared and can take whatever action is necessary.

710 Mark *one* answer
What does this sign mean?

☐ **A** Cyclists must dismount
☐ **B** Cycles are not allowed
☐ **C** Cycle route ahead
☐ **D** Cycle in single file

Where there's a cycle route ahead, a sign will show a bicycle in a red warning triangle. Watch out for children on bicycles and cyclists rejoining the main road.

711 Mark *one* answer
Which sign means that pedestrians may be walking along the road?

☐ A   ☐ B

☐ C   ☐ D

When you pass pedestrians in the road, leave plenty of room. You might have to use the right-hand side of the road, so look well ahead, as well as in your mirrors, before pulling out. Take great care if there is a bend in the road obscuring your view ahead.

712 Mark *one* answer
Which of these signs means there is a double bend ahead?

☐ A  ☐ B

☐ C  ☐ D

Triangular signs give you a warning of hazards ahead. They are there to give you time to prepare for the hazard, for example by adjusting your speed.

713 Mark *one* answer
What does this sign mean?

☐ A Wait at the barriers
☐ B Wait at the crossroads
☐ C Give way to trams
☐ D Give way to farm vehicles

Obey the 'give way' signs. Trams are unable to steer around you if you misjudge when it is safe to enter the junction.

714 Mark *one* answer
What does this sign mean?

☐ A Humpback bridge
☐ B Humps in the road
☐ C Entrance to tunnel
☐ D Soft verges

These have been put in place to slow the traffic down. They're usually found in residential areas. Slow down to an appropriate speed.

715 Mark *one* answer

Which of these signs means the end of a dual carriageway?

☐ **A**   ☐ **B**

☐ **C**   ☐ **D**

If you're overtaking make sure you move back safely into the left-hand lane before you reach the end of the dual carriageway.

716 Mark *one* answer

What does this sign mean?

☐ **A** End of dual carriageway
☐ **B** Tall bridge
☐ **C** Road narrows
☐ **D** End of narrow bridge

Don't leave moving into the left-hand lane until the last moment. Plan ahead and don't rely on other traffic letting you in.

717 Mark *one* answer

What does this sign mean?

☐ **A** Crosswinds
☐ **B** Road noise
☐ **C** Airport
☐ **D** Adverse camber

A warning sign with a picture of a windsock will indicate there may be strong crosswinds. This sign is often found on exposed roads.

718 Mark *one* answer

What does this traffic sign mean?

☐ **A** Slippery road ahead
☐ **B** Tyres liable to punctures ahead
☐ **C** Danger ahead
☐ **D** Service area ahead

This sign is there to alert you to the likelihood of danger ahead. It may be accompanied by a plate indicating the type of hazard. Be ready to reduce your speed and take avoiding action.

719 Mark *one* answer
You are about to overtake when you see this sign. You should

- ☐ **A** overtake the other driver as quickly as possible
- ☐ **B** move to the right to get a better view
- ☐ **C** switch your headlights on before overtaking
- ☐ **D** hold back until you can see clearly ahead

You won't be able to see any hazards that might be hidden in the dip. As well as oncoming traffic the dip may conceal
- cyclists
- horse riders
- parked vehicles
- pedestrians
in the road.

720 Mark *one* answer
What does this sign mean?

- ☐ **A** Level crossing with gate or barrier
- ☐ **B** Gated road ahead
- ☐ **C** Level crossing without gate or barrier
- ☐ **D** Cattle grid ahead

Some crossings have gates but no attendant or signals. You should stop, look both ways, listen and make sure that there is no train approaching. If there is a telephone, contact the signal operator to make sure that it's safe to cross.

721 Mark *one* answer
What does this sign mean?

- ☐ **A** No trams ahead
- ☐ **B** Oncoming trams
- ☐ **C** Trams crossing ahead
- ☐ **D** Trams only

This sign warns you to beware of trams. If you don't usually drive in a town where there are trams, remember to look out for them at junctions and look for tram rails, signs and signals.

722 Mark *one* answer
What does this sign mean?

- ☐ **A** Adverse camber
- ☐ **B** Steep hill downwards
- ☐ **C** Uneven road
- ☐ **D** Steep hill upwards

This sign will give you an early warning that the road ahead will slope downhill. Prepare to alter your speed and gear. Looking at the sign from left to right will show you whether the road slopes uphill or downhill.

723 Mark *one* answer
What does this sign mean?

- ☐ **A** Uneven road surface
- ☐ **B** Bridge over the road
- ☐ **C** Road ahead ends
- ☐ **D** Water across the road

This sign is found where a shallow stream crosses the road. Heavy rainfall could increase the flow of water. If the water looks too deep or the stream has spread over a large distance, stop and find another route.

---

724 Mark *one* answer
What does this sign mean?

- ☐ **A** Turn left for parking area
- ☐ **B** No through road on the left
- ☐ **C** No entry for traffic turning left
- ☐ **D** Turn left for ferry terminal

If you intend to take a left turn, this sign shows you that you can't get through to another route using the left-turn junction ahead.

725 Mark *one* answer
What does this sign mean?

- ☐ **A** T-junction
- ☐ **B** No through road
- ☐ **C** Telephone box ahead
- ☐ **D** Toilet ahead

You will not be able to find a through route to another road. Use this road only for access.

---

726 Mark *one* answer
Which sign means 'no through road'?

This sign is found at the entrance to a road that can only be used for access.

727 Mark *one* answer
Which is the sign for a ring road?

☐ **A**   ☐ **B**

☐ **C**   ☐ **D**

Ring roads are designed to relieve congestion in towns and city centres.

728 Mark *one* answer
What does this sign mean?

☐ **A** The right-hand lane ahead is narrow
☐ **B** Right-hand lane for buses only
☐ **C** Right-hand lane for turning right
☐ **D** The right-hand lane is closed

Yellow and black temporary signs may be used to inform you of roadworks or lane restrictions. Look well ahead. If you have to change lanes, do so in good time.

729 Mark *one* answer
What does this sign mean?

☐ **A** Change to the left lane
☐ **B** Leave at the next exit
☐ **C** Contraflow system
☐ **D** One-way street

If you use the right-hand lane in a contraflow system, you'll be travelling with no permanent barrier between you and the oncoming traffic. Observe speed limits and keep a good distance from the vehicle ahead.

730 Mark *one* answer
What does this sign mean?

☐ **A** Leave motorway at next exit
☐ **B** Lane for heavy and slow vehicles
☐ **C** All lorries use the hard shoulder
☐ **D** Rest area for lorries

Where there's a long, steep, uphill gradient on a motorway, a crawler lane may be provided. This helps the traffic to flow by diverting the slower heavy vehicles into a dedicated lane on the left.

731 Mark *one* answer
A red traffic light means

- ☐ **A** you should stop unless turning left
- ☐ **B** stop, if you are able to brake safely
- ☐ **C** you must stop and wait behind the stop line
- ☐ **D** proceed with caution

Make sure you learn and understand the sequence of traffic lights. Whatever light appears you will then know what light is going to appear next and be able to take the appropriate action. For example if amber is showing on its own you'll know that red will appear next, giving you ample time to slow and stop safely.

732 Mark *one* answer
At traffic lights, amber on its own means

- ☐ **A** prepare to go
- ☐ **B** go if the way is clear
- ☐ **C** go if no pedestrians are crossing
- ☐ **D** stop at the stop line .

When amber is showing on its own red will appear next. The amber light means STOP, unless you have already crossed the stop line or you are so close to it that pulling up might cause a collision.

733 Mark *one* answer
You are at a junction controlled by traffic lights. When should you NOT proceed at green?

- ☐ **A** When pedestrians are waiting to cross
- ☐ **B** When your exit from the junction is blocked
- ☐ **C** When you think the lights may be about to change
- ☐ **D** When you intend to turn right

As you approach the lights look into the road you wish to take. Only proceed if your exit road is clear. If the road is blocked hold back, even if you have to wait for the next green signal.

734 Mark *one* answer
You are in the left-hand lane at traffic lights. You are waiting to turn left. At which of these traffic lights must you NOT move on?

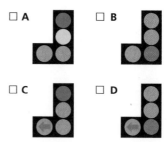

At some junctions there may be a separate signal for different lanes. These are called 'filter' lights. They're designed to help traffic flow at major junctions. Make sure that you're in the correct lane and proceed if the way is clear and the green light shows for your lane.

735 Mark *one* answer
What does this sign mean?

- ☐ **A** Traffic lights out of order
- ☐ **B** Amber signal out of order
- ☐ **C** Temporary traffic lights ahead
- ☐ **D** New traffic lights ahead

Where traffic lights are out of order you might see this sign. Proceed with caution as nobody has priority at the junction.

736 Mark *one* answer
When traffic lights are out of order, who has priority?

- ☐ **A** Traffic going straight on
- ☐ **B** Traffic turning right
- ☐ **C** Nobody
- ☐ **D** Traffic turning left

When traffic lights are out of order you should treat the junction as an unmarked crossroads. Be cautious as you may need to give way or stop. Keep a look out for traffic attempting to cross the junction at speed.

737 Mark *three* answers
These flashing red lights mean STOP. In which THREE of the following places could you find them?

- ☐ **A** Pelican crossings
- ☐ **B** Lifting bridges
- ☐ **C** Zebra crossings
- ☐ **D** Level crossings
- ☐ **E** Motorway exits
- ☐ **F** Fire stations

You must always stop when the red lights are flashing, whether or not the way seems to be clear.

738 Mark *one* answer
What do these zigzag lines at pedestrian crossings mean?

- ☐ **A** No parking at any time
- ☐ **B** Parking allowed only for a short time
- ☐ **C** Slow down to 20mph
- ☐ **D** Sounding horns is not allowed

The approach to, and exit from, a pedestrian crossing is marked with zigzag lines. You must not park on them or overtake the leading vehicle when approaching the crossing. Parking here would block the view for pedestrians and the approaching traffic.

739 Mark *one* answer

When may you cross a double solid white line in the middle of the road?

☐ **A** To pass traffic that is queuing back at a junction

☐ **B** To pass a car signalling to turn left ahead

☐ **C** To pass a road maintenance vehicle travelling at 10mph or less

☐ **D** To pass a vehicle that is towing a trailer

You may cross the solid white line to pass a stationary vehicle, pedal cycle, horse or road maintenance vehicle if they are travelling at 10mph or less. You may also cross the solid line to enter into a side road or access a property.

740 Mark *one* answer

What does this road marking mean?

☐ **A** Do not cross the line

☐ **B** No stopping allowed

☐ **C** You are approaching a hazard

☐ **D** No overtaking allowed

Road markings will warn you of a hazard ahead. A single, broken line along the centre of the road, with long markings and short gaps, is a hazard warning line. Don't cross it unless you can see that the road is clear well ahead.

741 Mark *one* answer

Where would you see this road marking?

☐ **A** At traffic lights

☐ **B** On road humps

☐ **C** Near a level crossing

☐ **D** At a box junction

Due to the dark colour of the road, changes in level aren't easily seen. White triangles painted on the road surface give you an indication of where there are road humps.

742 Mark *one* answer

Which is a hazard warning line?

You need to know the difference between the normal centre line and a hazard warning line. If there is a hazard ahead, the markings are longer and the gaps shorter. This gives you advanced warning of an unspecified hazard ahead.

743 Mark *one* answer
At this junction there is a stop sign with a solid white line on the road surface. Why is there a stop sign here?

- ☐ **A** Speed on the major road is de-restricted
- ☐ **B** It is a busy junction
- ☐ **C** Visibility along the major road is restricted
- ☐ **D** There are hazard warning lines in the centre of the road

If your view is restricted at a road junction you must stop. There may also be a 'stop' sign. Don't emerge until you're sure there's no traffic approaching.
IF YOU DON'T KNOW, DON'T GO.

744 Mark *one* answer
You see this line across the road at the entrance to a roundabout. What does it mean?

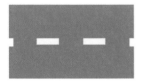

- ☐ **A** Give way to traffic from the right
- ☐ **B** Traffic from the left has right of way
- ☐ **C** You have right of way
- ☐ **D** Stop at the line

Slow down as you approach the roundabout and check for traffic from the right. If you need to stop and give way, stay behind the broken line until it is safe to emerge onto the roundabout.

745 Mark *one* answer
How will a police officer in a patrol vehicle normally get you to stop?

- ☐ **A** Flash the headlights, indicate left and point to the left
- ☐ **B** Wait until you stop, then approach you
- ☐ **C** Use the siren, overtake, cut in front and stop
- ☐ **D** Pull alongside you, use the siren and wave you to stop

You must obey signals given by the police. If a police officer in a patrol vehicle wants you to pull over they will indicate this without causing danger to you or other traffic.

746 Mark *one* answer
You approach a junction. The traffic lights are not working. A police officer gives this signal. You should

- ☐ **A** turn left only
- ☐ **B** turn right only
- ☐ **C** stop level with the officer's arm
- ☐ **D** stop at the stop line

If a police officer or traffic warden is directing traffic you must obey them. They will use the arm signals shown in The Highway Code. Learn what these mean and act accordingly.

747 Mark *one* answer

The driver of the car in front is giving this arm signal. What does it mean?

- ☐ **A** The driver is slowing down
- ☐ **B** The driver intends to turn right
- ☐ **C** The driver wishes to overtake
- ☐ **D** The driver intends to turn left

There might be an occasion where another driver uses an arm signal. This may be because the vehicle's indicators are obscured by other traffic. In order for such signals to be effective all drivers should know the meaning of them. Be aware that the 'left turn' signal might look similar to the 'slowing down' signal.

748 Mark *one* answer

Where would you see these road markings?

- ☐ **A** At a level crossing
- ☐ **B** On a motorway slip road
- ☐ **C** At a pedestrian crossing
- ☐ **D** On a single-track road

When driving on a motorway or slip road, you must not enter into an area marked with chevrons and bordered by a solid white line for any reason, except in an emergency.

749 Mark *one* answer

What does this motorway sign mean?

- ☐ **A** Change to the lane on your left
- ☐ **B** Leave the motorway at the next exit
- ☐ **C** Change to the opposite carriageway
- ☐ **D** Pull up on the hard shoulder

On the motorway, signs sometimes show temporary warnings due to traffic or weather conditions. They may be used to indicate
- lane closures
- temporary speed limits
- weather warnings.

750 Mark *one* answer

What does this motorway sign mean?

- ☐ **A** Temporary minimum speed 50mph
- ☐ **B** No services for 50 miles
- ☐ **C** Obstruction 50 metres (164 feet) ahead
- ☐ **D** Temporary maximum speed 50mph

Look out for signs above your lane or on the central reservation. These will give you important information or warnings about the road ahead. Due to the high speed of motorway traffic these signs may light up some distance from any hazard. Don't ignore the signs just because the road looks clear to you.

751 Mark *one* answer
What does this sign mean?

- ☐ **A** Through traffic to use left lane
- ☐ **B** Right-hand lane T-junction only
- ☐ **C** Right-hand lane closed ahead
- ☐ **D** 11 tonne weight limit

You should move into the lanes as directed by the sign. Here the right-hand lane is closed and the left-hand and centre lanes are available. Merging in turn is recommended when it's safe and traffic is going slowly, for example at road works or a road traffic incident. When vehicles are travelling at speed this is not advisable and you should move into the appropriate lane in good time.

752 Mark *one* answer
On a motorway this sign means

- ☐ **A** move over onto the hard shoulder
- ☐ **B** overtaking on the left only
- ☐ **C** leave the motorway at the next exit
- ☐ **D** move to the lane on your left

It is important to know and obey temporary signs on the motorway: they are there for a reason. You may not be able to see the hazard straight away, as the signs give warnings well in advance, due to the speed of traffic on the motorway.

753 Mark *one* answer
What does '25' mean on this motorway sign?

- ☐ **A** The distance to the nearest town
- ☐ **B** The route number of the road
- ☐ **C** The number of the next junction
- ☐ **D** The speed limit on the slip road

Before you set out on your journey use a road map to plan your route. When you see advance warning of your junction, make sure you get into the correct lane in plenty of time. Last-minute harsh braking and cutting across lanes at speed is extremely hazardous.

754 Mark *one* answer
The right-hand lane of a three-lane motorway is

- ☐ **A** for lorries only
- ☐ **B** an overtaking lane
- ☐ **C** the right-turn lane
- ☐ **D** an acceleration lane

You should stay in the left-hand lane of a motorway unless overtaking. The right-hand lane of a motorway is an overtaking lane and not a 'fast lane'.

After overtaking, move back to the left when it is safe to do so.

755 Mark *one* answer
Where can you find reflective amber studs on a motorway?

☐ **A** Separating the slip road from the motorway
☐ **B** On the left-hand edge of the road
☐ **C** On the right-hand edge of the road
☐ **D** Separating the lanes

At night or in poor visibility reflective studs on the road help you to judge your position on the carriageway.

756 Mark *one* answer
Where on a motorway would you find green reflective studs?

☐ **A** Separating driving lanes
☐ **B** Between the hard shoulder and the carriageway
☐ **C** At slip road entrances and exits
☐ **D** Between the carriageway and the central reservation

Knowing the colours of the reflective studs on the road will help you judge your position, especially at night, in foggy conditions or when visibility is poor.

757 Mark *one* answer
You are travelling along a motorway. You see this sign. You should

☐ **A** leave the motorway at the next exit
☐ **B** turn left immediately
☐ **C** change lane
☐ **D** move onto the hard shoulder

You'll see this sign if the motorway is closed ahead. Pull into the nearside lane as soon as it is safe to do so. Don't leave it to the last moment.

758 Mark *one* answer
What does this sign mean?

☐ **A** No motor vehicles
☐ **B** End of motorway
☐ **C** No through road
☐ **D** End of bus lane

When you leave the motorway make sure that you check your speedometer. You may be going faster than you realise. Slow down and look out for speed limit signs.

759 Mark *one* answer
Which of these signs means that the national speed limit applies?

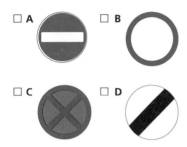

☐ A   ☐ B

☐ C   ☐ D

You should know the speed limit for the road on which you are travelling, and the vehicle that you are driving. The different speed limits are shown in The Highway Code.

760 Mark *one* answer
What is the maximum speed on a single carriageway road?

☐ **A** 50mph
☐ **B** 60mph
☐ **C** 40mph
☐ **D** 70mph

If you're travelling on a dual carriageway that becomes a single carriageway road, reduce your speed gradually so that you aren't exceeding the limit as you enter. There might not be a sign to remind you of the limit, so make sure you know what the speed limits are for different types of roads and vehicles.

761 Mark *one* answer
What does this sign mean?

☐ **A** End of motorway
☐ **B** End of restriction
☐ **C** Lane ends ahead
☐ **D** Free recovery ends

Temporary restrictions on motorways are shown on signs which have flashing amber lights. At the end of the restriction you will see this sign without any flashing lights.

762 Mark *one* answer
This sign is advising you to

☐ **A** follow the route diversion
☐ **B** follow the signs to the picnic area
☐ **C** give way to pedestrians
☐ **D** give way to cyclists

When a diversion route has been put in place, drivers are advised to follow a symbol which may be a triangle, square, circle or diamond shape on a yellow background.

763 Mark *one* answer
Why would this temporary speed limit sign be shown?

- ☐ **A** To warn of the end of the motorway
- ☐ **B** To warn you of a low bridge
- ☐ **C** To warn you of a junction ahead
- ☐ **D** To warn of road works ahead

In the interests of road safety, temporary speed limits are imposed at all major road works. Signs like this, giving advanced warning of the speed limit, are normally placed about three quarters of a mile ahead of where the speed limit comes into force.

764 Mark *one* answer
This traffic sign means there is

- ☐ **A** a compulsory maximum speed limit
- ☐ **B** an advisory maximum speed limit
- ☐ **C** a compulsory minimum speed limit
- ☐ **D** an advised separation distance

The sign gives you an early warning of a speed restriction. If you are travelling at a higher speed, slow down in good time. You could come across queuing traffic due to roadworks or a temporary obstruction.

765 Mark *one* answer
You see this sign at a crossroads. You should

- ☐ **A** maintain the same speed
- ☐ **B** carry on with great care
- ☐ **C** find another route
- ☐ **D** telephone the police

When traffic lights are out of order treat the junction as an unmarked crossroad. Be very careful as no one has priority and be prepared to stop.

766 Mark *one* answer
You are signalling to turn right in busy traffic. How would you confirm your intention safely?

- ☐ **A** Sound the horn
- ☐ **B** Give an arm signal
- ☐ **C** Flash your headlights
- ☐ **D** Position over the centre line

In some situations you may feel your indicators cannot be seen by other road users. If you think you need to make your intention more clearly seen, give the arm signal shown in The Highway Code.

767 Mark *one* answer
What does this sign mean?

☐ **A** Motorcycles only
☐ **B** No cars
☐ **C** Cars only
☐ **D** No motorcycles

You must comply with all traffic signs and be especially aware of those signs which apply specifically to the type of vehicle you are using.

768 Mark *one* answer
You are on a motorway. You see this sign on a lorry that has stopped in the right-hand lane. You should

☐ **A** move into the right-hand lane
☐ **B** stop behind the flashing lights
☐ **C** pass the lorry on the left
☐ **D** leave the motorway at the next exit

Sometimes work is carried out on the motorway without closing the lanes. When this happens, signs are mounted on the back of lorries to warn other road users of roadworks ahead.

769 Mark *one* answer
You are on a motorway. Red flashing lights appear above your lane only. What should you do?

☐ **A** Continue in that lane and look for further information
☐ **B** Move into another lane in good time
☐ **C** Pull onto the hard shoulder
☐ **D** Stop and wait for an instruction to proceed

Flashing red lights above your lane show that your lane is closed. You should move into another lane as soon as you can do so safely.

770 Mark *one* answer
A red traffic light means

☐ **A** you must stop behind the white stop line
☐ **B** you may go straight on if there is no other traffic
☐ **C** you may turn left if it is safe to do so
☐ **D** you must slow down and prepare to stop if traffic has started to cross

The white line is generally positioned so that pedestrians have room to cross in front of waiting traffic. Don't move off while pedestrians are crossing, even if the lights change to green.

771 Mark *one* answer
The driver of this car is giving an arm signal. What are they about to do?

☐ **A** Turn to the right
☐ **B** Turn to the left
☐ **C** Go straight ahead
☐ **D** Let pedestrians cross

In some situations drivers may need to give arm signals, in addition to indicators, to make their intentions clear. For arm signals to be effective, all road users should know their meaning.

---

772 Mark *one* answer
When may you sound the horn?

☐ **A** To give you right of way
☐ **B** To attract a friend's attention
☐ **C** To warn others of your presence
☐ **D** To make slower drivers move over

Never sound the horn aggressively. You MUST NOT sound it when driving in a built-up area between 11.30pm and 7am or when you are stationary, an exception to this is when another road user poses a danger. Do not scare animals by sounding your horn.

773 Mark *one* answer
You must not use your horn when you are stationary

☐ **A** unless a moving vehicle may cause you danger
☐ **B** at any time whatsoever
☐ **C** unless it is used only briefly
☐ **D** except for signalling that you have just arrived

When stationary only sound your horn if you think there is a risk of danger from another road user. Don't use it just to attract someone's attention. This causes unnecessary noise and could be misleading.

---

774 Mark *one* answer
What does this sign mean?

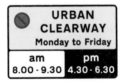

☐ **A** You can park on the days and times shown
☐ **B** No parking on the days and times shown
☐ **C** No parking at all from Monday to Friday
☐ **D** End of the urban clearway restrictions

Urban clearways are provided to keep traffic flowing at busy times. You may stop only briefly to set down or pick up passengers. Times of operation will vary from place to place so always check the signs.

775 Mark *one* answer
What does this sign mean?

☐ **A** Quayside or river bank
☐ **B** Steep hill downwards
☐ **C** Uneven road surface
☐ **D** Road liable to flooding

You should be careful in these locations as the road surface is likely to be wet and slippery. There may be a steep drop to the water, and there may not be a barrier along the edge of the road.

---

776 Mark *one* answer
Which sign means you have priority over oncoming vehicles?

☐ A    ☐ B

☐ C   ☐ D

Even though you have priority, be prepared to give way if other drivers don't. This will help to avoid congestion, confrontation or even a collision.

777 Mark *one* answer
A white line like this along the centre of the road is a

☐ **A** bus lane marking
☐ **B** hazard warning
☐ **C** give way marking
☐ **D** lane marking

The centre of the road is usually marked by a broken white line, with lines that are shorter than the gaps. When the lines become longer than the gaps this is a hazard warning line. Look well ahead for these, especially when you are planning to overtake or turn off.

778 Mark *one* answer
What is the reason for the yellow criss-cross lines painted on the road here?

- ☐ **A** To mark out an area for trams only
- ☐ **B** To prevent queuing traffic from blocking the junction on the left
- ☐ **C** To mark the entrance lane to a car park
- ☐ **D** To warn you of the tram lines crossing the road

Yellow 'box junctions' like this are often used where it's busy. Their purpose is to keep the junction clear for crossing traffic. Don't enter the painted area unless your exit is clear. The exception to this is when you are turning right and are only prevented from doing so by oncoming traffic or by other vehicles waiting to turn right.

779 Mark *one* answer
What is the reason for the area marked in red and white along the centre of this road?

- ☐ **A** It is to separate traffic flowing in opposite directions
- ☐ **B** It marks an area to be used by overtaking motorcyclists
- ☐ **C** It is a temporary marking to warn of the roadworks
- ☐ **D** It is separating the two sides of the dual carriageway

Areas of 'hatched markings' such as these are to separate traffic streams which could be a danger to each other. They are often seen on bends or where the road becomes narrow. If the area is bordered by a solid white line, you must not enter it except in an emergency.

780 Mark *one* answer
Other drivers may sometimes flash their headlights at you. In which situation are they allowed to do this?

- ☐ **A** To warn of a radar speed trap ahead
- ☐ **B** To show that they are giving way to you
- ☐ **C** To warn you of their presence
- ☐ **D** To let you know there is a fault with your vehicle

If other drivers flash their headlights this isn't a signal to show priority. The flashing of headlights has the same meaning as sounding the horn, it's a warning of their presence.

781 Mark *one* answer

In some narrow residential streets you may find a speed limit of

☐ **A** 20mph
☐ **B** 25mph
☐ **C** 35mph
☐ **D** 40mph

In some built-up areas, you may find the speed limit reduced to 20mph. Driving at a slower speed will help give you the time and space to see and deal safely with hazards such as pedestrians and parked cars.

782 Mark *one* answer

At a junction you see this signal. It means

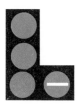

☐ **A** cars must stop
☐ **B** trams must stop
☐ **C** both trams and cars must stop
☐ **D** both trams and cars can continue

The white light shows that trams must stop, but the green light shows that other vehicles may go if the way is clear. You may not live in an area where there are trams but you should still learn the signs. You never know when you may go to a town with trams.

783 Mark *one* answer

Where would you find these road markings?

☐ **A** At a railway crossing
☐ **B** At a junction
☐ **C** On a motorway
☐ **D** On a pedestrian crossing

These markings show the direction in which the traffic should go at a mini-roundabout.

784 Mark *one* answer

There is a police car following you. The police officer flashes the headlights and points to the left. What should you do?

☐ **A** Turn left at the next junction
☐ **B** Pull up on the left
☐ **C** Stop immediately
☐ **D** Move over to the left

You must pull up on the left as soon as it's safe to do so and switch off your engine.

785 Mark *one* answer
You see this amber traffic light ahead. Which light or lights, will come on next?

☐ **A** Red alone
☐ **B** Red and amber together
☐ **C** Green and amber together
☐ **D** Green alone

At junctions controlled by traffic lights you must stop behind the white line until the lights change to green. Red and amber lights showing together also mean stop.

You may proceed when the light is green unless your exit road is blocked or pedestrians are crossing in front of you.

If you're approaching traffic lights that are visible from a distance and the light has been green for some time they are likely to change. Be ready to slow down and stop.

786 Mark *one* answer
This broken white line painted in the centre of the road means

☐ **A** oncoming vehicles have priority over you
☐ **B** you should give priority to oncoming vehicles
☐ **C** there is a hazard ahead of you
☐ **D** the area is a national speed limit zone

A long white line with short gaps means that you are approaching a hazard. If you do need to cross it, make sure that the road is clear well ahead.

787 Mark *one* answer
You see this signal overhead on the motorway. What does it mean?

☐ **A** Leave the motorway at the next exit
☐ **B** All vehicles use the hard shoulder
☐ **C** Sharp bend to the left ahead
☐ **D** Stop, all lanes ahead closed

You will see this sign if there has been an incident ahead and the motorway is closed. You MUST obey the sign. Make sure that you prepare to leave as soon as you see the warning sign.

Don't pull over at the last moment or cut across other traffic.

788 Mark *one* answer

What is the purpose of these yellow criss-cross lines on the road?

- ☐ **A** To make you more aware of the traffic lights
- ☐ **B** To guide you into position as you turn
- ☐ **C** To prevent the junction becoming blocked
- ☐ **D** To show you where to stop when the lights change

You MUST NOT enter a box junction until your exit road or lane is clear. The exception to this is if you want to turn right and are only prevented from doing so by oncoming traffic or by other vehicles waiting to turn right.

789 Mark *one* answer

What MUST you do when you see this sign?

- ☐ **A** Stop, only if traffic is approaching
- ☐ **B** Stop, even if the road is clear
- ☐ **C** Stop, only if children are waiting to cross
- ☐ **D** Stop, only if a red light is showing

STOP signs are situated at junctions where visibility is restricted or there is heavy traffic. They MUST be obeyed. You MUST stop.

Take good all-round observation before moving off.

790 Mark *one* answer

Which shape is used for a 'give way' sign?

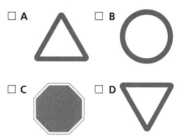

☐ **A** ☐ **B**

☐ **C** ☐ **D**

Other warning signs are the same shape and colour, but the 'give way' sign triangle points downwards. When you see this sign you MUST give way to traffic on the road which you are about to enter.

791 Mark *one* answer

What does this sign mean?

- ☐ **A** Buses turning
- ☐ **B** Ring road
- ☐ **C** Mini-roundabout
- ☐ **D** Keep right

When you see this sign, look out for any direction signs and judge whether you need to signal your intentions. Do this in good time so that other road users approaching the roundabout know what you're planning to do.

792 Mark *one* answer
What does this sign mean?

- ☐ **A** Two-way traffic straight ahead
- ☐ **B** Two-way traffic crosses a one-way road
- ☐ **C** Two-way traffic over a bridge
- ☐ **D** Two-way traffic crosses a two-way road

Be prepared for traffic approaching from junctions on either side of you. Try to avoid unnecessary changing of lanes just before the junction.

793 Mark *one* answer
What does this sign mean?

- ☐ **A** Two-way traffic ahead across a one-way road
- ☐ **B** Traffic approaching you has priority
- ☐ **C** Two-way traffic straight ahead
- ☐ **D** Motorway contraflow system ahead

This sign may be at the end of a dual carriageway or a one-way street. It is there to warn you of oncoming traffic.

794 Mark *one* answer
What does this sign mean?

- ☐ **A** Humpback bridge
- ☐ **B** Traffic-calming hump
- ☐ **C** Low bridge
- ☐ **D** Uneven road

You will need to slow down. At humpback bridges your view ahead will be restricted and the road will often be narrow on the bridge. If the bridge is very steep or your view is restricted sound your horn to warn others of your approach. Going too fast over the bridge is highly dangerous to other road users and could even cause your wheels to leave the road, with a resulting loss of control.

795 Mark *one* answer
Which of the following signs informs you that you are coming to a 'no through road'?

☐ A   ☐ B

☐ C   ☐ D

This sign is found at the entrance to a road that can only be used for access.

796 Mark *one* answer
What does this sign mean?

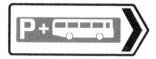

☐ **A** Direction to park-and-ride car park
☐ **B** No parking for buses or coaches
☐ **C** Directions to bus and coach park
☐ **D** Parking area for cars and coaches

To ease the congestion in town centres, some cities and towns provide park-and-ride schemes. These allow you to park in a designated area and ride by bus into the centre.
   Park-and-ride schemes are usually cheaper and easier than car parking in the town centre.

797 Mark *one* answer
You are approaching traffic lights. Red and amber are showing. This means

☐ **A** pass the lights if the road is clear
☐ **B** there is a fault with the lights – take care
☐ **C** wait for the green light before you cross the stop line
☐ **D** the lights are about to change to red

Be aware that other traffic might still be clearing the junction. Make sure the way is clear before continuing.

798 Mark *one* answer
This marking appears on the road just before a

☐ **A** 'no entry' sign
☐ **B** 'give way' sign
☐ **C** 'stop' sign
☐ **D** 'no through road' sign

Where you see this road marking you should give way to traffic on the main road. It might not be used at junctions where there is relatively little traffic. However, if there is a double broken line across the junction the 'give way' rules still apply.

799 Mark *one* answer
At a railway level crossing the red light signal continues to flash after a train has gone by. What should you do?

☐ **A** Phone the signal operator
☐ **B** Alert drivers behind you
☐ **C** Wait
☐ **D** Proceed with caution

You MUST always obey red flashing stop lights. If a train passes but the lights continue to flash, another train will be passing soon. Cross only when the lights go off and the barriers open.

800 Mark *one* answer
You are in a tunnel and you see this sign. What does it mean?

- ☐ **A** Direction to emergency pedestrian exit
- ☐ **B** Beware of pedestrians, no footpath ahead
- ☐ **C** No access for pedestrians
- ☐ **D** Beware of pedestrians crossing ahead

If you have to leave your vehicle in a tunnel and leave by an emergency exit, do so as quickly as you can. Follow the signs directing you to the nearest exit point. If there are several people using the exit, don't panic but try to leave in a calm and orderly manner.

---

801 Mark *one* answer
Which of these signs shows that you are entering a one-way system?

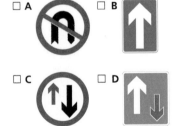

☐ A ☐ B

☐ C ☐ D

If the road has two lanes you can use either lane and overtake on either side. Use the lane that's more convenient for your destination unless signs or road markings indicate otherwise.

802 Mark *one* answer
What does this sign mean?

- ☐ **A** With-flow bus and cycle lane
- ☐ **B** Contraflow bus and cycle lane
- ☐ **C** No buses and cycles allowed
- ☐ **D** No waiting for buses and cycles

Buses and cycles can travel in this lane. In this case they will flow in the same direction as other traffic. If it's busy they may be passing you on the left, so watch out for them. Times on the sign will show its hours of operation. No times shown, or no sign at all, means it's 24 hours. In some areas other vehicles, such as taxis and motorcycles, are allowed to use bus lanes. The sign will show these.

---

803 Mark *one* answer
Which of these signs warns you of a zebra crossing?

☐ A   ☐ B

☐ C   ☐ D

Look well ahead and check the pavements and surrounding areas for pedestrians. Look for anyone walking towards the crossing. Check your mirrors for traffic behind, in case you have to slow down or stop.

804 Mark *one* answer
What does this sign mean?

- ☐ **A** No footpath
- ☐ **B** No pedestrians
- ☐ **C** Zebra crossing
- ☐ **D** School crossing

You need to be aware of the various signs that relate to pedestrians. Some of the signs look similar but have very different meanings. Make sure you know what they all mean and be ready for any potential hazard.

805 Mark *one* answer
What does this sign mean?

- ☐ **A** School crossing patrol
- ☐ **B** No pedestrians allowed
- ☐ **C** Pedestrian zone – no vehicles
- ☐ **D** Zebra crossing ahead

Look well ahead and be ready to stop for any pedestrians crossing, or about to cross, the road. Also check the pavements for anyone who looks like they might step or run into the road.

806 Mark *one* answer
Which sign means there will be two-way traffic crossing your route ahead?

☐ **A**   ☐ **B**

☐ **C**   ☐ **D**

This sign is found in or at the end of a one-way system. It warns you that traffic will be crossing your path from both directions.

807 Mark *one* answer
Which arm signal tells you that the car you are following is going to pull up?

☐ **A**   ☐ **B**

☐ **C**   ☐ **D**

There may be occasions when drivers need to give an arm signal to confirm an indicator. This could include in bright sunshine, at a complex road layout, when stopping at a pedestrian crossing or when turning right just after passing a parked vehicle. You should understand what each arm signal means. If you give arm signals, make them clear, correct and decisive.

808 Mark *one* answer

Which of these signs means turn left ahead?

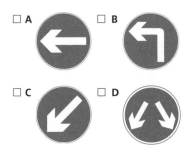

☐ A ☐ B ☐ C ☐ D

Blue circles tell you what you must do and this sign gives a clear instruction to turn left ahead. You should be looking out for signs at all times and know what they mean.

809 Mark *one* answer

Which sign shows that traffic can only travel in one direction on the road you're on?

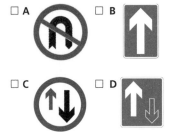

☐ A ☐ B ☐ C ☐ D

This sign means that traffic can only travel in one direction. The others show different priorities on a two-way road.

810 Mark *one* answer

You have just driven past this sign. You should be aware that

☐ **A** it is a single track road
☐ **B** you cannot stop on this road
☐ **C** there is only one lane in use
☐ **D** all traffic is going one way

In a one-way system traffic may be passing you on either side. Always be aware of all traffic signs and understand their meaning. Look well ahead and react to them in good time.

811 Mark *one* answer

You are approaching a red traffic light. What will the signal show next?

☐ **A** Red and amber
☐ **B** Green alone
☐ **C** Amber alone
☐ **D** Green and amber

If you know which light is going to show next you can plan your approach accordingly. This can help prevent excessive braking or hesitation at the junction.

812 Mark *one* answer
What does this sign mean?

☐ **A** Low bridge ahead
☐ **B** Tunnel ahead
☐ **C** Ancient monument ahead
☐ **D** Traffic danger spot ahead

When approaching a tunnel switch on your dipped headlights. Be aware that your eyes might need to adjust to the sudden darkness. You may need to reduce your speed.

813 Mark *one* answer
You are approaching a zebra crossing where pedestrians are waiting. Which arm signal might you give?

☐ A   ☐ B

☐ C   ☐ D

A 'slowing down' signal will indicate your intentions to oncoming and following vehicles. Be aware that pedestrians might start to cross as soon as they see this signal.

814 Mark *one* answer
The white line along the side of the road

☐ **A** shows the edge of the carriageway
☐ **B** shows the approach to a hazard
☐ **C** means no parking
☐ **D** means no overtaking

A continuous white line is used on many roads to indicate the edge of the carriageway. This can be useful when visibility is restricted. The line is discontinued at junctions, lay-bys and entrances and exits from private drives.

815 Mark *one* answer
You see this white arrow on the road ahead. It means

☐ **A** entrance on the left
☐ **B** all vehicles turn left
☐ **C** keep left of the hatched markings
☐ **D** road bending to the left

Don't attempt to overtake here, as there might be unseen hazards over the brow of the hill. Keep to the left.

816 Mark *one* answer
How should you give an arm signal to turn left?

☐ **A** ☐ **B**

☐ **C** ☐ **D**

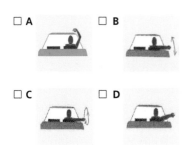

There may be occasions where other road users are unable to see your indicator, such as in bright sunlight or at a busy, complicated junction. In these cases a hand signal will help others to understand your intentions.

817 Mark *one* answer
You are waiting at a T-junction. A vehicle is coming from the right with the left signal flashing. What should you do?

☐ **A** Move out and accelerate hard
☐ **B** Wait until the vehicle starts to turn in
☐ **C** Pull out before the vehicle reaches the junction
☐ **D** Move out slowly

Other road users may give misleading signals. When you're waiting at a junction don't emerge until you're sure of their intentions.

818 Mark *one* answer
When may you use hazard warning lights when driving?

☐ **A** Instead of sounding the horn in a built-up area between 11.30pm and 7am
☐ **B** On a motorway or unrestricted dual carriageway, to warn of a hazard ahead
☐ **C** On rural routes, after a warning sign of animals
☐ **D** On the approach to toucan crossings where cyclists are waiting to cross

When there's queuing traffic ahead and you have to slow down or even stop, showing your hazard warning lights will alert following traffic to the hazard. Don't forget to switch them off as the queue forms behind you.

819 Mark *one* answer
You are driving on a motorway. There is a slow-moving vehicle ahead. On the back you see this sign. You should

☐ **A** pass on the right
☐ **B** pass on the left
☐ **C** leave at the next exit
☐ **D** drive no further

If a vehicle displaying this sign is in your lane you will have to pass it on the left. Use your mirrors and signal. When it's safe move into the lane on your left. You should always look well ahead so that you can spot any hazards early, giving yourself time to react safely.

820 Mark *one* answer

You should NOT normally stop on these markings near schools

- ☐ **A** except when picking up children
- ☐ **B** under any circumstances
- ☐ **C** unless there is nowhere else available
- ☐ **D** except to set down children

At schools you should not stop on yellow zigzag lines for any length of time, not even to set down or pick up children or other passengers.

821 Mark *one* answer

Why should you make sure that your indicators are cancelled after turning?

- ☐ **A** To avoid flattening the battery
- ☐ **B** To avoid misleading other road users
- ☐ **C** To avoid dazzling other road users
- ☐ **D** To avoid damage to the indicator relay

Leaving your indicators on could confuse other road users and may even lead to a crash. Be aware that if you haven't taken a sharp turn your indicators may not self-cancel and you will need to turn them off manually.

822 Mark *one* answer

You are driving in busy traffic. You want to pull up on the left just after a junction on the left. When should you signal?

- ☐ **A** As you are passing or just after the junction
- ☐ **B** Just before you reach the junction
- ☐ **C** Well before you reach the junction
- ☐ **D** It would be better not to signal at all

You need to signal to let other drivers know your intentions. However, if you indicate too early they may think you are turning left into the junction. Correct timing of the signal is very important to avoid misleading others.

823 Mark *one* answer
An MOT certificate is normally valid for

☐ **A** three years after the date it was issued
☐ **B** 10,000 miles
☐ **C** one year after the date it was issued
☐ **D** 30,000 miles

Make a note of the date that your MOT certificate expires. Some garages remind you that your vehicle is due an MOT but not all do. You may take your vehicle for MOT up to one month in advance and have the certificate post dated.

824 Mark *one* answer
A cover note is a document issued before you receive your

☐ **A** driving licence
☐ **B** insurance certificate
☐ **C** registration document
☐ **D** MOT certificate

Sometimes an insurance company will issue a temporary insurance certificate called a cover note. It gives you the same insurance cover as your certificate, but lasts for a limited period, usually one month.

825 Mark *two* answers
You have just passed your practical test. You do not hold a full licence in another category. Within two years you get six penalty points on your licence. What will you have to do?

☐ **A** Retake only your theory test
☐ **B** Retake your theory and practical tests
☐ **C** Retake only your practical test
☐ **D** Reapply for your full licence immediately
☐ **E** Reapply for your provisional licence

If you accumulate six or more penalty points within two years of gaining your first full licence it will be revoked. The six or more points include any gained due to offences you committed before passing your test. If this happens you may only drive as a learner until you pass both the theory and practical tests again.

826 Mark *one* answer
How long will a Statutory Off Road Notification (SORN) last for?

☐ **A** 12 months
☐ **B** 24 months
☐ **C** 3 years
☐ **D** 10 years

A SORN declaration allows you to keep a vehicle off road and untaxed for 12 months. If you want to keep your vehicle off road beyond that you must send a further SORN form to DVLA, or DVA in Northern Ireland. If the vehicle is sold SORN will end and the new owner becomes responsible immediately.

827 Mark *one* answer NI
What is a Statutory Off Road Notification (SORN) declaration?

☐ **A** A notification to tell VOSA that a vehicle does not have a current MOT
☐ **B** Information kept by the police about the owner of the vehicle
☐ **C** A notification to tell DVLA that a vehicle is not being used on the road
☐ **D** Information held by insurance companies to check the vehicle is insured

If you want to keep a vehicle off the public road you must declare SORN. It is an offence not to do so. You then won't have to pay road tax. If you don't renew the SORN declaration or re-license the vehicle, you will incur a penalty.

828 Mark *one* answer NI
A Statutory Off Road Notification (SORN) declaration is

☐ **A** to tell DVLA that your vehicle is being used on the road but the MOT has expired
☐ **B** to tell DVLA that you no longer own the vehicle
☐ **C** to tell DVLA that your vehicle is not being used on the road
☐ **D** to tell DVLA that you are buying a personal number plate

This will enable you to keep a vehicle off the public road for 12 months without having to pay road tax. You must send a further SORN declaration after 12 months.

829 Mark *one* answer
A Statutory Off Road Notification (SORN) is valid

☐ **A** for as long as the vehicle has an MOT
☐ **B** for 12 months only
☐ **C** only if the vehicle is more than 3 years old
☐ **D** provided the vehicle is insured

If you want to keep a vehicle off the public road you must declare SORN. It is an offence not to do so. You then won't have to pay road tax for that vehicle. You will incur a penalty after 12 months if you don't renew the SORN declaration, or re-license the vehicle. If you sell the vehicle the SORN declaration ends and the new owner should declare SORN or re-license the vehicle.

830 Mark *one* answer
A Statutory Off Road Notification (SORN) will last

☐ **A** for the life of the vehicle
☐ **B** for as long as you own the vehicle
☐ **C** for 12 months only
☐ **D** until the vehicle warranty expires

If you are keeping a vehicle, or vehicles, off road and don't want to pay road tax you must declare SORN. You must still do this even if the vehicle is incapable of being used, for example it may be under restoration or being stored. After 12 months you must send another SORN declaration or re-license your vehicle. You will be fined if you don't do this. The SORN will end if you sell the vehicle and the new owner will be responsible immediately.

831 Mark *one* answer
What is the maximum specified fine for driving without insurance?

☐ **A** £50
☐ **B** £500
☐ **C** £1000
☐ **D** £5000

It is a serious offence to drive without insurance. As well as a heavy fine you may be disqualified or incur penalty points.

832 Mark *one* answer
Who is legally responsible for ensuring that a Vehicle Registration Certificate (V5C) is updated?

☐ **A** The registered vehicle keeper
☐ **B** The vehicle manufacturer
☐ **C** Your insurance company
☐ **D** The licensing authority

It is your legal responsibility to keep the details of your Vehicle Registration Certificate (V5C) up to date. You should tell the licensing authority of any changes. These include your name, address, or vehicle details. If you don't do this you may have problems when you sell your vehicle.

833 Mark *one* answer
For which of these MUST you show your insurance certificate?

☐ **A** When making a SORN declaration
☐ **B** When buying or selling a vehicle
☐ **C** When a police officer asks you for it
☐ **D** When having an MOT inspection

You MUST be able to produce your valid insurance certificate when requested by a police officer. If you can't do this immediately you may be asked to take it to a police station. Other documents you may be asked to produce are your driving licence and MOT certificate.

834 Mark *one* answer
You must have valid insurance before you can

☐ **A** make a SORN declaration
☐ **B** buy or sell a vehicle
☐ **C** apply for a driving licence
☐ **D** obtain a tax disc

You MUST have valid insurance before you can apply for a tax disc. Your vehicle will also need to have a valid MOT certificate, if applicable. You can apply online, at certain post offices or by post. It is illegal and can be dangerous to drive without valid insurance or an MOT.

835 Mark *one* answer
Your vehicle needs a current MOT certificate. Until you have one you will NOT be able to

☐ **A** renew your driving licence
☐ **B** change your insurance company
☐ **C** renew your road tax disc
☐ **D** notify a change of address

If your vehicle is required to have an MOT certificate you will need to make sure this is current before you are able to renew your tax disc (also known as vehicle excise duty). You can renew online, by phone or by post.

836 Mark *three* answers
Which THREE of these do you need before you can use a vehicle on the road legally?

☐ **A** A valid driving licence
☐ **B** A valid tax disc clearly displayed
☐ **C** Proof of your identity
☐ **D** Proper insurance cover
☐ **E** Breakdown cover
☐ **F** A vehicle handbook

Using a vehicle on the road illegally carries a heavy fine and can lead to penalty points on your licence. Things you MUST have include a valid driving licence, a current valid tax disc, and proper insurance cover.

837 Mark *one* answer
When you apply to renew your Vehicle Excise Duty (tax disc) you must have

☐ **A** valid insurance
☐ **B** the old tax disc
☐ **C** the handbook
☐ **D** a valid driving licence

Tax discs can be renewed at post offices, vehicle registration offices, online, or by post. When applying make sure you have all the relevant valid documents, including MOT where applicable.

838 Mark *one* answer
A police officer asks to see your documents. You do not have them with you. You may be asked to take them to a police station within

☐ **A** 5 days
☐ **B** 7 days
☐ **C** 14 days
☐ **D** 21 days

You don't have to carry the documents for your vehicle around with you. If a police officer asks to see them and you don't have them with you, you may be asked to produce them at a police station within seven days.

839 Mark *one* answer

When you apply to renew your vehicle excise licence (tax disc) what must you have?

☐ **A** Valid insurance
☐ **B** The old tax disc
☐ **C** The vehicle handbook
☐ **D** A valid driving licence

Tax discs can be renewed online, at most post offices, your nearest vehicle registration office or by post to the licensing authority. Make sure you have or take all the relevant documents with your application.

840 Mark *one* answer

When should you update your Vehicle Registration Certificate?

☐ **A** When you pass your driving test
☐ **B** When you move house
☐ **C** When your vehicle needs an MOT
☐ **D** When you have a collision

As the registered keeper of a vehicle it is up to you to inform DVLA (DVA in Northern Ireland) of any changes in your vehicle or personal details, for example, change of name or address. You do this by completing the relevant section of the Registration Certificate and sending it to them.

841 Mark *one* answer

To drive on the road learners MUST

☐ **A** have NO penalty points on their licence
☐ **B** have taken professional instruction
☐ **C** have a signed, valid provisional licence
☐ **D** apply for a driving test within 12 months

Before you drive on the road you MUST have a valid provisional licence, for the category of vehicle that you're driving. It must show your signature, it isn't valid without it.

842 Mark *one* answer

Before driving anyone else's motor vehicle you should make sure that

☐ **A** the vehicle owner has third party insurance cover
☐ **B** your own vehicle has insurance cover
☐ **C** the vehicle is insured for your use
☐ **D** the owner has left the insurance documents in the vehicle

Driving a vehicle without insurance cover is illegal. If you cause injury to anyone or damage to property, it could be very expensive and you could also be subject to a criminal prosecution. You can arrange insurance cover with an insurance company, a broker and some motor manufacturers or dealers.

843 Mark *one* answer
Your car needs an MOT certificate. If you drive without one this could invalidate your

☐ **A** vehicle service record
☐ **B** insurance
☐ **C** road tax disc
☐ **D** vehicle registration document

If your vehicle requires an MOT certificate, it's illegal to drive it without one. The only exceptions are that you may drive to a pre-arranged MOT test appointment, or to a garage for repairs required for the test. As well as being illegal, the vehicle may also be unsafe for use on the road and could endanger you, any passengers, and other road users.

844 Mark *one* answer
How old must you be to supervise a learner driver?

☐ **A** 18 years old ☐ **B** 19 years old
☐ **C** 20 years old ☐ **D** 21 years old

As well as being at least 21 years old you must hold a full EC/EEA driving licence for the category of vehicle being driven and have held that licence for at least three years.

845 Mark *one* answer
A newly qualified driver must

☐ **A** display green 'L' plates
☐ **B** not exceed 40mph for 12 months
☐ **C** be accompanied on a motorway
☐ **D** have valid motor insurance

It is your responsibility to make sure you are properly insured for the vehicle you are driving.

846 Mark *three* answers
You have third party insurance. What does this cover?

☐ **A** Damage to your own vehicle
☐ **B** Damage to your vehicle by fire
☐ **C** Injury to another person
☐ **D** Damage to someone's property
☐ **E** Damage to other vehicles
☐ **F** Injury to yourself

Third party insurance doesn't cover damage to your own vehicle or injury to yourself. If you have a crash and your vehicle is damaged you might have to carry out the repairs at your own expense.

847 Mark *one* answer
Vehicle excise duty is often called 'Road Tax' or 'The Tax Disc'. You must

☐ **A** keep it with your registration document
☐ **B** display it clearly on your vehicle
☐ **C** keep it concealed safely in your vehicle
☐ **D** carry it on you at all times

The tax disc should be displayed at the bottom of the windscreen on the nearside (left-hand side). This allows it to be easily seen from the kerbside. It must be current, and you can't transfer the disc from vehicle to vehicle.

848 Mark *one* answer
Your vehicle needs a current MOT certificate. You do not have one. Until you do have one you will not be able to renew your

- ☐ **A** driving licence
- ☐ **B** vehicle insurance
- ☐ **C** road tax disc
- ☐ **D** vehicle registration document

When you renew your road tax disc you need to produce a current, valid MOT certificate for your vehicle.

849 Mark *three* answers
Which THREE pieces of information are found on a vehicle registration document?

- ☐ **A** Registered keeper
- ☐ **B** Make of the vehicle
- ☐ **C** Service history details
- ☐ **D** Date of the MOT
- ☐ **E** Type of insurance cover
- ☐ **F** Engine size

Every vehicle used on the road has a registration certificate. This is issued by the Driver and Vehicle Licensing Agency (DVLA) or Driver and Vehicle Agency (DVA) in Northern Ireland. The document shows vehicle details including date of first registration, registration number, previous keeper, registered keeper, make of vehicle, engine size and chassis number, year of manufacture and colour.

850 Mark *three* answers
You have a duty to contact the licensing authority when

- ☐ **A** you go abroad on holiday
- ☐ **B** you change your vehicle
- ☐ **C** you change your name
- ☐ **D** your job status is changed
- ☐ **E** your permanent address changes
- ☐ **F** your job involves travelling abroad

The licensing authority need to keep their records up to date. They send out a reminder when your road tax is due and need your current address to send this to you. Every vehicle in the country is registered, so it's possible to trace its history.

851 Mark *three* answers
You must notify the licensing authority when

- ☐ **A** your health affects your driving
- ☐ **B** your eyesight does not meet a set standard
- ☐ **C** you intend lending your vehicle
- ☐ **D** your vehicle requires an MOT certificate
- ☐ **E** you change your vehicle

The Driver and Vehicle Licensing Agency (DVLA) hold the records of all vehicles and drivers in Great Britain (DVA in Northern Ireland). They need to know of any change in circumstances so that they can keep their records up to date. Your health might affect your ability to drive safely. Don't risk endangering your own safety or that of other road users.

852 Mark *one* answer [NI]
The cost of your insurance may reduce if you

☐ **A** are under 25 years old
☐ **B** do not wear glasses
☐ **C** pass the driving test first time
☐ **D** take the Pass Plus scheme

The cost of insurance varies with your age and how long you have been driving. Usually, the younger you are the more expensive it is, especially if you are under 25 years of age.

The Pass Plus scheme provides additional training to newly qualified drivers. Pass Plus is recognised by many insurance companies and taking this extra training could give you reduced insurance premiums, as well as improving your skills and experience.

853 Mark *one* answer [NI]
Which of the following may reduce the cost of your insurance?

☐ **A** Having a valid MOT certificate
☐ **B** Taking a Pass Plus course
☐ **C** Driving a powerful car
☐ **D** Having penalty points on your licence

The aim of the Pass Plus course is to build up your skills and experience. It is recognised by some insurance companies, who reward people completing the scheme with cheaper insurance premiums.

854 Mark *two* answers
To supervise a learner driver you must

☐ **A** have held a full licence for at least 3 years
☐ **B** be at least 21 years old
☐ **C** be an approved driving instructor
☐ **D** hold an advanced driving certificate

Don't just take someone's word that they are qualified to supervise you. The person who sits alongside you while you are learning should be a responsible adult and an experienced driver.

855 Mark *one* answer [NI]
When is it legal to drive a car over three years old without an MOT certificate?

☐ **A** Up to seven days after the old certificate has run out
☐ **B** When driving to an MOT centre to arrange an appointment
☐ **C** Just after buying a second-hand car with no MOT
☐ **D** When driving to an appointment at an MOT centre

Any car over three years old MUST have a valid MOT certificate before it can be used on the road. Exceptionally, you may drive to a pre-arranged test appointment or to a garage for repairs required for the test. However, you should check this with your insurance company. Driving an unroadworthy vehicle may invalidate your insurance.

856 Mark *one* answer [NI]
Motor cars must first have an MOT test certificate when they are

☐ **A** one year old
☐ **B** three years old
☐ **C** five years old
☐ **D** seven years old

The vehicle you drive MUST be roadworthy and in good condition. If it's over three years old it MUST have a valid MOT test certificate. The MOT test ensures that a vehicle meets minimum legal standards in terms of safety, components and environmental impact at the time it is tested.

857 Mark *one* answer [NI]
The Pass Plus scheme has been created for new drivers. What is its main purpose?

☐ **A** To allow you to drive faster
☐ **B** To allow you to carry passengers
☐ **C** To improve your basic skills
☐ **D** To let you drive on motorways

New drivers are far more vulnerable on the road and more likely to be involved in incidents and collisions. The Pass Plus scheme has been designed to improve new drivers' basic skills and help widen their driving experience.

858 Mark *two* answers
Your vehicle is insured third party only. This covers

☐ **A** damage to your vehicle
☐ **B** damage to other vehicles
☐ **C** injury to yourself
☐ **D** injury to others
☐ **E** all damage and injury

This type of insurance cover is usually cheaper than comprehensive. However, it does not cover any damage to your own vehicle or property. It only covers damage and injury to others.

859 Mark *one* answer
What is the legal minimum insurance cover you must have to drive on public roads?

☐ **A** Third party, fire and theft
☐ **B** Comprehensive
☐ **C** Third party only
☐ **D** Personal injury cover

The minimum insurance required by law is third party cover. This covers others involved in a collision but not damage to your vehicle. Basic third party insurance won't cover theft or fire damage. Check with your insurance company for advice on the best cover for you and make sure that you read the policy carefully.

860 Mark *one* answer

You claim on your insurance to have your car repaired. Your policy has an excess of £100. What does this mean?

- ☐ **A** The insurance company will pay the first £100 of any claim
- ☐ **B** You will be paid £100 if you do not claim within one year
- ☐ **C** Your vehicle is insured for a value of £100 if it is stolen
- ☐ **D** You will have to pay the first £100 of the cost of repair to your car

Having an excess on your policy will help to keep down the premium, but if you make a claim you will have to pay the excess yourself, in this case £100.

861 Mark *one* answer   NI

The Pass Plus scheme is designed to

- ☐ **A** give you a discount on your MOT
- ☐ **B** improve your basic driving skills
- ☐ **C** increase your mechanical knowledge
- ☐ **D** allow you to drive anyone else's vehicle

After passing your practical driving test you can take further training. This is known as the Pass Plus scheme. It is designed to improve your basic driving skills and involves a series of modules including night time and motorway driving. The sort of things you may not have covered whilst learning.

862 Mark *one* answer   NI

By taking part in the Pass Plus scheme you will

- ☐ **A** never get any points on your licence
- ☐ **B** be able to service your own car
- ☐ **C** allow you to drive anyone else's vehicle
- ☐ **D** improve your basic driving skills

The Pass Plus scheme can be taken after you've passed your practical driving test. Ask your ADI for details. It is designed to improve your basic driving skills. By successfully completing the course you may get a discount on your insurance.

863 Mark *one* answer   NI

The Pass Plus scheme is aimed at all newly qualified drivers. It enables them to

- ☐ **A** widen their driving experience
- ☐ **B** supervise a learner driver
- ☐ **C** increase their insurance premiums
- ☐ **D** avoid mechanical breakdowns

The Pass Plus scheme was created by DSA for newly qualified drivers. It aim's to widen their driving experience and improve basic skills. After passing the practical driving test additional professional training can be taken with an Approved Driving Instructor (ADI). Some insurance companies also offer discounts to holders of a Pass Plus certificate.

864 Mark *two* answers [NI]
New drivers can take further training after passing the practical test. A Pass Plus course will help to

☐ **A** improve your basic skills
☐ **B** widen your experience
☐ **C** increase your insurance premiums
☐ **D** get cheaper road tax

Novice drivers are in much more danger than experienced drivers. They can often be involved in collisions soon after passing their test, sometimes with tragic results. The Pass Plus scheme gives structured training to help new drivers improve basic skills and widen their experience. Approved Driving Instructors (ADIs) will be able to advise of the benefits.

865 Mark *one* answer [NI]
The Pass Plus Scheme is operated by DSA for newly qualified drivers. It is intended to

☐ **A** improve your basic skills
☐ **B** reduce the cost of your driving licence
☐ **C** prevent you from paying congestion charges
☐ **D** allow you to supervise a learner driver

The Pass Plus scheme provides a wide range of driving experience accompanied by a qualified instructor. There is no test and when completed you may get a reduction in insurance costs. It can help to improve basic skills, reduce the risk of having a collision and make you a safer driver.

866 Mark *one* answer
For which of these must you show your motor insurance certificate?

☐ **A** When you are taking your driving test
☐ **B** When buying or selling a vehicle
☐ **C** When a police officer asks you for it
☐ **D** When having an MOT inspection

When you take out motor insurance you'll be issued with a certificate. This contains details explaining who and what is insured. If a police officer asks to see your insurance certificate you must produce it at the time or at a police station within a specified period. You also need to have current valid insurance when renewing your vehicle excise duty (road tax).

867 Mark *three* answers
Which THREE of these do you need before you can drive legally?

☐ **A** A valid driving licence
☐ **B** A valid tax disc displayed on your vehicle
☐ **C** A vehicle service record
☐ **D** Proper insurance cover
☐ **E** Breakdown cover
☐ **F** A vehicle handbook

Make sure that you have a valid driving licence and proper insurance cover before driving any vehicle. These are legal requirements, as is displaying a valid tax disc in the vehicle.

868 Mark *one* answer

A friend wants to help you learn to drive. They must be

☐ **A** at least 21 and have held a full licence for at least one year

☐ **B** over 18 and hold an advanced driver's certificate

☐ **C** over 18 and have fully comprehensive insurance

☐ **D** at least 21 and have held a full licence for at least three years

Helping someone to drive is a responsible task. Before learning to drive you're advised to find a qualified Approved Driving Instructor (ADI) to teach you. This will ensure that you're taught the correct procedures from the start.

869 Mark *one* answer

Your motor insurance policy has an excess of £100. What does this mean?

☐ **A** The insurance company will pay the first £100 of any claim

☐ **B** You will be paid £100 if you do not have a crash

☐ **C** Your vehicle is insured for a value of £100 if it is stolen

☐ **D** You will have to pay the first £100 of any claim

This is a method used by insurance companies to keep annual premiums down. Generally, the higher the excess you choose to pay, the lower the annual premium you will be charged.

870 Mark *one* answer
You see a car on the hard shoulder of a motorway with a HELP pennant displayed. This means the driver is most likely to be

- ☐ **A** a disabled person
- ☐ **B** first aid trained
- ☐ **C** a foreign visitor
- ☐ **D** a rescue patrol person

If a disabled driver's vehicle breaks down and they are unable to walk to an emergency phone, they are advised to stay in their car and switch on the hazard warning lights. They may also display a 'Help' pennant in their vehicle.

871 Mark *two* answers
For which TWO should you use hazard warning lights?

- ☐ **A** When you slow down quickly on a motorway because of a hazard ahead
- ☐ **B** When you have broken down
- ☐ **C** When you wish to stop on double yellow lines
- ☐ **D** When you need to park on the pavement

Hazard warning lights are fitted to all modern cars and some motorcycles. They should only be used to warn other road users of a hazard ahead.

872 Mark *one* answer
When are you allowed to use hazard warning lights?

- ☐ **A** When stopped and temporarily obstructing traffic
- ☐ **B** When travelling during darkness without headlights
- ☐ **C** When parked for shopping on double yellow lines
- ☐ **D** When travelling slowly because you are lost

You must not use hazard warning lights when moving, except when slowing suddenly on a motorway or unrestricted dual carriageway to warn the traffic behind.
   Never use hazard warning lights to excuse dangerous or illegal parking.

873 Mark *one* answer
You are going through a congested tunnel and have to stop. What should you do?

- ☐ **A** Pull up very close to the vehicle in front to save space
- ☐ **B** Ignore any message signs as they are never up to date
- ☐ **C** Keep a safe distance from the vehicle in front
- ☐ **D** Make a U-turn and find another route

It's important to keep a safe distance from the vehicle in front at all times. This still applies in congested tunnels even if you are moving very slowly or have stopped. If the vehicle in front breaks down you may need room to manoeuvre past it.

874 Mark *one* answer

On the motorway, the hard shoulder should be used

☐ **A** to answer a mobile phone
☐ **B** when an emergency arises
☐ **C** for a short rest when tired
☐ **D** to check a road atlas

Pull onto the hard shoulder and use the emergency telephone to report your problem. This lets the emergency services know your exact location so they can send help. Never cross the carriageway to use the telephone on the other side.

875 Mark *one* answer

You arrive at the scene of a crash. Someone is bleeding badly from an arm wound. There is nothing embedded in it. What should you do?

☐ **A** Apply pressure over the wound and keep the arm down
☐ **B** Dab the wound
☐ **C** Get them a drink
☐ **D** Apply pressure over the wound and raise the arm

If possible, lay the casualty down. Check for anything that may be in the wound. Apply firm pressure to the wound using clean material, without pressing on anything which might be in it. Raising the arm above the level of the heart will also help to stem the flow of blood.

876 Mark *one* answer

You are at an incident where a casualty is unconscious. Their breathing should be checked. This should be done for at least

☐ **A** 2 seconds   ☐ **B** 10 seconds
☐ **C** 1 minute   ☐ **D** 2 minutes

Once the airway is open, check breathing. Listen and feel for breath. Do this by placing your cheek over their mouth and nose, and look to see if the chest rises. This should be done for up to 10 seconds.

877 Mark *one* answer

Following a collision someone has suffered a burn. The burn needs to be cooled. What is the shortest time it should be cooled for?

☐ **A** 5 minutes   ☐ **B** 10 minutes
☐ **C** 15 minutes   ☐ **D** 20 minutes

Check the casualty for shock and if possible try to cool the burn for at least ten minutes. Use a clean, cold non-toxic liquid preferably water.

878 Mark *one* answer

After a collision someone has suffered a burn. The burn needs to be cooled. What is the shortest time it should be cooled for?

☐ **A** 30 seconds   ☐ **B** 60 seconds
☐ **C** 5 minutes   ☐ **D** 10 minutes

It's important to cool a burn for at least ten minutes. Use a clean, cold non-toxic liquid preferably water. Bear in mind the person may also be in shock.

879 Mark *one* answer
A casualty is not breathing normally. Chest compressions should be given. At what rate?

☐ **A** 50 per minute
☐ **B** 100 per minute
☐ **C** 200 per minute
☐ **D** 250 per minute

If a casualty is not breathing normally chest compressions may be needed to maintain circulation. Place two hands on the centre of the chest and press down about 4-5 centimetres, at the rate of 100 per minute.

880 Mark *one* answer
A person has been injured. They may be suffering from shock. What are the warning signs to look for?

☐ **A** Flushed complexion
☐ **B** Warm dry skin
☐ **C** Slow pulse
☐ **D** Pale grey skin

The effects of shock may not be immediately obvious. Warning signs are rapid pulse, sweating, pale grey skin and rapid shallow breathing.

881 Mark *one* answer
You suspect that an injured person may be suffering from shock. What are the warning signs to look for?

☐ **A** Warm dry skin ☐ **B** Sweating
☐ **C** Slow pulse ☐ **D** Skin rash

Sometimes you may not realise that someone is in shock. The signs to look for are rapid pulse, sweating, pale grey skin and rapid shallow breathing.

882 Mark *one* answer
An injured person has been placed in the recovery position. They are unconscious but breathing normally. What else should be done?

☐ **A** Press firmly between the shoulders
☐ **B** Place their arms by their side
☐ **C** Give them a hot sweet drink
☐ **D** Check the airway is clear

After a casualty has been placed in the recovery position, their airway should be checked to make sure it's clear. Don't leave them alone until medical help arrives. Where possible do NOT move a casualty unless there's further danger.

883 Mark *one* answer
An injured motorcyclist is lying unconscious in the road. You should always

☐ **A** remove the safety helmet
☐ **B** seek medical assistance
☐ **C** move the person off the road
☐ **D** remove the leather jacket

If someone has been injured, the sooner proper medical attention is given the better. Send someone to phone for help or go yourself. An injured person should only be moved if they're in further danger. An injured motorcyclist's helmet should NOT be removed unless it is essential.

884 Mark *one* answer

You are on a motorway. A large box falls onto the road from a lorry. The lorry does not stop. You should

☐ **A** go to the next emergency telephone and report the hazard
☐ **B** catch up with the lorry and try to get the driver's attention
☐ **C** stop close to the box until the police arrive
☐ **D** pull over to the hard shoulder, then remove the box

Lorry drivers can be unaware of objects falling from their vehicles. If you see something fall onto a motorway look to see if the driver pulls over. If they don't stop, do not attempt to retrieve it yourself. Pull on to the hard shoulder near an emergency telephone and report the hazard. You will be connected to the police or a Highways Agency control centre.

885 Mark *one* answer

You are going through a long tunnel. What will warn you of congestion or an incident ahead?

☐ **A** Hazard warning lines
☐ **B** Other drivers flashing their lights
☐ **C** Variable message signs
☐ **D** Areas marked with hatch markings

Follow the instructions given by the signs or by tunnel officials.

In congested tunnels a minor incident can soon turn into a major one with serious or even fatal results.

886 Mark *one* answer

An adult casualty is not breathing. To maintain circulation, compressions should be given. What is the correct depth to press?

☐ **A** 1 to 2 centimetres
☐ **B** 4 to 5 centimetres
☐ **C** 10 to 15 centimetres
☐ **D** 15 to 20 centimetres

An adult casualty is not breathing normally. To maintain circulation place two hands on the centre of the chest. Then press down 4 to 5 centimetres at a rate of 100 times per minute.

887 Mark *two* answers

You are the first to arrive at the scene of a crash. Which TWO of these should you do?

☐ **A** Leave as soon as another motorist arrives
☐ **B** Make sure engines are switched off
☐ **C** Drag all casualties away from the vehicles
☐ **D** Call the emergency services promptly

At a crash scene you can help in practical ways, even if you aren't trained in first aid. Make sure you do not put yourself or anyone else in danger. The safest way to warn other traffic is by switching on your hazard warning lights.

888 Mark *one* answer
At the scene of a traffic incident you should

- ☐ **A** not put yourself at risk
- ☐ **B** go to those casualties who are screaming
- ☐ **C** pull everybody out of their vehicles
- ☐ **D** leave vehicle engines switched on

It's important that people at the scene of a collision do not create further risk to themselves or others. If the incident is on a motorway or major road, traffic will be approaching at speed. Do not put yourself at risk when trying to help casualties or warning other road users.

889 Mark *three* answers
You are the first person to arrive at an incident where people are badly injured. Which THREE should you do?

- ☐ **A** Switch on your own hazard warning lights
- ☐ **B** Make sure that someone telephones for an ambulance
- ☐ **C** Try and get people who are injured to drink something
- ☐ **D** Move the people who are injured clear of their vehicles
- ☐ **E** Get people who are not injured clear of the scene

If you're the first to arrive at a crash scene the first concerns are the risk of further collision and fire. Ensuring that vehicle engines are switched off will reduce the risk of fire. Use hazard warning lights so that other traffic knows there's a need for caution. Make sure the emergency services are contacted, don't assume this has already been done.

890 Mark *one* answer
You arrive at the scene of a motorcycle crash. The rider is injured. When should the helmet be removed?

- ☐ **A** Only when it is essential
- ☐ **B** Always straight away
- ☐ **C** Only when the motorcyclist asks
- ☐ **D** Always, unless they are in shock

DO NOT remove a motorcyclist's helmet unless it is essential. Remember they may be suffering from shock. Don't give them anything to eat or drink but do reassure them confidently.

891 Mark *three* answers
You arrive at a serious motorcycle crash. The motorcyclist is unconscious and bleeding. Your THREE main priorities should be to

- ☐ **A** try to stop the bleeding
- ☐ **B** make a list of witnesses
- ☐ **C** check their breathing
- ☐ **D** take the numbers of other vehicles
- ☐ **E** sweep up any loose debris
- ☐ **F** check their airways

Further collisions and fire are the main dangers immediately after a crash. If possible get others to assist you and make the area safe. Help those involved and remember DR ABC, Danger, Response, Airway, Breathing, Compressions. This will help when dealing with any injuries.

892 Mark *one* answer

You arrive at an incident. A motorcyclist is unconscious. Your FIRST priority is the casualty's

□ **A** breathing
□ **B** bleeding
□ **C** broken bones
□ **D** bruising

At the scene of an incident always be aware of danger from further collisions or fire. The first priority when dealing with an unconscious person is to ensure they can breathe. This may involve clearing their airway if you can see an obstruction, or if they're having difficulty breathing.

893 Mark *three* answers

At an incident a casualty is unconscious. Which THREE of these should you check urgently?

□ **A** Circulation
□ **B** Airway
□ **C** Shock
□ **D** Breathing
□ **E** Broken bones

Remember DR ABC. An unconscious casualty may have difficulty breathing. Check that their airway is clear by tilting the head back gently and unblock it if necessary. Then make sure they are breathing. If there is bleeding, stem the flow by placing clean material over any wounds but without pressing on any objects in the wound. Compressions may need to be given to maintain circulation.

894 Mark *three* answers

You arrive at the scene of an incident. It has just happened and someone is unconscious. Which THREE of these should be given urgent priority to help them?

□ **A** Clear the airway and keep it open
□ **B** Try to get them to drink water
□ **C** Check that they are breathing
□ **D** Look for any witnesses
□ **E** Stop any heavy bleeding
□ **F** Take the numbers of vehicles involved

Make sure that the emergency services are called immediately. Once first aid has been given, stay with the casualty.

895 Mark *three* answers

At an incident someone is unconscious. Your THREE main priorities should be to

□ **A** sweep up the broken glass
□ **B** take the names of witnesses
□ **C** count the number of vehicles involved
□ **D** check the airway is clear
□ **E** make sure they are breathing
□ **F** stop any heavy bleeding

Remember this procedure by saying DR ABC. This stands for Danger, Response, Airway, Breathing, Compressions.

896 Mark *three* answers
You have stopped at an incident to give help. Which THREE things should you do?

- ☐ **A** Keep injured people warm and comfortable
- ☐ **B** Keep injured people calm by talking to them reassuringly
- ☐ **C** Keep injured people on the move by walking them around
- ☐ **D** Give injured people a warm drink
- ☐ **E** Make sure that injured people are not left alone

There are a number of things you can do to help, even without expert training. Be aware of further danger and fire, make sure the area is safe. People may be in shock. Don't give them anything to eat or drink. Keep them warm and comfortable and reassure them. Don't move injured people unless there is a risk of further danger.

897 Mark *three* answers
You arrive at an incident. It has just happened and someone is injured. Which THREE should be given urgent priority?

- ☐ **A** Stop any severe bleeding
- ☐ **B** Give them a warm drink
- ☐ **C** Check they are breathing
- ☐ **D** Take numbers of vehicles involved
- ☐ **E** Look for witnesses
- ☐ **F** Clear their airway and keep it open

The first priority with a casualty is to make sure their airway is clear and they are breathing. Any wounds should be checked for objects and then bleeding stemmed using clean material. Ensure the emergency services are called, they are the experts. If you're not first aid trained consider getting training. It might save a life.

898 Mark *one* answer
Which of the following should you NOT do at the scene of a collision?

- ☐ **A** Warn other traffic by switching on your hazard warning lights
- ☐ **B** Call the emergency services immediately
- ☐ **C** Offer someone a cigarette to calm them down
- ☐ **D** Ask drivers to switch off their engines

Keeping casualties or witnesses calm is important, but never offer a cigarette because of the risk of fire. Bear in mind they may be in shock. Don't offer an injured person anything to eat or drink. They may have internal injuries or need surgery.

899 Mark *two* answers
There has been a collision. A driver is suffering from shock. What TWO of these should you do?

- ☐ **A** Give them a drink
- ☐ **B** Reassure them
- ☐ **C** Not leave them alone
- ☐ **D** Offer them a cigarette
- ☐ **E** Ask who caused the incident

Be aware they could have an injury that is not immediately obvious. Ensure the emergency services are called. Reassure and stay with them until the experts arrive.

900 Mark *one* answer

You have to treat someone for shock at the scene of an incident. You should

☐ **A** reassure them constantly
☐ **B** walk them around to calm them down
☐ **C** give them something cold to drink
☐ **D** cool them down as soon as possible

Stay with the casualty and talk to them quietly and firmly to calm and reassure them. Avoid moving them unnecessarily in case they are injured. Keep them warm, but don't give them anything to eat or drink.

901 Mark *one* answer

You arrive at the scene of a motorcycle crash. No other vehicle is involved. The rider is unconscious and lying in the middle of the road. The FIRST thing you should do is

☐ **A** move the rider out of the road
☐ **B** warn other traffic
☐ **C** clear the road of debris
☐ **D** give the rider reassurance

The motorcyclist is in an extremely vulnerable position, exposed to further danger from traffic. Approaching vehicles need advance warning in order to slow down and safely take avoiding action or stop. Don't put yourself or anyone else at risk. Use the hazard warning lights on your vehicle to alert other road users to the danger.

902 Mark *one* answer

At an incident a small child is not breathing. To restore normal breathing you should breathe into their mouth

☐ **A** sharply
☐ **B** gently
☐ **C** heavily
☐ **D** rapidly

If a young child has stopped breathing, first check that the airway is clear. Then give compressions to the chest using one hand (two fingers for an infant) and begin mouth-to-mouth resuscitation. Breathe very gently and continue the procedure until they can breathe without help.

903 Mark *three* answers

At an incident a casualty is not breathing. To start the process to restore normal breathing you should

☐ **A** tilt their head forward
☐ **B** clear the airway
☐ **C** turn them on their side
☐ **D** tilt their head back gently
☐ **E** pinch the nostrils together
☐ **F** put their arms across their chest

It's important to ensure that the airways are clear before you start mouth to mouth resuscitation. Gently tilt their head back and use your finger to check for and remove any obvious obstruction in the mouth.

904 Mark *one* answer

You arrive at an incident. There has been an engine fire and someone's hands and arms have been burnt. You should NOT

- ☐ **A** douse the burn thoroughly with clean cool non-toxic liquid
- ☐ **B** lay the casualty down on the ground
- ☐ **C** remove anything sticking to the burn
- ☐ **D** reassure them confidently and repeatedly

This could cause further damage and infection to the wound. Your first priority is to cool the burn with a clean, cool, non-toxic liquid, preferably water. Don't forget the casualty may be in shock.

905 Mark *one* answer

You arrive at an incident where someone is suffering from severe burns. You should

- ☐ **A** apply lotions to the injury
- ☐ **B** burst any blisters
- ☐ **C** remove anything stuck to the burns
- ☐ **D** douse the burns with clean cool non-toxic liquid

Use a liquid that is clean, cold and non-toxic, preferably water. Its coolness will help take the heat out of the burn and relieve the pain. Keep the wound doused for at least ten minutes. If blisters appear don't attempt to burst them as this could lead to infection.

906 Mark *two* answers

You arrive at an incident. A pedestrian has a severe bleeding leg wound. It is not broken and there is nothing in the wound. What TWO of these should you do?

- ☐ **A** Dab the wound to stop bleeding
- ☐ **B** Keep both legs flat on the ground
- ☐ **C** Apply firm pressure to the wound
- ☐ **D** Raise the leg to lessen bleeding
- ☐ **E** Fetch them a warm drink

First check for anything that may be in the wound such as glass. If there's nothing in it apply a pad of clean cloth or bandage. Raising the leg will lessen the flow of blood. Don't tie anything tightly round the leg. This will restrict circulation and can result in long-term injury.

907 Mark *one* answer

At an incident a casualty is unconscious but still breathing. You should only move them if

- ☐ **A** an ambulance is on its way
- ☐ **B** bystanders advise you to
- ☐ **C** there is further danger
- ☐ **D** bystanders will help you to

Do not move a casualty unless there is further danger, for example, from other traffic or fire. They may have unseen or internal injuries. Moving them unnecessarily could cause further injury. Do NOT remove a motorcyclist's helmet unless it's essential.

908 Mark *one* answer

At a collision you suspect a casualty has back injuries. The area is safe. You should

☐ **A** offer them a drink
☐ **B** not move them
☐ **C** raise their legs
☐ **D** not call an ambulance

Talk to the casualty and keep them calm. Do not attempt to move them as this could cause further injury. Call an ambulance at the first opportunity.

909 Mark *one* answer

At an incident it is important to look after any casualties. When the area is safe, you should

☐ **A** get them out of the vehicle
☐ **B** give them a drink
☐ **C** give them something to eat
☐ **D** keep them in the vehicle

When the area is safe and there's no danger from other traffic or fire it's better not to move casualties. Moving them may cause further injury.

910 Mark *one* answer

A tanker is involved in a collision. Which sign shows that it is carrying dangerous goods?

☐ **A**   ☐ **B**

☐ **C**   ☐ **D**

There will be an orange label on the side and rear of the tanker. Look at this carefully and report what it says when you phone the emergency services. Details of hazard warning plates are given in The Highway Code.

911 Mark *three* answers

You are involved in a collision. Because of this which THREE of these documents may the police ask you to produce?

☐ **A** Vehicle registration document
☐ **B** Driving licence
☐ **C** Theory test certificate
☐ **D** Insurance certificate
☐ **E** MOT test certificate
☐ **F** Vehicle service record

You MUST stop if you have been involved in a collision which results in injury or damage. The police may ask to see your documents at the time or later at a police station.

912 Mark *one* answer

After a collision someone is unconscious in their vehicle. When should you call the emergency services?

- ☐ **A** Only as a last resort
- ☐ **B** As soon as possible
- ☐ **C** After you have woken them up
- ☐ **D** After checking for broken bones

It is important to make sure that emergency services arrive on the scene as soon as possible. When a person is unconscious, they could have serious injuries that are not immediately obvious.

913 Mark *one* answer

A casualty has an injured arm. They can move it freely but it is bleeding. Why should you get them to keep it in a raised position?

- ☐ **A** Because it will ease the pain
- ☐ **B** It will help them to be seen more easily
- ☐ **C** To stop them touching other people
- ☐ **D** It will help to reduce the blood flow

If a casualty is bleeding heavily, raise the limb to a higher position. This will help to reduce the blood flow. Before raising the limb you should make sure that it is not broken.

914 Mark *one* answer

You are going through a tunnel. What systems are provided to warn of any incidents, collisions or congestion?

- ☐ **A** Double white centre lines
- ☐ **B** Variable message signs
- ☐ **C** Chevron 'distance markers'
- ☐ **D** Rumble strips

Take notice of any instructions given on variable message signs or by tunnel officials. They will warn you of any incidents or congestion ahead and advise you what to do.

915 Mark *one* answer

A collision has just happened. An injured person is lying in a busy road. What is the FIRST thing you should do to help?

- ☐ **A** Treat the person for shock
- ☐ **B** Warn other traffic
- ☐ **C** Place them in the recovery position
- ☐ **D** Make sure the injured person is kept warm

The most immediate danger is further collisions and fire. You could warn other traffic by displaying an advance warning triangle or sign (but not on a motorway), switching on hazard warning lights or by any other means that does not put you or others at risk.

916 Mark *two* answers
At an incident a casualty has stopped breathing. You should

☐ **A** remove anything that is blocking the mouth
☐ **B** keep the head tilted forwards as far as possible
☐ **C** raise the legs to help with circulation
☐ **D** try to give the casualty something to drink
☐ **E** tilt the head back gently to clear the airway

Unblocking the airway and gently tilting the head back will help the casualty to breathe. They will then be in the correct position if mouth-to-mouth resuscitation is required. Don't move a casualty unless there's further danger.

917 Mark *four* answers
You are at the scene of an incident. Someone is suffering from shock. You should

☐ **A** reassure them constantly
☐ **B** offer them a cigarette
☐ **C** keep them warm
☐ **D** avoid moving them if possible
☐ **E** avoid leaving them alone
☐ **F** give them a warm drink

The signs of shock may not be immediately obvious. Prompt treatment can help to minimise the effects. Lay the casualty down, loosen tight clothing, call an ambulance and check their breathing and pulse.

918 Mark *one* answer
There has been a collision. A motorcyclist is lying injured and unconscious. Unless it's essential, why should you usually NOT attempt to remove their helmet?

☐ **A** Because they may not want you to
☐ **B** This could result in more serious injury
☐ **C** They will get too cold if you do this
☐ **D** Because you could scratch the helmet

When someone is injured, any movement which is not absolutely necessary should be avoided since it could make injuries worse. Unless it is essential, it's generally safer to leave a motorcyclist's helmet in place.

919 Mark *one* answer
You have broken down on a two-way road. You have a warning triangle. You should place the warning triangle at least how far from your vehicle?

☐ **A** 5 metres (16 feet)
☐ **B** 25 metres (82 feet)
☐ **C** 45 metres (147 feet)
☐ **D** 100 metres (328 feet)

Advance warning triangles fold flat and don't take up much room. Use it to warn other road users if your vehicle has broken down or there's been an incident. Place it at least 45 metres (147 feet) behind your vehicle or incident on the same side of the road or verge. Place it further back if the scene is hidden by, for example, a bend, hill or dip in the road. Don't use them on motorways.

920 Mark *three* answers

You break down on a level crossing. The lights have not yet begun to flash. Which THREE things should you do?

- ☐ **A** Telephone the signal operator
- ☐ **B** Leave your vehicle and get everyone clear
- ☐ **C** Walk down the track and signal the next train
- ☐ **D** Move the vehicle if a signal operator tells you to
- ☐ **E** Tell drivers behind what has happened

If your vehicle breaks down on a level crossing, your first priority is to get everyone out of the vehicle and clear of the crossing. Then use the railway telephone, if there is one, to tell the signal operator. If you have time before the train arrives, move the vehicle clear of the crossing, but only do this if alarm signals are not on.

921 Mark *two* answers

Your tyre bursts while you are driving. Which TWO things should you do?

- ☐ **A** Pull on the handbrake
- ☐ **B** Brake as quickly as possible
- ☐ **C** Pull up slowly at the side of the road
- ☐ **D** Hold the steering wheel firmly to keep control
- ☐ **E** Continue on at a normal speed

A tyre bursting can lead to a loss of control, especially if you're travelling at high speed. Using the correct procedure should help you to stop the vehicle safely.

922 Mark *two* answers

Which TWO things should you do when a front tyre bursts?

- ☐ **A** Apply the handbrake to stop the vehicle
- ☐ **B** Brake firmly and quickly
- ☐ **C** Let the vehicle roll to a stop
- ☐ **D** Hold the steering wheel lightly
- ☐ **E** Grip the steering wheel firmly

Try not to react by applying the brakes harshly. This could lead to further loss of steering control. Indicate your intention to pull up at the side of the road and roll to a stop.

923 Mark *one* answer

Your vehicle has a puncture on a motorway. What should you do?

- ☐ **A** Drive slowly to the next service area to get assistance
- ☐ **B** Pull up on the hard shoulder. Change the wheel as quickly as possible
- ☐ **C** Pull up on the hard shoulder. Use the emergency phone to get assistance
- ☐ **D** Switch on your hazard lights. Stop in your lane

Pull up on the hard shoulder and make your way to the nearest emergency telephone to call for assistance.

Do not attempt to repair your vehicle while it is on the hard shoulder because of the risk posed by traffic passing at high speeds.

924 Mark *one* answer
You have stalled in the middle of a level crossing and cannot restart the engine. The warning bell starts to ring. You should

☐ **A** get out and clear of the crossing
☐ **B** run down the track to warn the signal operator
☐ **C** carry on trying to restart the engine
☐ **D** push the vehicle clear of the crossing

Try to stay calm, especially if you have passengers on board. If you can't restart your engine before the warning bells ring, leave the vehicle and get yourself and any passengers well clear of the crossing.

925 Mark *two* answers
You are on a motorway. When can you use hazard warning lights?

☐ **A** When a vehicle is following too closely
☐ **B** When you slow down quickly because of danger ahead
☐ **C** When you are towing another vehicle
☐ **D** When driving on the hard shoulder
☐ **E** When you have broken down on the hard shoulder

Hazard warning lights will warn the traffic travelling behind you that there is a hazard ahead.

926 Mark *three* answers
You have broken down on a motorway. When you use the emergency telephone you will be asked

☐ **A** for the number on the telephone that you are using
☐ **B** for your driving licence details
☐ **C** for the name of your vehicle insurance company
☐ **D** for details of yourself and your vehicle
☐ **E** whether you belong to a motoring organisation

Have these details ready before you use the emergency telephone and be sure to give the correct information. For your own safety always face the traffic when you speak on a roadside telephone.

927 Mark *one* answer
Before driving through a tunnel what should you do?

☐ **A** Switch your radio off
☐ **B** Remove any sunglasses
☐ **C** Close your sunroof
☐ **D** Switch on windscreen wipers

If you are wearing sunglasses you should remove them before driving into a tunnel. If you don't, your vision will be restricted, even in tunnels that appear to be well-lit.

928 Mark *one* answer

You are driving through a tunnel and the traffic is flowing normally. What should you do?

☐ **A** Use parking lights
☐ **B** Use front spot lights
☐ **C** Use dipped headlights
☐ **D** Use rear fog lights

Before entering a tunnel you should switch on your dipped headlights, as this will allow you to see and be seen. In many tunnels it is a legal requirement.

Don't wear sunglasses while driving in a tunnel. You may wish to tune your radio into a local channel.

929 Mark *one* answer

You are driving through a tunnel. Your vehicle breaks down. What should you do?

☐ **A** Switch on hazard warning lights
☐ **B** Remain in your vehicle
☐ **C** Wait for the police to find you
☐ **D** Rely on CCTV cameras seeing you

If your vehicle breaks down in a tunnel it could present a danger to other traffic. First switch on your hazard warning lights and then call for help from an emergency telephone point.

Don't rely on being found by the police or being seen by a CCTV camera. The longer the vehicle stays in an exposed position, the more danger it poses to other drivers.

930 Mark *one* answer

When driving through a tunnel you should

☐ **A** Look out for variable message signs
☐ **B** Use your air conditioning system
☐ **C** Switch on your rear fog lights
☐ **D** Always use your windscreen wipers

A minor incident in a tunnel can quickly turn into a major disaster. Variable message signs are provided to warn of any incidents or congestion. Follow their advice.

931 Mark *two* answers

What TWO safeguards could you take against fire risk to your vehicle?

☐ **A** Keep water levels above maximum
☐ **B** Carry a fire extinguisher
☐ **C** Avoid driving with a full tank of petrol
☐ **D** Use unleaded petrol
☐ **E** Check out any strong smell of petrol
☐ **F** Use low octane fuel

The fuel in your vehicle can be a dangerous fire hazard. Never
• use a naked flame near the vehicle if you can smell fuel
• smoke when refuelling your vehicle.

932 Mark *one* answer
You are on the motorway. Luggage falls from your vehicle. What should you do?

☐ **A** Stop at the next emergency telephone and contact the police
☐ **B** Stop on the motorway and put on hazard lights while you pick it up
☐ **C** Walk back up the motorway to pick it up
☐ **D** Pull up on the hard shoulder and wave traffic down

If any object falls onto the motorway carriageway from your vehicle pull over onto the hard shoulder near an emergency telephone and phone for assistance.
You will be connected to the police or a Highways Agency control centre. Don't stop on the carriageway or attempt to retrieve anything.

---

933 Mark *one* answer
While driving, a warning light on your vehicle's instrument panel comes on. You should

☐ **A** continue if the engine sounds all right
☐ **B** hope that it is just a temporary electrical fault
☐ **C** deal with the problem when there is more time
☐ **D** check out the problem quickly and safely

Make sure you know what the different warning lights mean. An illuminated warning light could mean that your car is unsafe to drive. Don't take risks. If you aren't sure about the problem get a qualified mechanic to check it.

934 Mark *one* answer
You have broken down on a two-way road. You have a warning triangle. It should be displayed

☐ **A** on the roof of your vehicle
☐ **B** at least 150 metres (492 feet) behind your vehicle
☐ **C** at least 45 metres (147 feet) behind your vehicle
☐ **D** just behind your vehicle

If you need to display a warning triangle make sure that it can be clearly seen by other road users. Place it on the same side of the road as the broken down vehicle and away from any obstruction that would make it hard to see.

---

935 Mark *one* answer
Your engine catches fire. What should you do first?

☐ **A** Lift the bonnet and disconnect the battery
☐ **B** Lift the bonnet and warn other traffic
☐ **C** Call a breakdown service
☐ **D** Call the fire brigade

If you suspect a fire in the engine compartment you should pull up as safely and as quickly as possible. DO NOT open the bonnet as this will fuel the fire further. Get any passengers out of the vehicle and dial 999 immediately to contact the fire brigade.

936 Mark *one* answer

Your vehicle breaks down in a tunnel. What should you do?

☐ **A** Stay in your vehicle and wait for the police
☐ **B** Stand in the lane behind your vehicle to warn others
☐ **C** Stand in front of your vehicle to warn oncoming drivers
☐ **D** Switch on hazard lights then go and call for help immediately

A broken-down vehicle in a tunnel can cause serious congestion and danger to other road users. If your vehicle breaks down, get help without delay. Switch on your hazard warning lights, then go to an emergency telephone point to call for help.

937 Mark *one* answer

Your vehicle catches fire while driving through a tunnel. It is still driveable. What should you do?

☐ **A** Leave it where it is with the engine running
☐ **B** Pull up, then walk to an emergency telephone point
☐ **C** Park it away from the carriageway
☐ **D** Drive it out of the tunnel if you can do so

If it's possible, and you can do so without causing further danger, it may be safer to drive a vehicle which is on fire out of a tunnel. The greatest danger in a tunnel fire is smoke and suffocation.

938 Mark *one* answer

You are driving through a tunnel. Your vehicle catches fire. What should you do?

☐ **A** Continue through the tunnel if you can
☐ **B** Turn your vehicle around immediately
☐ **C** Reverse out of the tunnel
☐ **D** Carry out an emergency stop

The main dangers in a tunnel fire are suffocation and smoke. If you can do so safely it's better to drive a burning vehicle out of a tunnel. If you can't do this, pull over, switch off the engine, use hazard warning lights and phone immediately for help. It may be possible to put out a small fire but if it seems large do NOT tackle it!

939 Mark *two* answers

You are in a tunnel. Your vehicle is on fire and you CANNOT drive it. What should you do?

☐ **A** Stay in the vehicle and close the windows
☐ **B** Switch on hazard warning lights
☐ **C** Leave the engine running
☐ **D** Try and put out the fire
☐ **E** Switch off all of your lights
☐ **F** Wait for other people to phone for help

It's usually better to drive a burning vehicle out of a tunnel. If you can't do this pull over and stop at an emergency point if possible. Switch off the engine, use hazard warning lights, and leave the vehicle immediately. Call for help from the nearest emergency point. If you have an extinguisher it may help to put out a small fire but do NOT try to tackle a large one.

940 Mark *one* answer
When approaching a tunnel it is good advice to

☐ **A** put on your sunglasses and use the sun visor
☐ **B** check your tyre pressures
☐ **C** change down to a lower gear
☐ **D** make sure your radio is tuned to the frequency shown

On the approach to tunnels a sign will usually show a local radio channel. It should give a warning of any incidents or congestion in the tunnel ahead. Many radios can be set to automatically pick up traffic announcements and local frequencies. If you have to tune the radio manually don't be distracted while doing so. Incidents in tunnels can lead to serious casualties. The greatest hazard is fire. Getting an advance warning of problems could save your life and others.

941 Mark *one* answer
Your vehicle has broken down on an automatic railway level crossing. What should you do FIRST?

☐ **A** Get everyone out of the vehicle and clear of the crossing
☐ **B** Telephone your vehicle recovery service to move it
☐ **C** Walk along the track to give warning to any approaching trains
☐ **D** Try to push the vehicle clear of the crossing as soon as possible

Firstly get yourself and anyone else well away from the crossing. If there's a railway phone use that to get instructions from the signal operator. Then if there's time move the vehicle clear of the crossing.

942 Mark *three* answers
Which THREE of these items should you carry for use in the event of a collision?

☐ **A** Road map
☐ **B** Can of petrol
☐ **C** Jump leads
☐ **D** Fire extinguisher
☐ **E** First aid kit
☐ **F** Warning triangle

Used correctly, these items can provide invaluable help in the event of a collision or breakdown. They could even save a life.

943 Mark *one* answer
You have a collision whilst your car is moving. What is the FIRST thing you must do?

☐ **A** Stop only if someone waves at you
☐ **B** Call the emergency services
☐ **C** Stop at the scene of the incident
☐ **D** Call your insurance company

If you are in a collision that causes damage or injury to any other person, vehicle, animal or property, by law you MUST STOP. Give your name, the vehicle owner's name and address, and the vehicle's registration number to anyone who has reasonable grounds for requiring them.

944 Mark *four* answers

You are in collision with another moving vehicle. Someone is injured and your vehicle is damaged. Which FOUR of the following should you find out?

- ☐ **A** Whether the driver owns the other vehicle involved
- ☐ **B** The other driver's name, address and telephone number
- ☐ **C** The make and registration number of the other vehicle
- ☐ **D** The occupation of the other driver
- ☐ **E** The details of the other driver's vehicle insurance
- ☐ **F** Whether the other driver is licensed to drive

Try to keep calm and don't rush. Ensure that you have all the details before you leave the scene. If possible take pictures and note the positions of all the vehicles involved.

945 Mark *one* answer   NI

You lose control of your car and damage a garden wall. No one is around. What must you do?

- ☐ **A** Report the incident to the police within 24 hours
- ☐ **B** Go back to tell the house owner the next day
- ☐ **C** Report the incident to your insurance company when you get home
- ☐ **D** Find someone in the area to tell them about it immediately

If the property owner is not available at the time, you MUST inform the police of the incident. This should be done as soon as possible, and within 24 hours.

946 Mark *one* answer

You are in a collision on a two-way road. You have a warning triangle with you. At what distance before the obstruction should you place the warning triangle?

- ☐ **A** 25 metres (82 feet)
- ☐ **B** 45 metres (147 feet)
- ☐ **C** 100 metres (328 feet)
- ☐ **D** 150 metres (492 feet)

This is the minimum distance to place the triangle from the obstruction. If there's a bend or hump in the road place it so that approaching traffic has plenty of time to react to the warning and slow down. You may also need to use your hazard warning lights, especially in poor visibility or at night.

947 Mark *one* answer

You have a collision while driving through a tunnel. You are not injured but your vehicle cannot be driven. What should you do FIRST?

- ☐ **A** Rely on other drivers phoning for the police
- ☐ **B** Switch off the engine and switch on hazard lights
- ☐ **C** Take the names of witnesses and other drivers
- ☐ **D** Sweep up any debris that is in the road

If you are involved in a collision in a tunnel be aware of the danger this can cause to other traffic. The greatest danger is fire. Put on your hazard warning lights straight away and switch off your engine. Then call for help from an emergency telephone point.

948 Mark *one* answer

You are driving through a tunnel. There has been a collision and the car in front is on fire and blocking the road. What should you do?

☐ **A** Overtake and continue as quickly as you can

☐ **B** Lock all the doors and windows

☐ **C** Switch on hazard warning lights

☐ **D** Stop, then reverse out of the tunnel

If the vehicle in front is on fire, you should pull over to the side and stop. Switch on your warning lights and switch off your engine. If you can locate a fire extinguisher use it to put out the fire, taking great care. Do NOT open the bonnet. Always call for help from the nearest emergency point and if possible give first aid to anyone who is injured.

949 Mark *two* answers
You are towing a small trailer on a busy three-lane motorway. All the lanes are open. You must

☐ **A** not exceed 60mph
☐ **B** not overtake
☐ **C** have a stabiliser fitted
☐ **D** use only the left and centre lanes

You should be aware of the motorway regulations for vehicles towing trailers. These state that a vehicle towing a trailer must not
- use the right-hand lane of a three-lane motorway unless directed to do so, for example, at roadworks or due to a lane closure
- exceed 60mph.

950 Mark *one* answer
If a trailer swerves or snakes when you are towing it you should

☐ **A** ease off the accelerator and reduce your speed
☐ **B** let go of the steering wheel and let it correct itself
☐ **C** brake hard and hold the pedal down
☐ **D** increase your speed as quickly as possible

Strong winds or buffeting from large vehicles can cause a trailer or caravan to snake or swerve. If this happens, ease off the accelerator. Don't brake harshly, steer sharply or increase your speed.

951 Mark *one* answer
How can you stop a caravan snaking from side to side?

☐ **A** Turn the steering wheel slowly to each side
☐ **B** Accelerate to increase your speed
☐ **C** Stop as quickly as you can
☐ **D** Slow down very gradually

Keep calm and don't brake harshly or you could lose control completely. Ease off the accelerator until the unit is brought back under control. The most dangerous time is on long downhill gradients.

952 Mark *two* answers
On which TWO occasions might you inflate your tyres to more than the recommended normal pressure?

☐ **A** When the roads are slippery
☐ **B** When driving fast for a long distance
☐ **C** When the tyre tread is worn below 2mm
☐ **D** When carrying a heavy load
☐ **E** When the weather is cold
☐ **F** When the vehicle is fitted with anti-lock brakes

Check the vehicle handbook. This should give you guidance on the correct tyre pressures for your vehicle and when you may need to adjust them. If you are carrying a heavy load you may need to adjust the headlights as well. Most cars have a switch on the dashboard to do this.

953 Mark *one* answer
A heavy load on your roof rack will

☐ **A** improve the road holding
☐ **B** reduce the stopping distance
☐ **C** make the steering lighter
☐ **D** reduce stability

A heavy load on your roof rack will reduce the stability of the vehicle because it moves the centre of gravity away from that designed by the manufacturer. Be aware of this when you negotiate bends and corners.

If you change direction at speed, your vehicle and/or load could become unstable and you could lose control.

954 Mark *one* answer
You are towing a caravan along a motorway. The caravan begins to swerve from side to side. What should you do?

☐ **A** Ease off the accelerator slowly
☐ **B** Steer sharply from side to side
☐ **C** Do an emergency stop
☐ **D** Speed up very quickly

Try not to brake or steer heavily as this will only make matters worse and you could lose control altogether. Keep calm and regain control by easing off the accelerator.

955 Mark *two* answers
Overloading your vehicle can seriously affect the

☐ **A** gearbox
☐ **B** steering
☐ **C** handling
☐ **D** battery life
☐ **E** journey time

Any load will have an effect on the handling of your vehicle and this becomes worse as you increase the load. Any change in the centre of gravity or weight the vehicle is carrying will affect its braking and handling on bends.

You need to be aware of this when carrying passengers, heavy loads, fitting a roof rack or towing a trailer.

956 Mark *one* answer
Who is responsible for making sure that a vehicle is not overloaded?

☐ **A** The driver of the vehicle
☐ **B** The owner of the items being carried
☐ **C** The person who loaded the vehicle
☐ **D** The licensing authority

Your vehicle must not be overloaded. Carrying heavy loads will affect control and handling characteristics. If your vehicle is overloaded and it causes a crash, you'll be held responsible.

957 Mark *one* answer
You are planning to tow a caravan. Which of these will mostly help to aid the vehicle handling?

☐ **A** A jockey wheel fitted to the tow bar
☐ **B** Power steering fitted to the towing vehicle
☐ **C** Anti-lock brakes fitted to the towing vehicle
☐ **D** A stabiliser fitted to the towbar

Towing a caravan or trailer affects the way the tow vehicle handles. It is highly recommended that you take a caravan manoeuvring course. These are provided by various organisations for anyone wishing to tow a trailer.

958 Mark *one* answer
Are passengers allowed to ride in a caravan that is being towed?

☐ **A** Yes, if they are over fourteen
☐ **B** No, not at any time
☐ **C** Only if all the seats in the towing vehicle are full
☐ **D** Only if a stabiliser is fitted

Riding in a towed caravan is highly dangerous. The safety of the entire unit is dependent on the stability of the trailer. Moving passengers would make the caravan unstable and could cause loss of control.

959 Mark *one* answer
A trailer must stay securely hitched up to the towing vehicle. What additional safety device can be fitted to the trailer braking system?

☐ **A** Stabiliser
☐ **B** Jockey wheel
☐ **C** Corner steadies
☐ **D** Breakaway cable

In the event of a tow bar failure the cable activates the trailer brakes, then snaps. This allows the towing vehicle to get free of the trailer and out of danger.

960 Mark *one* answer
Why would you fit a stabiliser before towing a caravan?

☐ **A** It will help with stability when driving in crosswinds
☐ **B** It will allow heavy items to be loaded behind the axle
☐ **C** It will help you to raise and lower the jockey wheel
☐ **D** It will allow you to tow without the breakaway cable

Fitting a stabiliser to your tow bar will help to reduce snaking by the caravan especially where there are crosswinds. However, this does not take away your responsibility to ensure that your vehicle/caravan combination is loaded correctly.

961 Mark *one* answer

You wish to tow a trailer. Where would you find the maximum noseweight of your vehicle's tow ball?

☐ **A** In the vehicle handbook
☐ **B** In The Highway Code
☐ **C** In your vehicle registration certificate
☐ **D** In your licence documents

You must know how to load your trailer or caravan so that the hitch exerts a downward force onto the tow ball. This information can be found in your vehicle handbook or from your vehicle manufacturer's agent.

962 Mark *one* answer

Any load that is carried on a roof rack should be

☐ **A** securely fastened when driving
☐ **B** loaded towards the rear of the vehicle
☐ **C** visible in your exterior mirror
☐ **D** covered with plastic sheeting

The safest way to carry items on the roof is in a specially designed roof box. This will help to keep your luggage secure and dry, and also has less wind resistance than loads carried on a roof rack.

963 Mark *one* answer

You are carrying a child in your car. They are under three years of age. Which of these is a suitable restraint?

☐ **A** A child seat
☐ **B** An adult holding a child
☐ **C** An adult seat belt
☐ **D** An adult lap belt

It's your responsibility to ensure that all children in your car are secure. Suitable restraints include a child seat, baby seat, booster seat or booster cushion. It's essential that any restraint used should be suitable for the child's size and weight, and fitted to the manufacturers instructions.

Glossary

Accelerate

To make the vehicle move faster by pressing the right-hand pedal.

Advanced stop lines

A marked area on the road at traffic lights, which permits cyclists or buses to wait in front of other traffic.

Adverse weather

Bad weather that makes driving difficult or dangerous.

Alert

Quick to notice possible hazards.

Anticipation

Looking out for hazards and taking action before a problem starts.

Anti-lock brakes

Brakes that stop the wheels locking so that you are less likely to skid on a slippery road.

Aquaplane

To slide out of control on a wet road surface.

Articulated vehicle

A long vehicle that is divided into two or more sections joined by cables.

Attitude

The way you think or feel, which affects the way you drive. Especially, whether you are patient and polite, or impatient and aggressive.

Automatic

A vehicle with gears that change by themselves as you speed up or slow down.

Awareness

Taking notice of the road and traffic conditions around you at all times.

Black ice

An invisible film of ice that forms over the road surface, creating very dangerous driving conditions.

Blind spot

The section of road behind you which you cannot see in your mirrors. You 'cover' your blind spot by looking over your shoulder before moving off or overtaking.

Brake fade

Loss of power to the brakes when you have been using them for a long time without taking your foot off the brake pedal. For example, when driving down a steep hill. The brakes will overheat and not work properly.

Braking distance

The distance you must allow to slow the vehicle in order to come to a stop.

Brow

The highest point of a hill.

Built-up area

A town, or place with lots of buildings.

Carriageway

One side of a road or motorway. A 'dual carriageway' has a central reservation.

Catalytic converter

A piece of equipment fitted in the exhaust system that changes harmful gases into less harmful ones.

Chicane

A sharp double bend that has been put into a road to make traffic slow down.

Child restraint

A child seat or special seat belt for children. It keeps them safe and stops them moving around in the car.

Clearway

A road where no stopping is allowed at any time. The sign for a clearway is a red cross in a red circle on a blue background.

Coasting

Driving a vehicle without using any of the gears. That is, with your foot on the clutch pedal and the car in neutral.

Commentary driving

Talking to yourself about what you see on the road ahead and what action you are going to take – an aid to concentration.

Comprehensive insurance

A motor insurance policy that pays for all repairs even if you cause an accident.

Concentration

Keeping all your attention on your driving.

Conditions

How good or bad the road surface is, volume of traffic on the road, and what the weather is like.

Congestion

Heavy traffic that makes it difficult to get to where you want to go.

Consideration

Thinking about other road users and not just yourself. For example, letting another driver go first at a junction, or stopping at a zebra crossing to let pedestrians cross over.

Contraflow

When traffic on a motorway follows signs to move to the opposite carriageway for a short distance because of roadworks. (During a contraflow, there is traffic driving in both directions on the same side of the motorway.)

Coolant

Liquid in the radiator that removes heat from the engine.

Defensive driving

Driving safely without taking risks, looking out for hazards and thinking for others.

Disqualified

Stopped from doing something (eg driving) by law, because you have broken the law.

Distraction

Anything that stops you concentrating on your driving, such as chatting to passengers or on your mobile phone.

Document

An official paper or card, eg your driving licence.

Dual carriageway

A road or motorway with a central reservation.

Engine braking – see also gears

Using the low gears to keep your speed down. For example, when you are driving down a steep hill and you want to stop the vehicle running away. Using the gears instead of braking will help to prevent brake fade.

Environment

The world around us and the air we breathe.

Equestrian crossing

An unusual kind of crossing. It has a button high up for horse riders to push.

Exceed

Go higher than an upper limit.

Exhaust emissions

Gases that come out of the exhaust pipe to form part of the outside air.

Field of vision

How far you can see in front and around you when you are driving.

Filler cap

Provides access to the vehicle's fuel tank, for filling up with petrol or diesel.

Fog lights

Extra bright rear (and sometimes front) lights which may be switched on in conditions of very poor visibility. You must remember to switch them off when visibility improves, as they can dazzle and distract other drivers.

Ford

A place in a stream or river which is shallow enough to drive across with care.

Four-wheel drive (4WD)

On a conventional vehicle, steering and engine speed affect just two 'drive' wheels. On 4WD, they affect all four wheels, ensuring optimum grip on loose ground.

Frustration

Feeling annoyed because you cannot drive as fast as you want to because of other drivers or heavy traffic.

Fuel consumption

The amount of fuel (petrol or diesel) that your vehicle uses. Different vehicles have different rates of consumption. Increased fuel consumption means using more fuel. Decreased fuel consumption means using less fuel.

Fuel gauge

A display or dial on the instrument panel that tells you how much fuel (petrol or diesel) you have left.

Gantry

An overhead platform like a high narrow bridge that displays electric signs on a motorway.

Gears

Control the speed of the engine in relation to the vehicle's speed. May be hand operated (manual) or automatically controlled. In a low gear (such as first or second) the engine runs more slowly. In a high gear (such as fourth or fifth), it runs more quickly. Putting the car into a lower gear as you drive can create the effect of engine braking – forcing the engine to run more slowly.

Handling

How well your vehicle moves or responds when you steer or brake.

Harass

To drive in away that makes other road users afraid.

Hard shoulder

The single lane to the left of the inside lane on a motorway, which is for emergency use only. You should not drive on the hard shoulder except in an emergency, or when there are signs telling you to use the hard shoulder because of roadworks.

Harsh braking (or harsh acceleration)

Using the brake or accelerator too hard so as to cause wear on the engine.

Hazard warning lights

Flashing amber lights which you should use only when you have broken down. On a motorway you can use them to warn other drivers behind of a hazard ahead.

High-sided vehicle

A van or truck with tall sides, or a tall trailer such as a caravan or horse-box, that is at risk of being blown off-course in strong winds.

Impatient

Not wanting to wait for pedestrians and other road users.

Inflate

To blow up – to put air in your tyres until they are at the right pressures.

Instrument panel

The car's electrical controls and gauges, set behind the steering wheel. Also called the dashboard.

Intimidate

To make someone feel afraid.

Involved

Being part of something. For example, being one of the drivers in an accident.

Jump leads

A pair of thick electric cables with clips at either end. You use it to charge a flat battery by connecting it to the live battery in another vehicle.

Junction

A place where two or more roads join.

Liability

Being legally responsible.

Manoeuvre

Using the controls to make your car move in a particular direction. For example turning, reversing or parking.

Manual

By hand. In a car that is a 'manual' or has manual gears, you have to change the gears yourself.

Maximum

The largest possible; 'maximum speed' is the highest speed allowed.

Minimum

The smallest possible.

Mirrors

Modern cars have a minimum of three rear view mirrors: one in the centre of the windscreen, and one on each front door. Additional mirrors may be required on longer vehicles, or when towing a high trailer such as a caravan. Some mirrors may be curved (convex or concave) to increase the field of vision. The mirror on the windscreen can be turned to anti-dazzle position, if glare from headlights behind creates a distraction.

Mobility

The ability to move around easily.

Monotonous

Boring. For example, a long stretch of motorway with no variety and nothing interesting to see.

MOT

The test that proves your car is safe to drive. Your MOT certificate is one of the important documents for your vehicle.

Motorway

A fast road that has two or more lanes on each side and a hard shoulder. Drivers must join or leave it on the left, via a motorway junction. Many kinds of slower vehicles – such as bicycles – are not allowed on motorways.

Multiple-choice questions

Questions with several possible answers where you have to try to choose the right one.

Observation

The ability to notice important information, such as hazards developing ahead.

Obstruct

To get in the way of another road user.

Octagonal

Having eight sides.

Oil level

The amount of oil needed for the engine to run effectively. The oil level should be checked as part of your regular maintenance routine, and the oil replaced as necessary.

Pedestrian

A person walking.

Pelican crossing

A crossing with traffic lights that pedestrians can use by pushing a button. Cars must give way to pedestrians on the crossing while the amber light is flashing. You must give pedestrians enough time to get to the other side of the road.

Perception

Seeing or noticing (as in Hazard Perception).

Peripheral vision

The area around the edges of your field of vision.

Positive attitude

Being sensible and obeying the law when you drive.

Priority

The vehicle or other road user that is allowed by law to go first is the one that has priority.

Provisional licence

A first driving licence. all learner drivers must get one before they start having lessons.

Puffin crossing

A type of pedestrian crossing that does not have a flashing amber light phase.

Reaction time

The amount of time it takes you to see a hazard and decide what to do about it.

Red route

You see these in London and some other cities. Double red lines at the edge of the road tell you that you must not stop or park there at any time. Single red lines have notices with times when you must not stop or park. Some red routes have marked bays for either parking or loading at certain times.

Red warning triangle

An item of safety equipment to carry in your car in case you break down. You can place the triangle 45m behind your car on the same side of the road. It warns traffic that your vehicle is causing an obstruction. (Do not use these on motorways.)

Residential areas

Areas of housing where people live. The speed limit is 30mph or sometimes 20mph.

Road hump

A low bump built across the road to slow vehicles down. Also called 'sleeping policemen'.

Rumble strips

Raised strips across the road near a roundabout or junction that change the sound the tyres make on the road surface, warning drivers to slow down. They are also used on motorways to separate the main carriageway from the hard shoulder.

Safety margin

The amount of space you need to leave between your vehicle and the one in front so that you are not in danger of crashing into it if the driver slows down suddenly or stops. Safety margins have to be longer in wet or icy conditions.

Separation distance

The amount of space you need to leave between your vehicle and the one in front so that you are not in danger of crashing into it if the driver slows down suddenly or stops. The separation distance must be longer in wet or icy conditions.

Security coded radio

To deter thieves, a radio or CD unit which requires a security code (or pin number) to operate it.

Single carriageway

Generally, a road with one lane in each direction.

Skid

When the tyres fail to grip the surface of the road, the subsequent loss of control of the vehicle's movement is called a skid. Usually caused by harsh or fierce braking, steering or acceleration.

Snaking

Moving from side to side. This sometimes happens with caravans or trailers when you drive too fast, or they are not properly loaded.

Staggered junction

Where you drive cross another road. Instead of going straight across, you have to go a bit to the right or left.

Steering

Control of the direction of the vehicle. May be affected by road surface conditions: when the steering wheel turns very easily, steering is 'light', and when you have to pull hard on the wheel it is described as 'heavy'.

Sterile

Clean and free from bacteria.

Stopping distance

The time it takes for you to stop your vehicle – made up of 'thinking distance' and 'braking distance'.

Supervisor

Someone who sits in the passenger seat with a learner driver. They must be over 21 and have held a full driving licence for at least three years.

Tailgating

Driving too closely behind another vehicle – either to harass the driver in front or to help you in thick fog.

Tax disc

The disc you display on your windscreen to show that you have taxed your car (see Vehicle Excise Duty, below).

Thinking distance

The time it takes you to notice something and take the right action. You need to add thinking distance to your braking distance to make up your total stopping distance.

Third party insurance

An insurance policy that insures you against any claim by passengers or other persons for damage or injury to their person or property.

Toucan crossing

A type of pedestrian crossing that does not have a flashing amber light phase, and cyclists are allowed to ride across.

Tow

To pull something behind your vehicle. It could be a caravan or trailer.

Traffic-calming measures

Speed humps, chicanes and other devices placed in roads to slow traffic down.

Tram

A public transport vehicle which moves along the streets on fixed rails, usually electrically powered by overhead lines.

Tread depth

The depth of the grooves in a car's tyres that help them grip the road surface. The grooves must all be at least 1.6mm deep.

Turbulence

Strong movement of air. For example, when a large vehicle passes a much smaller one.

Two-second rule

In normal driving, the ideal minimum distance between you and the vehicle in front can be timed using the 'two-second' rule. As the vehicle in front passes a fixed object (such as a signpost), say to yourself 'Only a fool breaks the two second rule'. It takes two seconds to say it. If you have passed the same object before you finish, you are too close – pull back.

Tyre pressures

The amount of air which must be pumped into a tyre in order for it to be correctly blown up.

Vehicle Excise Duty

The tax you pay for your vehicle so that you may drive it on public roads.

Vehicle Registration Certificate

A record of details about a vehicle and its owner, also known as a log book.

Vehicle watch scheme

A system for identifying vehicles that may have been stolen.

Vulnerable

At risk of harm or injury.

Waiting restrictions

Times when you may not park or load your vehicle in a particular area.

Wheel balancing

To ensure smooth rotation at all speeds, wheels need to be 'balanced' correctly. This is a procedure done at a garage or tyre centre, when each wheel is removed for testing. Balancing may involve minor adjustment with the addition of small weights, to avoid wheel wobble.

Wheel-spin

When the vehicle's wheels spin round out of control with no grip on the road surface.

Zebra crossing

A pedestrian crossing without traffic lights. It has an orange light, and is marked by black and white stripes on the road. Drivers must stop for pedestrians to cross.

Answers to
Questions

Answers to Questions

Section 1 – Alertness

1 C	2 BDF	3 D	4 C	5 C	6 C	7 C	8 B	9 C
10 B	11 A	12 AC	13 ABCD	14 AD	15 AB	16 AB	17 ABCD	18 B
19 B	20 ABE	21 C	22 B	23 B	24 C	25 D	26 D	27 D
28 B	29 D	30 B	31 D	32 C	33 C	34 A	35 D	36 B
37 D								

Section 2 – Attitude

38 D	39 A	40 C	41 D	42 D	43 B	44 BCD	45 ABE	46 A
47 D	48 B	49 A	50 B	51 A	52 A	53 C	54 A	55 D
56 D	57 D	58 A	59 B	60 C	61 B	62 A	63 B	64 C
65 A	66 C	67 A	68 C	69 C	70 DE	71 B	72 D	73 B
74 C	75 A	76 A	77 B	78 A	79 A	80 B	81 B	82 C
83 AB	84 D	85 D	86 C	87 C				

Section 3 – Safety and Your Vehicle

88 AB	89 C	90 ACF	91 C	92 B	93 D	94 C	95 D	96 D
97 D	98 A	99 AE	100 D	101 B	102 B	103 ABF	104 BEF	105 D
106 A	107 A	108 B	109 C	110 D	111 A	112 B	113 C	114 D
115 A	116 B	117 A	118 B	119 B	120 B	121 D	122 D	123 BC
124 BC	125 A	126 D	127 A	128 B	129 D	130 D	131 D	132 B
133 B	134 B	135 D	136 ABF	137 ABC	138 ABC	139 BDF	140 ADE	141 B
142 CDE	143 B	144 B	145 B	146 DE	147 C	148 B	149 D	150 D
151 B	152 A	153 D	154 C	155 AB	156 A	157 B	158 BCD	159 C
160 CD	161 A	162 A	163 D	164 C	165 B	166 B	167 ABE	168 ADE
169 D	170 B	171 BD	172 C	173 A	174 D	175 C	176 B	177 A
178 B	179 D	180 B	181 C	182 D	183 D	184 B	185 A	186 D
187 B	188 C	189 D	190 D	191 C	192 D	193 B	194 B	195 C
196 A	197 A	198 A	199 D					

Section 4 – Safety Margins

200 D	201 D	202 D	203 A	204 B	205 BC	206 B	207 D	208 C
209 C	210 B	211 B	212 C	213 A	214 C	215 A	216 D	217 ACD
218 B	219 A	220 B	221 AE	222 C	223 BDEF	224 B	225 D	226 A
227 C	228 AD	229 C	230 B	231 B	232 C	233 B	234 BC	235 C
236 C	237 B	238 D	239 BC	240 D	241 D	242 A	243 D	244 BD
245 D	246 A	247 D	248 A	249 A	250 C	251 B	252 C	253 B
254 B	255 B	256 C	257 D	258 ACE				

Section 5 – Hazard Awareness

259 CD	260 C	261 A	262 D	263 ACE	264 C	265 C	266 D	267 B
268 A	269 A	270 A	271 C	272 C	273 B	274 A	275 C	276 D
277 B	278 B	279 C	280 A	281 D	282 D	283 C	284 B	285 BF
286 B	287 A	288 A	289 AE	290 C	291 A	292 D	293 B	294 CD
295 ACE	296 ABD	297 B	298 B	299 B	300 B	301 A	302 D	303 A
304 B	305 C	306 B	307 B	308 B	309 C	310 D	311 C	312 CD
313 AC	314 AB	315 A	316 A	317 B	318 ABC	319 C	320 C	321 C
322 ABE	323 C	324 D	325 D	326 C	327 C	328 D	329 ABC	330 D
331 C	332 B	333 B	334 CD	335 D	336 ACE	337 ABE	338 A	339 D
340 D	341 D	342 A	343 B	344 CD	345 D	346 AE	347 BC	348 AB
349 A	350 B	351 D	352 A	353 B	354 A			

Section 6 – Vulnerable Road Users

355 D	356 D	357 C	358 C	359 B	360 D	361 D	362 C	363 D
364 A	365 D	366 D	367 B	368 D	369 D	370 AC	371 C	372 C
373 A	374 D	375 C	376 D	377 ABC	378 C	379 AC	380 D	381 A
382 D	383 C	384 C	385 D	386 D	387 B	388 A	389 C	390 D
391 C	392 C	393 A	394 D	395 A	396 A	397 B	398 B	399 A
400 A	401 C	402 B	403 D	404 A	405 D	406 D	407 D	408 A
409 C	410 ABD	411 B	412 D	413 B	414 B	415 D	416 C	417 C
418 B	419 C	420 AE	421 C	422 C	423 B	424 B	425 D	426 D
427 B	428 B	429 B	430 C	431 D	432 A	433 D	434 C	435 D

Section 7 – Other Types of Vehicle

436 A	437 A	438 B	439 B	440 D	441 B	442 BC	443 A	444 C
445 B	446 D	447 B	448 D	449 D	450 A	451 D	452 A	453 A
454 A	455 B	456 B	457 AC	458 B	459 D	460 B	461 BD	462 D

Section 8 – Vehicle Handling

463 ACE	464 A	465 CD	466 D	467 A	468 C	469 C	470 DE	471 C
472 D	473 D	474 C	475 BDF	476 C	477 B	478 B	479 D	480 BD
481 B	482 C	483 C	484 D	485 A	486 A	487 C	488 B	489 A
490 D	491 B	492 B	493 ACD	494 B	495 A	496 C	497 B	498 A
499 C	500 A	501 C	502 D	503 B	504 D	505 ABD	506 D	507 C
508 C	509 C	510 D	511 D	512 A	513 CE	514 A	515 A	516 AB
517 C	518 B	519 BD	520 ABDF	521 D	522 C	523 B	524 BD	

Answers to Questions

Section 9 – Motorway Rules

525 D	526 D	527 D	528 A	529 C	530 C	531 C	532 A	533 C
534 C	535 C	536 C	537 C	538 C	539 B	540 B	541 A	542 B
543 D	544 C	545 ADEF	546 ADEF	547 D	548 B	549 A	550 A	551 C
552 B	553 B	554 D	555 A	556 A	557 B	558 D	559 D	560 B
561 D	562 D	563 C	564 D	565 C	566 D	567 A	568 CDF	569 D
570 C	571 B	572 D	573 B	574 D	575 B	576 D	577 C	578 D
579 A	580 B	581 B	582 D	583 A	584 D	585 C	586 B	587 C
588 D	589 A	590 B	591 A					

Section 10 – Rules of the Road

592 C	593 D	594 B	595 A	596 C	597 D	598 ADF	599 A	600 B
601 A	602 B	603 A	604 D	605 A	606 D	607 C	608 A	609 ACE
610 C	611 D	612 BD	613 B	614 A	615 C	616 A	617 B	618 CDE
619 B	620 AE	621 B	622 A	623 ABD	624 A	625 A	626 D	627 A
628 AD	629 D	630 B	631 C	632 B	633 B	634 B	635 C	636 D
637 D	638 C	639 D	640 D	641 D	642 D	643 D	644 C	645 C
646 D	647 A	648 A	649 C	650 B	651 A	652 D	653 A	654 A
655 D	656 B	657 D	658 D	659 A	660 A	661 A	662 D	663 D
664 AB	665 A	666 ABC						

Section 11 – Road and Traffic Signs

667 D	668 D	669 A	670 A	671 B	672 A	673 D	674 B	675 D
676 D	677 D	678 A	679 C	680 B	681 D	682 C	683 B	684 A
685 B	686 B	687 C	688 C	689 A	690 C	691 B	692 C	693 D
694 D	695 C	696 C	697 D	698 A	699 D	700 D	701 B	702 A
703 A	704 A	705 B	706 B	707 A	708 D	709 ACEF	710 C	711 A
712 B	713 C	714 B	715 D	716 A	717 A	718 C	719 D	720 A
721 C	722 B	723 D	724 B	725 B	726 C	727 C	728 D	729 C
730 B	731 C	732 D	733 B	734 A	735 A	736 C	737 BDF	738 A
739 C	740 C	741 B	742 A	743 C	744 A	745 A	746 D	747 D
748 B	749 A	750 D	751 C	752 D	753 C	754 B	755 C	756 C
757 A	758 B	759 D	760 B	761 B	762 A	763 D	764 A	765 B
766 B	767 D	768 C	769 B	770 A	771 B	772 C	773 A	774 B
775 A	776 C	777 B	778 B	779 A	780 C	781 A	782 B	783 B
784 B	785 A	786 C	787 A	788 C	789 B	790 D	791 C	792 B
793 C	794 A	795 C	796 A	797 C	798 B	799 C	800 A	801 B
802 A	803 A	804 C	805 D	806 B	807 B	808 B	809 B	810 D
811 A	812 B	813 A	814 A	815 C	816 C	817 B	818 B	819 B
820 B	821 B	822 A						

Section 12 – Documents

823 C	824 B	825 BE	826 A	827 C	828 C	829 B	830 C	831 D
832 A	833 C	834 D	835 C	836 ABD	837 A	838 B	839 A	840 B
841 C	842 C	843 B	844 D	845 D	846 CDE	847 B	848 C	849 ABF
850 BCE	851 ABE	852 D	853 B	854 AB	855 D	856 B	857 C	858 BD
859 C	860 D	861 B	862 D	863 A	864 AB	865 A	866 C	867 ABD
868 D	869 D							

Section 13 – Incidents, Accidents and Emergencies

870 A	871 AB	872 A	873 C	874 B	875 D	876 B	877 B	878 D
879 B	880 D	881 B	882 D	883 B	884 A	885 C	886 B	887 BD
888 A	889 ABE	890 A	891 ACF	892 A	893 ABD	894 ACE	895 DEF	896 ABE
897 ACF	898 C	899 BC	900 A	901 B	902 B	903 BDE	904 C	905 D
906 CD	907 C	908 B	909 D	910 B	911 BDE	912 B	913 D	914 B
915 B	916 AE	917 ACDE	918 B	919 C	920 ABD	921 CD	922 CE	923 C
924 A	925 BE	926 ADE	927 B	928 C	929 A	930 A	931 BE	932 A
933 D	934 C	935 D	936 D	937 D	938 A	939 BD	940 D	941 A
942 DEF	943 C	944 ABCE	945 A	946 B	947 B	948 C		

Section 14 – Vehicle Loading

949 AD	950 A	951 D	952 BD	953 D	954 A	955 BC	956 A	957 D
958 B	959 D	960 A	961 A	962 A	963 A			

Personal Information

My driver number

Driving instructor's name and
phone number

Driving instructor's number

Theory Test date and time

Theory Test pass date

Theory Test certificate number

Driving school code

Practical Test date and time